FOOTBALL COACHING STRATEGIES

AMERICAN FOOTBALL COACHES ASSOCIATION

Human Kinetics

Library of Congress Cataloging-in-Publication Data

Football coaching strategies / American Football Coaches Association.
    p.   cm.
  ISBN 0-87322-869-3
  1. Football--Coaching.   I. American Football Coaches Association.
  GV954.4.F66 1995
  796.332'07'7--dc20   95-8140
                                             CIP

ISBN: 0-87322-869-3

All articles used and adapted with permission of the lead authors. The article by Woody Hayes used and adapted with permission of Mrs. Anne Hayes.

Expert Consultants: Jim Butterfield, Jerry Claiborne, Joe Restic, and Vic Rowen; **Managing Editor:** Dawn Roselund; **Assistant Editor:** Henry Woolsey; **Editorial Assistance:** Andrew Starr and Wendy Gossett; **Copyeditor:** Bob Replinger; **Proofreader:** Jim Burns; **Typesetter:** Francine Hamerski; **Text Design and Layout:** Robert M. Reuther; **Cover Designer:** Jack Davis; **Illustrators:** Craig Ronto, Jennifer Delmotte, Tara Welsch, and Denise Lowry; **Printer:** United Graphics

Human Kinetics books are available at special discounts for bulk purchase. Special editions or book excerpts can also be created to specification. For details, contact the Special Sales Manager at Human Kinetics.

Printed in the United States of America   10

Human Kinetics
Web site: www.HumanKinetics.com

United States: Human Kinetics, P.O. Box 5076, Champaign, IL 61825-5076
800-747-4457
e-mail: humank@hkusa.com

Canada: Human Kinetics, 475 Devonshire Road, Unit 100, Windsor, ON N8Y 2L5
800-465-7301 (in Canada only)
e-mail: orders@hkcanada.com

Europe: Human Kinetics, 107 Bradford Road, Stanningley
Leeds LS28 6AT, United Kingdom
+44 (0) 113 255 5665
e-mail: hk@hkeurope.com

Australia: Human Kinetics, 57A Price Avenue, Lower Mitcham, South Australia 5062
08 8277 1555
e-mail: liahka@senet.com.au

New Zealand: Human Kinetics, P.O. Box 105-231, Auckland Central
09-523-3462
e-mail: hkp@ihug.co.nz

CONTENTS

PART I

Offense

Run Offense

Pass Offense

Run and Pass Offense

Situational Offense

PART II

Defense

Team Defense

Emphasis on Defense

PART III

Special Teams

PART IV
Philosophy, Motivation, and Management

FOREWORD

In 36 years of coaching football I relied heavily on finding the right kind of players, a loyal dedicated coaching staff, and good information about the game of football. Football coaches are the most sharing group of professionals I know. They're willing to divulge how they achieved success and the fundamentals they've used to improve the skills of their players and the teaching of leadership and motivational techniques.

Coaches listen to lectures, watch videos, and spend endless hours talking by phone and in confidential conversations with friends in the coaching profession. But through the years, the one constant in disseminating information on the game of football has been articles and books.

I wholeheartedly recommend this collection of outstanding articles that have appeared in AFCA publications over the years. In reading these articles anew, I have found the information to be just as pertinent and timely today as it was the day it was written.

Grant Teaff
Executive Director
American Football Coaches Association

INTRODUCTION

Football, like no other sport, combines a rich history with the most recent innovations. Our fondest memories of plays, games, players, and coaches somehow make the modern game more meaningful and more enjoyable.

What now works on the gridiron does so because of the many lessons shared by coaches and players from practices, games, and seasons gone by. Today's sophisticated video and computer technology, players' equipment, training tables, conditioning programs, and sports medicine services are valuable only when they coexist with the oldest football principles of all—organization, teaching, blocking, tackling, teamwork, effort, and sacrifice.

Innovation and tradition; young, bright aspiring coaches and old, wise veteran coaches; upstart teams breaking into the top 25, and perennial powers that seem to never leave it. No other sport is so high-tech and yet so deeply rooted in the lessons of the past; so ready to change with the times and yet so set in its ways; so ready to hail today's stars as the greatest of all time and yet so appreciative of the legends who preceded them.

Rarely do we have the opportunity to present, in one book, insights from football's past and present as we do in *Football Coaching Strategies*. We get this chance only because so many successful coaches have taken the time to share their teaching and practice methods, tactical approaches, and philosophies during the past 25 years.

The proceedings from the American Football Coaches Association's annual convention and articles for the AFCA Summer Manual since 1970 capture both the creative genius and the enduring principles that have shaped the modern game. What Woody Hayes, John McKay, and Darrell Royal told us a quarter century ago is as important as what Dick Tomey, Dennis Green, and Steve Spurrier have to say today. And you'll be able to read passages from all six of these fine coaches and many others in this book.

Football Coaching Strategies presents much of the most important tactical thinking in football. From the Wishbone to the Eagle, the book describes and illustrates a wide selection of popular offensive and defensive formations, schemes, and plays. Also included are time-tested, effective attacks for the all-important kicking game. In all, more than 300 detailed diagrams of formations and plays are shown.

But success in football isn't achieved through Xs and Os alone. Proper philosophy, motivation, and management are equally important, and these subjects are addressed at length in Part IV.

The book includes 67 articles contributed by many of the greatest football coaches the game has ever known, all addressing topics in which they have special expertise or interest. We wanted to include the most coaches and the most strategies possible. To do that, we had to abridge and revise the original articles—in some cases, considerably—without eliminating the substance of the coaches' messages.

Among the primary considerations in our selection process were to

- distribute the articles across the 25-year time period (1970–1994), but to emphasize more recent works;
- present a variety of topics within each of four categories: offense; defense; special teams; and philosophy, motivation, and management;
- include at least one coach from the high school, junior college, each NCAA division, and professional levels;
- feature coaches presenting on their area of expertise;
- fit as much information in as we possibly could, given the book's page allowance; and
- make the book highly readable, useful, and entertaining.

Regrettably, we had to omit many very worthy articles presented by hundreds of great coaches. But all of you understand that when you're tied, and it's 4th-and-goal with little time remaining, you have to make the tough call. And together with Human Kinetics we had to make several of them during the course of the book's development.

Football Coaching Strategies is for the veteran coach who continues to add to his knowledge base, for the less experienced coach who is still learning many facets of football and how to coach it, for the player who is looking to improve his understanding and performance, for the student of the game who wants an inside look at the sport's nuances, and for the fan who wants to be a more informed spectator. For all of you, the book's blend of the best lessons of the past with the most current thinking in today's game should make next football season and the seasons that follow all the more special.

KEY TO DIAGRAMS

Offensive players:

Wide receiver = X, SE, WR, ◯

Flanker = Z, WB, F, ◯

Tight end = Y, TE, ◯

Tackles and guards = ◯

Center = ☐

Quarterback = QB, ◯

Fullback = FB, B, ◯

Running back = RB, HB, A, ◯

Defensive players:

End = E, V

Tackle = T, ST, G, V

Nose tackle = N, V

Inside linebacker = M, B, LB, V

Outside linebacker = S, W, B, LB, ⊗, V

Safeties = S, FS, SS, R, V

Cornerbacks = C, V, WC, SC

Special teams:

Kicker = K

Punter = P

Holder = H

Kick returner = KR

Punt returner = PR

Primary ball-carrier and receiver = ●

Primary options as ball-carriers and receivers = ◯

Handoff = ⊥↑

Pitch = ----⊥↑

Pass = •••↑

Block = ⊣

Optional paths to run = ——⟨

Continued path after block = ⊣→

Motion before snap, less than full speed running, or backpedal = ∿∿ or ∧∧∧

Quarterback dropback, less than full speed running, or backpedal = ∿∿ or ——

Quarterback set-up to pass or point of release = ∿∿• or ——•

Quarterback release point or set-up point for read by defender = •

Defensive player coverage assignment = ------

Offense

Run Offense

Pass Offense

Run and Pass Offense

Situational Offense

Bread-and-Butter Running Plays

JOHN McKAY

In all the clinics that I've attended over the years, when a coach wins anything, everybody comes and takes the diagrams he puts up and says, "That's it." The last couple of years it's been the Wishbone.

We don't use the Wishbone, but just to get in the swing of things, we changed the name of our offense from the I to the I-Bone. The offense is the same, and just the name is changed.

For years, we wanted to run right at you with the blast play and find out where you were, and establish the fact that we were as strong, physically, as you were. After we established the blast, we went to our pitch play, or, as it's also called, "student body left or right." This year, we started with the pitch and ran it until you stopped it, and then we'd go to the blast. We run the pitch awhile, then go to the blast, and back to the pitch.

We really are pretty simple. Over the years, we've found out that players win, not plays. Our attack is based on multiple sets, using motion and shifting. We start out with sixteen different sets, and by using motion and shifting, we can add greatly to the number of things we do. It's pretty complicated for the opponent, but it's simple to us, and out of it come our two basic plays, the pitch and the blast.

The Pitch

We start by running the pitch play, until you put so many people outside that we can make our inside offense go. We start every offensive set to run the ball outside. If we go outside to the tight end side, we ask the tight end to block the outside man on the line. We don't care where you line him up, we feel we can block him. We ask him to block the defensive man high up in his face, and his main job is to keep the defender on the line, and, if possible, hook the man. If the defender fights to the outside fast, then we ask him to drive him to the sideline, but to stay up on him and keep him on the line.

Here are our blocking assignments between the tackles. We tell our tackle to hook the defensive

tackle, to stay up, to never go to his knees. He should stay up and block him as high as he can, keep pushing on him. If the defensive man slants inside, our tackle just goes on to the linebacker. The center's job is to reach to the onside, unless he is covered, and then take that man. We tell the guard to block the onside linebacker. We ask him to pull around the tight end for the linebacker. If the linebacker shoots, the guard just stops and takes him. So it's imperative that the guard keeps his eyes on the linebacker all the time (see Figure 1). We tell the offside guard to pull and go through the first opening he can find. The offside tackle's assignment is the same as the guard's.

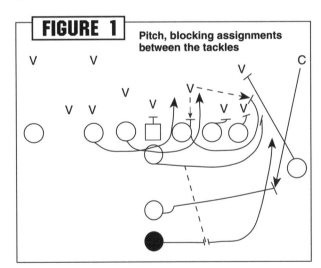

FIGURE 1 Pitch, blocking assignments between the tackles

Our quarterback, at times, leads this play. If we ask him to lead, assuming we're going to the right, he should step right with his right foot, and then reverse pivot. He shouldn't reverse pivot first; if he does, he will be behind the play. Then, he just leads around the end and looks inside. We ask him to fall at the feet of the defender. We don't want him to body block him or get tough with other people. Our quarterbacks make a lot of good blocks that way.

We tell our fullback to take a slight step forward, and then go parallel to the line and annihilate the cornerback. We don't want him to body block—just run right over him.

Our Z-back's (flanker's) job changes, depending on where he is set. If he is set wide, we ask him to crack back on the first man inside, usually the strong safety. If he is set in the Power-I position, then he leads outside the tight end, and helps him with the defensive end. If our tight end has his man, then Z leads straight up for the safety man.

Our tailback's job is to open step toward the sideline, catch the pitch from the quarterback, and run as fast as he can for the outside, always keeping his eyes up the field. If he can get all the way outside, then we want him to run off the fullback's block on the corner. If there's a funnel there, we tell him to turn upfield and go (see Figure 2).

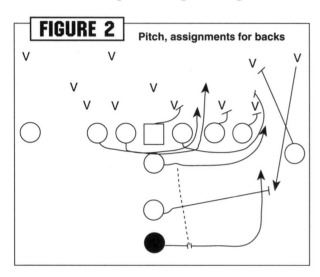

FIGURE 2   Pitch, assignments for backs

If the defensive end, or rover (R in the diagrams), ever gets upfield or outside too fast, then our tailback will cut up inside and pick up the blocks of our backside pullers (see Figure 3).

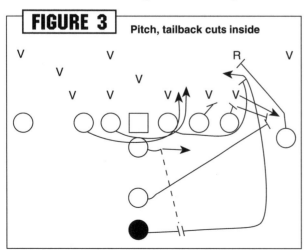

FIGURE 3   Pitch, tailback cuts inside

If people are overplaying this play with an unbalanced defense, we will shift, or motion, our Z-back to balance up or take advantage of the defense. This year, for example, we faced a rover defense, which put two men on the line outside our tight end or Z-back (see Figure 4). So we put our Z-back in motion through the backfield, and ran the pitch away from the rover, as shown in Figure 5.

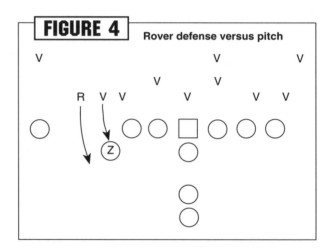

FIGURE 4   Rover defense versus pitch

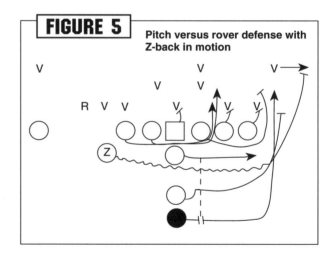

FIGURE 5   Pitch versus rover defense with Z-back in motion

The Blast

Now, we get to the blast play (see Figure 6). One coaching point on this play is extremely important: We want our backs to stay deep. The fullback should be at least 4 1/2 to 5 yards deep, and the tailback should be 6 to 6 1/2 yards deep, so that they can option run versus all the potential stunts we may see. Where you line up is as important as where you wind up. If you want to crowd up, it means you're too slow to play in the backfield.

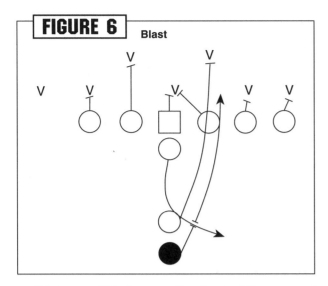

FIGURE 6   Blast

It's impossible for an offensive tackle or guard to keep a defender, if he's lined up head-on, from going inside. If you're stubborn enough to say you're going to run the ball through any one hole, then certain stunts will wipe this play out.

Someone made the comment to me the other day that he was amazed that we kept our tailback at 7 yards during the entire game against Ohio State in the Rose Bowl. I said, "Yep, that's what we want when the defense stunts on us." We want him back where he can see.

We ask our backs to key the first defensive lineman to the onside. As they approach the hole, they will run away from the direction the lineman slants. If the defensive lineman slants in, it's obvious the linebacker is coming to the outside. Our tackle will just block the defensive tackle the way he wants to go, and our fullback will "kick out" the linebacker the way he is going. If the tail-

back stays back away from the fullback, there's an alley between those blocks that he can hit. The rest of the blocking is pretty simple.

The quarterback gives the tailback the ball as deep as possible. I don't believe you can run as hard when you get the ball close to the line of scrimmage. The first thing any back thinks of is possession, possession first. "I must have the ball," he says, "then I can think about the other things." So, we ask our quarterback to reverse pivot and get the ball deep.

This play can be a great goal-line play, provided the back is willing to go "over the top" versus the gap defenses. If we face a goal-line or gap set, we tell our tailback to be ready to dive over the line. Again, he must line up deep to have time to secure the ball and then get up in the air. He takes off about a yard back and a good diver can go about 5 or 6 yards. Now, what you have got to do is convince the diver. We tell the diver this, "They'll probably catch you, and that's the best thing that can happen to you. Now, if we block well, you'll hit the ground, and that's the worst thing that can happen to you, because you're going to hit approximately right on your head."

People ask, "how do you practice this play?" We don't. But I'll give you a little stat. In the first six games this year and the last two games, 37 times we had short-yardage or goal-line situations, and we either made it or scored on all but one. Proper execution and the threat of the blast play was a big reason why.

I don't think theories win; players win. Down through the years, we haven't changed much. The things we do best are those things we know best and have taught for years.

—*1973 Proceedings. Coach McKay was head coach at the University of Southern California.*

Big Plays From the I-Formation
TOM OSBORNE

I would like to present the most consistent big play we've had for many years, and its companion pass play. It's important that you consider both the run and the pass together, as separately they won't be nearly as effective.

We've had several seasons where the counter sweep has averaged 7 to 11 yards per carry. And the counter sweep bootleg has done just as well as a companion play. We run the counter sweep with a variety of runners from a variety of formations; however, the basic blocking is always the same.

Counter Sweep

Figure 1, a and b, illustrates the basic counter sweep run from the I-Pro formation versus 50 and 43 defenses.

Assignments for each offensive player are as follows:

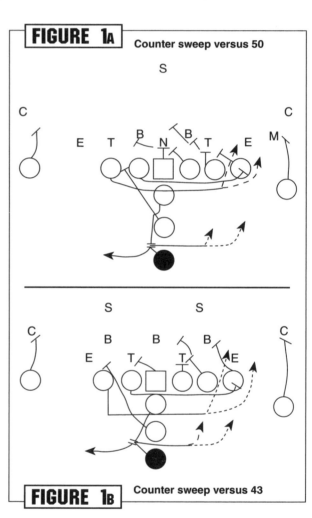

FIGURE 1A   Counter sweep versus 50

FIGURE 1B   Counter sweep versus 43

Flanker—Blocks first deep defender.

Tight end—Blocks outside hip of defensive tackle. If tackle slants inside and crosses offensive tackle's face, tight end scrapes to LB. If offensive tackle is uncovered, TE blocks first LB inside.

Right tackle—Steps with inside foot and blocks inside half of defensive tackle. If DT slants inside, tackle locks on DT. If DT doesn't slant, tackle releases for outside LB and then on to backside LB if onside LB flows. If uncovered, tackle blocks inside.

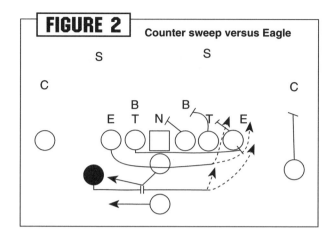

FIGURE 2 Counter sweep versus Eagle

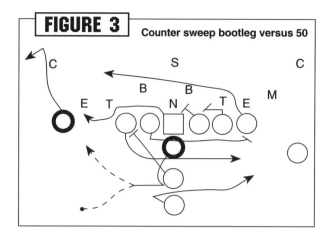

FIGURE 3 Counter sweep bootleg versus 50

Right guard—If uncovered, blocks nose-guard. If NG slants away, guard scrapes to LB. If covered, blocks man on.

Center—If covered, pops middle guard and turns back for plugging LB or slant tackle. If uncovered, blocks back to cover pulling guard.

Left guard—Pulls right and blocks defensive end. Logs DE inside if DE remains on line. Kicks DE out if DE crosses line of scrimmage.

Left tackle—Pulls right, getting a little more depth than left guard, and reads left guard's block. If left guard logs DE, tackle reads around DE and blocks strong safety. If left guard blocks DE out, tackle turns inside DE and finds strong safety.

Split end—Blocks first deep defender.

Fullback—Blocks first man to show behind pulling left tackle.

I-Back—Takes three quick steps toward left tackle area, then counters right as he receives handoff. I-back reads block of left guard (not left tackle). Both the left tackle and I-back react to the block of the left guard.

Quarterback—Opens left, hands ball to I-back and fakes bootleg around left end.

We run the counter sweep from a variety of formations using a variety of ball-carriers. In Figure 2 you can see how we might run the play versus an Eagle defense.

Counter Sweep Bootleg

The counter sweep bootleg puts a great deal of stress on linebackers and slows down pursuit of the counter sweep. See Figure 3 for how we run this play versus a 50 defense.

Blocking is the same as the counter sweep except for the center, who, after popping the nose-guard, releases to the weakside flat and acts as personal interferer for the quarterback. The quarterback's first option is to run; his second option is to throw to the crossing tight end; and his third option is to hit the split end running a deep comeback pattern.

—1987 Proceedings. Coach Osborne was head coach at the University of Nebraska.

Running Options From the I-Formation
ROY KIDD

Our offense has been very productive both in yardage gained and points scored. Much of the success has been due to the athletes we've been able to recruit and because these young men are sold on the I-formation and our offensive philosophy. We are an option-oriented football team. In recent years we've utilized our fullback more to enhance productivity but have not gone away from our basic I-formation principles.

We believe the I-formation gives us a mirrored offense where we can run all our plays to either side. It cuts down on our teaching time because our fullback is always the dive back or blocking back, and our tailback is always the pitch back on option plays, allowing both to get many more repetitions in a given period of time. We like the option course that we get from the I and feel that we can get on the corner easier than Split-Back or Wishbone teams. The I also allows us to run the isolation and sprint draw series, which have been extremely important in our success the last two years.

The past seven years we've led the Ohio Valley Conference in scoring and six of those seven years we've also led the conference in rushing.

Isolation

One of the first plays we put in our offense each fall is the isolation. With it, we're trying to play one-on-one football and give our tailback the opportunity to run to daylight. Figures 1 and 2 show the ways we block the isolation strong versus a 50 defense and weak versus an overshift.

The quarterback drop sets to the call side, reverse pivots, and hands the ball as deep as possible to the tailback. He then fakes a quick screen pass opposite the play.

The fullback lead steps to the play-call side and blocks the linebacker at the point of attack. His key is the first down lineman past the center, and he blocks opposite his charge.

The tailback drop steps with the foot opposite the call side, keys the first down lineman past the center, and runs to daylight opposite his charge after receiving the ball.

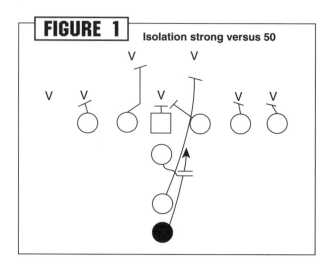

FIGURE 1 — Isolation strong versus 50

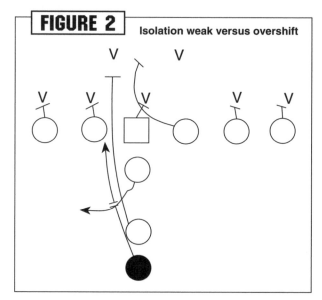

FIGURE 2 — Isolation weak versus overshift

Sprint Draw

The sprint draw is a change-of-pace play for us and is the basic backfield action for most of our passing attack. It has been a big play for us in passing situations, and because of the success we've had running the play, it helps us hold the linebackers when we throw off this action. Figure 3 shows our basic manner of blocking this play versus a 50 defense.

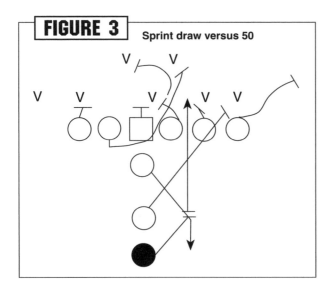

FIGURE 3 Sprint draw versus 50

The quarterback open steps at six o'clock and sprints, getting width and depth at a 45-degree angle. He hands off to the tailback on his third step and drops straight back faking a pass.

The fullback lead steps to the tail of the tackle to the play-call side and blocks inside out on the defensive end.

The tailback lead steps to the play-call side, gradually gaining ground until the third step. On the third step he plants his foot, squares his shoulders to the line of scrimmage, receives the ball, and runs to daylight opposite the block on the first down lineman past the center.

Dive Options

We run basically three types of options. Two have dive plays to the fullback that complement them and a third is our speed or straight-down-the-line option.

Figures 4 and 5 show our dive and dive-option plans and the blocking schemes we use strong versus a 50 defense.

Our backs use the same steps on the dive and the dive option, giving us added repetition and making the plays look the same to people who read our backs.

The quarterback open steps at three o'clock to the play-call side and reaches the ball as deep as possible to the fullback. He takes an adjustment step with the foot nearest to the line of scrimmage and gives or keeps the ball according to the play called. He steps around the fullback with the foot away from the line of scrimmage and attacks the inside shoulder of the defensive end, keeping or pitching off the defensive end's reaction if the option has been called.

The fullback steps with the near foot to the outside hip of the guard to the play-call side. He receives the ball during his third step (if the dive is called), reads the guard's block, and runs to daylight. There is a possibility versus a 50 defense that the fullback may break behind an angling middle guard. On the option he remains on track and blocks the first off-colored jersey that shows.

The tailback lead steps and turns his shoulders to the play-call side. He sprints to a point on the line of scrimmage 10 yards outside of the tight end's alignment.

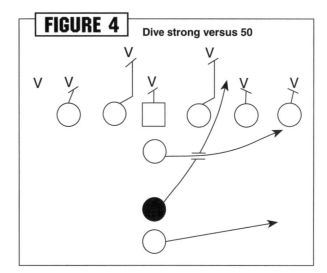

FIGURE 4 Dive strong versus 50

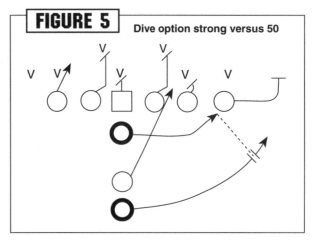

FIGURE 5 Dive option strong versus 50

Trap Option

The trap and trap option has been one of the major series in our offense the last few years. It gives us a misdirection play that helps hold our opponent's linebackers and enables us to get outside. We block the trap several ways depending on the front and the type of stunts we're seeing.

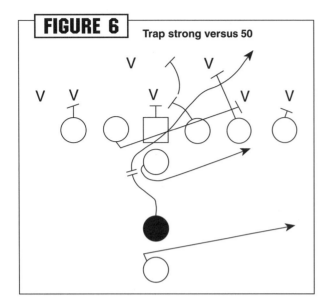

FIGURE 6   Trap strong versus 50

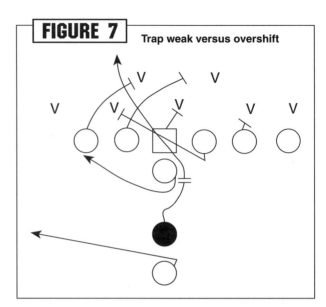

FIGURE 7   Trap weak versus overshift

Figure 6 shows how we would block trap running strong versus a 50 defense. Figure 7 shows how we run it to the weak side versus an overshift.

The steps for the backs are the same for the trap series as they are for the dive and dive-option series. The quarterback open steps deep to six o'clock turning his back to the hole called. He takes an adjustment step with his pivot foot to allow the guard to clear and the fullback to cut back. He hands the ball to the fullback (if the dive is called), reverse pivots, and attacks the inside shoulder of the defensive end, keeping or pitching off his reaction if the option is called.

—1981 Proceedings. Coach Kidd is head coach at Eastern Kentucky University.

The Freeze Option Series

DICK MacPHERSON

When we needed to improve our offensive productivity, we chose option football. We did so for these four reasons:

- *It's the best way for us to get the football outside the perimeter of the defense.* In today's football, it has become increasingly difficult to establish a sweep or toss play as an outside play. However, the option gives us a chance to get our skill people at running back and quarterback loose in the open field.
- *You don't need dominant offensive linemen to have success in an option defense.* The finesse and deception of option football allow you the luxury of not having to knock people off the ball on every snap. You can read some defenders rather than block them. Also, the angle blocks and double teams of option football help your linemen.
- *It makes the defense play assignment football.* In defending the option on every play, the defense will assign a man each to the dive, QB, and pitch phase of our option on both sides of our formation. This makes them play assignment football rather than reaction football.
- *The option will help your pass offense dramatically because of the defensive*

structures that you'll face. The defenses we see to stop our option include 8-man blitzes, 2-deep zones, and tight end rotated coverages.

Our option offense uses multiple formations and motions to run the same options. The I-formation allows the speed back at tailback to catch the pitch and run outside, and the fullback to be the inside runner. We want to make the defense constrict on the fullback, so we try to establish the fullback game inside.

We have a play-action pass off all our options. We also employ the dropback game to prevent defenses from ganging up on the option game.

Setting Up the Freeze Option

The heart and soul of our option attack has been the "freeze option" series that was established at Wichita State and really refined and popularized at East Carolina. This series gave us the inside fullback game we were looking for, with an excellent option game complementing it. As defenses adjusted to take away our freeze option, we would immediately go to the other complementary options in our package that were now available.

One of the first ways we'd attack is up the middle with the fullback. The tight fullback dive is a quick-hitting play in which the fullback can run off the block of the offensive center versus the 5-2 defense (see Figure 1). It's a base-blocking concept up front.

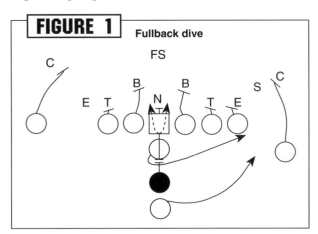

FIGURE 1   Fullback dive

Quarterback—Step back off the midline and stretch the ball back to the fullback. Gather your second step and hand the ball off to the fullback. Continue the option fake off the football until you get to the outside leg of the guard, then attack downhill.

Fullback—Take a lead step and run the midline. Run off the block of the center. Once cut is made, get your shoulders square.

Tailback—Freeze on the snap of the ball. Once the QB's second step hits the ground, sprint into pitch relationship.

The second way we'd run the fullback is the FB trap off the tight dive action. Realize the backfield mechanics are the same as the tight dive, except the FB must now get in phase inside the trapping guard (see Figure 2).

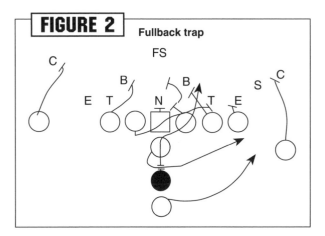

FIGURE 2   Fullback trap

The Freeze Option

The freeze option is one of our favorite option series. It became the heart and soul of our offense. It's a play that can be run both to the TE side and the SE side (see Figures 3a, b).

Freeze Option Rules

Onside tackle—Inside for LB.

Onside guard—Down on nose.

Center—Slam nose and block A gap back side.

Offside guard—Pull and read the tackle area. Fight to get to LB.

Offside tackle—Gap seal hinge.

Tight end—Option to: Block primary run support; option away: Gap seal hinge.

Split end—Option to: Block primary run support; option away: Block inside number of near halfback.

Flanker—Option to: Block nonprimary run support; option away: Block inside number on near halfback.

Fullback—Run through the midline of the center. Get a great mesh and drive to backside linebacker.

Quarterback—Step back off the midline and stretch the ball back to the fullback. Gather

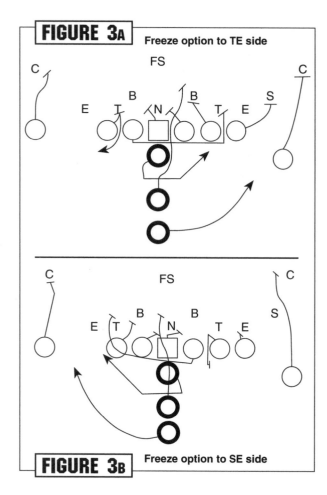

FIGURE 3A Freeze option to TE side

FIGURE 3B Freeze option to SE side

of certain coverages that can give you an advantage in the perimeter, without changes for your people up front.

Play-Action off of Freeze Option

The importance of the play-action pass off the option action must be noted. It's crucial that the defensive support people be placed in a pass-run bind in order to slow down their option support. Figure 4, a and b, shows how we run play-action off the option to the tight end and split end sides, respectively.

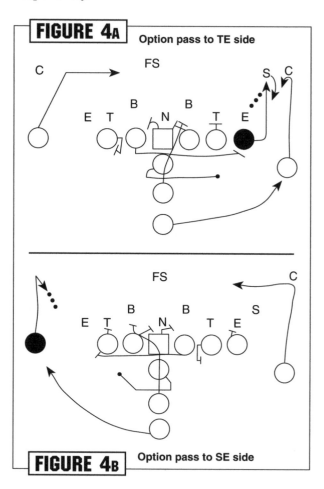

FIGURE 4A Option pass to TE side

FIGURE 4B Option pass to SE side

your second step and ride the fullback to your front hip. Stay off the ball until the outside leg of the guard, then drive downhill and option the No. 3 man.

Tailback—Freeze on the snap. When the QB's second step hits the ground, sprint to pitch relationship. Keep a 4-yard by 4-yard relationship with the quarterback.

The use of multiple formations and motions can provide you with definite advantages in attacking the perimeter with the freeze option series. The rules for your linemen and backs are consistent, regardless of the formation used. The motion can change the defensive support system

—1986 Summer Manual. Coach MacPherson was head coach at Syracuse University.

The Wishbone-T Triple Option
DARRELL ROYAL

The Wishbone-T formation is not an original idea with the University of Texas. It's a combination of offensive concepts we pulled together.

Homer Rice fooled around with something similar years back. Then the University of Houston had fantastic success with the triple option. And we noticed Texas A&M's success running a form of triple option with a tight fullback. So we took a little bit here, and a little bit there, and came up with an offense that worked well for our personnel.

Some writers have asked us what we called it and we said, "Well, actually we don't have a name for it. We don't call it anything." They said, "Well, don't you think you ought to call it something?" "Well, I guess it is a good idea to call it something, but I don't know what to call it." They said, "Why don't you call it a Y. Your backfield is like that." Then someone else said, "Why don't you call it a Wishbone. It's the shape of a wishbone." And I said, "That's good enough." So that's the way the Wishbone-T got its name.

Choosing the Wishbone

There are three reasons why we use this formation. First, we wanted to maintain at least one split receiver at all times. We wanted a player in the offense who was a threat to run pass routes and catch the football. Thus, our line of scrimmage was to be a balanced line with one end split and the other end in tight alignment.

The next thing we had to decide was how to develop a sound running game toward the split end side. The play that was decided on was the triple option.

The third thing we needed to decide was the alignment of the backs. Our personnel was such that we wanted to utilize the running abilities of the backs that we had, none of which were wingback types. We also wanted to establish a basic offense that was mirrored (which posed a constant threat to both sides) and balanced so that the abilities of all our backs could complement one another. Since the option was to be our basic play,

we aligned the backs in the positions we thought would be the most conducive to consistent execution of the triple option. Thus, we came up with the formation that is commonly referred to as the Wishbone-T (see Figure 1). The line splits are very important for the triple option to be successful.

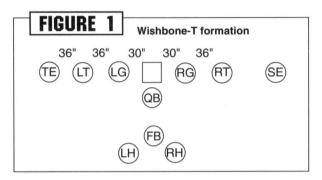

FIGURE 1 Wishbone-T formation

Guards—2' constant split (four-point stance)
Tackles—2' to 4' variable split (four-point stance)
Tight end—2' to 4' variable split (four-point stance; will flip-flop)
Split end—8 to 14 yards variable split (three-point stance; will flip-flop)
Fullback—directly behind center, heels 13' from ball (four-point stance)
Halfbacks—18" right and left of fullback and 15" deep to fullback (three-point stance)

Variations

To supplement our basic formation we decided on what we call the "counter" formation (see Figure 2). We know there are times when we'd want more than one deployed receiver. Our backs were se-

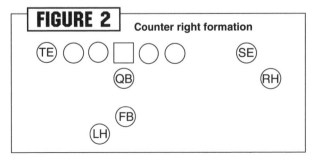

FIGURE 2 Counter right formation

lected as runners and blockers, not as receivers, but this alignment forced defenses to honor them as receivers, without our having to teach them to run a lot of routes or be dependent on them as primary receivers. From this formation we could still maintain the triple option to both sides.

We also decided on a third formation—a pro formation, shown in Figure 3. Against certain defenses this formation allowed us to get our split end on a 3-deep halfback one-on-one and still keep our running attack as a constant threat.

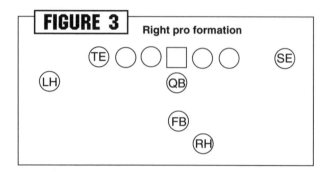

FIGURE 3   Right pro formation

Our Basic Triple Option

Here are the basic assignments on our triple option play:

Ends—Force. Always responsible for No. 1 (the man covering the deep third).
Tackles—Inside.
Guards—No. 1 LOS inside tackle.
Center—Base.
Lead halfback—Arc at 8 or 9. No. 2 from outside (the man who must take the pitch). Break straight laterally for the first three steps and start arc for the outside leg of No. 2. Takes as aggressive an angle as possible.
Trailing halfback—Break straight parallel at maximum speed, ride the outside hip of the lead halfback, and cut off his block.
Fullback—Break at maximum speed on direct path for guard-tackle gap. As ball is placed in your stomach, take a soft hold on the ball and continue on veer course. If quarterback leaves ball, run with it. If he takes ball out of pocket, continue on course and become a blocker on inside pursuit. Path must always be outside the block of the OT.

Quarterback—Open step with near foot on 45-degree angle. Pick up fullback with split vision, and place ball in fullback's pocket at earliest point. Stay down and work with extended arm. First option takes place on ride with the fullback from right to left (decision area). Key the first man inside the defensive end and react as follows: (a) key doesn't take the fullback—leave ball with the fullback, and (b) key takes the fullback—pull ball out and go to outside option. The outside option key is the defensive end, and react as follows: freeze, force, and pitch the ball (see Figure 4) or take the obvious keep.

These assignments hold true in most situations. Different defenses will force us to block differently. We'll make calls and adjust at the line of scrimmage. Whatever we call, for the play to be successful our linemen must create a lane between guard and tackle.

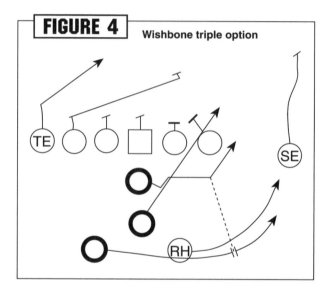

FIGURE 4   Wishbone triple option

If we're having trouble reading keys for the option, we call the fullback handoff play with blocking. Or, if we want the outside option, we call it and go to the outside, faking first to the fullback, then optioning the outside man with the keep or pitch. The fullback knows that he will not get the ball, so he should be a key blocker on the linebacker.

—1970 Proceedings. Coach Royal was head coach at the University of Texas.

Wishbone Trap and Trap Option Package

CHARLIE TAAFFE

We're a Wishbone team on offense, which means we primarily run the football, and approximately 60 to 65% of our rushing attack is based on the triple option. The triple option is where our offense begins, but we've also felt the need to develop a package that complements our base offense.

It's imperative to prevent the defense from scheming methods to remove our fullback as a running threat. In the Wishbone, the fullback *must* run with the ball. Over the years, we have had to devise ways for our fullback to be a factor in the offense—the triple option is not enough! The trap and trap-option series has given us a consistent method of keeping the fullback involved.

The Fullback Trap

The FB trap is a consistent play that can be executed against most defenses. Generally, we will trap the first defensive lineman past the center and have the ability to change the direction of the play at the LOS based on the alignment of the defensive front (see Figure 1, a and b). We don't prefer to trap a four-defender side.

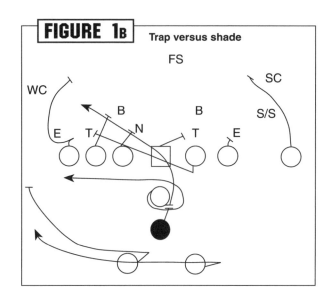

FIGURE 1B — Trap versus shade

If we elect to trap an A gap defender, we add the term "goal line" to our trap play (see Figure 2). This play allows us to trap most goal-line defenses and to assist the fullback in knowing where the trap will occur.

The fullback aligns with his heels 5 1/2 yards from the front tip of the ball. This could vary

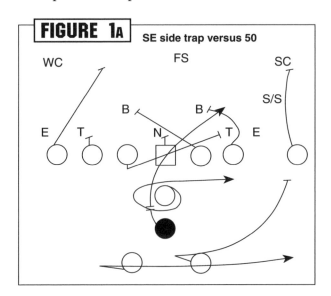

FIGURE 1A — SE side trap versus 50

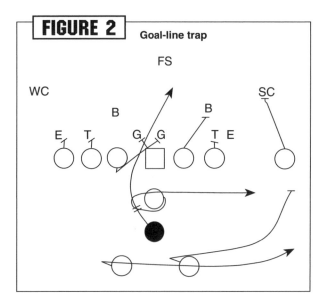

FIGURE 2 — Goal-line trap

slightly, depending on the speed of the fullback. The fullback should know prior to the snap where the trap will occur, based on the defensive alignments. On the snap, the fullback will run an S course, putting the playside foot in front of the offside foot (crossover). It's important that the fullback does not step outside the offside foot. We'd like the FB to stay tight to any down block—stay inside out of the trap block and break off the block on the playside LB.

The quarterback executes a full turn (360 degrees), or "whirlybird" action. We prefer this action because of the holding effect it has on the linebackers and FS. On the snap, the QB will reverse pivot slightly past six o'clock. His second step (balance step) must insure that his shoulders will be perpendicular to the LOS. The third step is a ride and follow the fullback—turn to the inside, sink the mesh, and carry out the option fake.

The Trap Option

Once the trap has been established and LBs begin to step up on play recognition, the defense makes itself vulnerable to the trap option. The QB action and subsequent mesh with the FB has the potential to freeze the LBs and FS. When this occurs, it's time to run the option off the trap fake. The backfield action is identical to the trap —everything must look the same (see Figure 3, a and b).

A good coaching point for the QB is to sneak a peak at the pitch key on the first step. The whirlybird action allows the QB to accomplish this, since he doesn't have his back to the pitch key on the first step. This is particularly helpful to the open end side!

The pitch back can also assist the QB by recognizing hard pressure and making a call to the QB as the stunt is recognized. The line blocking is identical to the trap—on the trap option, we "log" the same defender who is trapped on the trap play. This has the potential to create conflict for the defensive lineman.

The trap option gives us a misdirection type of option play that has an excellent "freeze" effect on the LBs and free safety. It's imperative to establish the FB trap in order for the trap option to be successful.

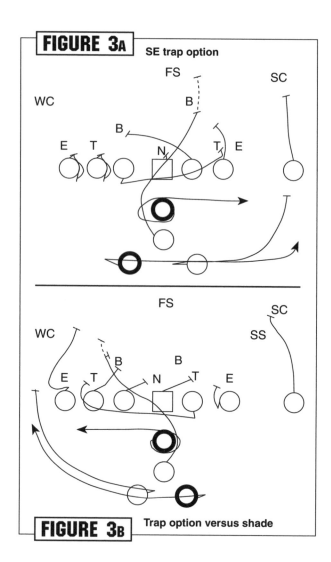

FIGURE 3A   SE trap option

FIGURE 3B   Trap option versus shade

The Trap-Option Pass

This is an excellent series because the pass look is identical to the trap and trap option. When we throw off the trap-option series, we have specific ideas in mind—we want to control the pitch support on the option and take advantage of a fast flow LB. Two routes that accomplish these objectives are shown in Figure 4, a and b.

This series has been a supplement to our Wishbone triple option attack. The trap has kept our fullback as a threat in the offense; the trap option provides a misdirection option with tremendous freeze potential on the LB and FS, and the trap-option pass has taken advantage of a secondary which aggressively supports against the option phases of the series.

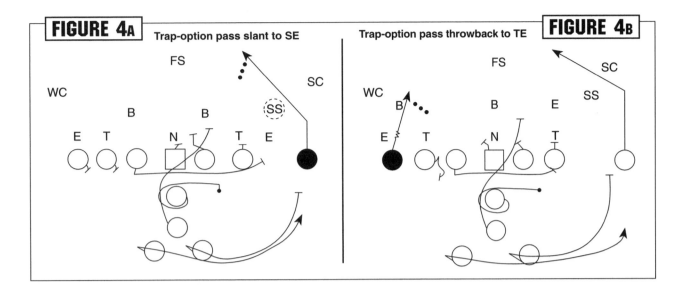

FIGURE 4A Trap-option pass slant to SE

FIGURE 4B Trap-option pass throwback to TE

—1993 Summer Manual. Coach Taaffe is assistant coach for the Montreal Alouettes.

The Flexbone Offense
FISHER DeBERRY

Without good players, it makes no difference what offensive formation you line up in. For whatever success we've had, we're indebted to our players, their execution, and their belief in our offense.

There's no magic in the term "Flexbone." The origin of this term came from our Sports Information Department two years ago when Coach Ken Hatfield remarked at a preseason press conference that we would try to be more "flexible" in our attack from the Wishbone. Actually, the Flexbone is nothing but the 3-back, 2-split end Wishbone offense, with the halfbacks positioned one yard behind and one yard outside of our tackles.

The Wishbone has been criticized for not being a good pass formation, particularly in long-yardage situations. Under my former head coach, Jim Brakefield, at Appalachian State University, we used this set for our long-yardage and 2-minute offense, because it gave us four quick receivers on the line of scrimmage and it tended to spread the defense out a little more and diverted their concentration from the run game to the pass game. Therefore, when we started to toy with this formation at the Academy, we felt we could incorporate our run offense from it just as well as our pass offense.

Being an old secondary coach, I've always felt that play-action passing was the toughest to defend. Therefore, the concept was to use this attack to run our base offense and, hopefully, make the defense a little softer for the run. The offense could also make our pass offense look exactly like our running plays, and give us more opportunities on third-and-long (hopefully, running the Wishbone you won't be in this situation too often) and in our hurry-up offense.

Reasons for Option Offense

We believe in the option offense because it's:

- unique in a pass-oriented league,
- difficult for our opponents to gain familiarity with in a week's preparation time, and
- an offense that doesn't require you to knock everybody off the line of scrimmage, but allows you to "read" the defense's commitment.

For these reasons the offense gives our players an excellent chance to be successful, because normally we don't measure up to the physical standards of our opponents. We must depend on speed and quickness.

If you don't "read" the offense almost every snap, then you're defeating the purpose of using it. Repetition is the key to being successful in the execution of *any* offense, and we don't have a lot of meeting time with our players, due to their heavy academic demands. Therefore, the offense suits our limited practice time because we don't have to make a lot of changes from week to week.

The triple option, shown in Figure 1, is our base play. We read the first man outside our guard. Versus a 50, 6-1, or offset defense, we'd read the defensive tackle. Against a 4-3 defense, we'd read the defensive end for the handoff key to our FB. The real key to the execution of this play is the timing of the slotbacks getting into the same relationship as they would be from the regular Wishbone.

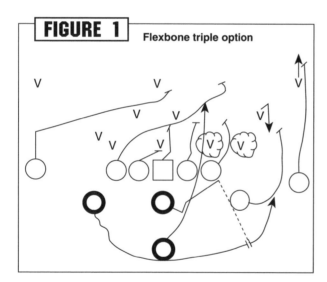

FIGURE 1 Flexbone triple option

If you overshift your defense, our QB will be alert to run away from your strength, and we might also employ one of our eight-man front blocking schemes and carry the second option into the secondary. There are several ways you can block the front and we adjust game to game.

Play-Action Pass

We want to establish play-action passes from all our base plays, because we're going to be primarily a rushing team, and this type of passing is the toughest to defend if you're having to defend the run so hard. We want the pass from the base op-

tion play to look *exactly* like the run, and we feel this creates a lot of one-on-one coverage, which is all you ever want in any passing game. This attack also allows us to use only one pass protection, thus reducing our practice time on pass protection.

The slotback run-or-pass option complements the base option and will really put the rover or cornerback in no-man's-land (see Figure 2). The slot simply reads the coverage and its reaction to

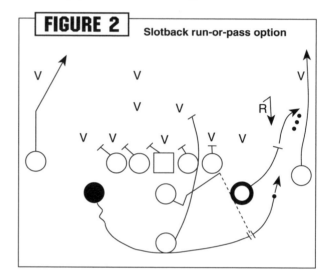

FIGURE 2 Slotback run-or-pass option

the support of the option. If the support hangs, he runs it; if the support comes, he merely drops it over his head. You can designate who to throw the ball to by adding the term HB or X to the call, and that way if the deep coverage is releasing fast on the potential run, you have a deep pass with blocking support in front of the passer.

The down-the-line frontside hook route in Figure 3 is one of our favorites. You're almost assured of having one-on-one coverage on the split

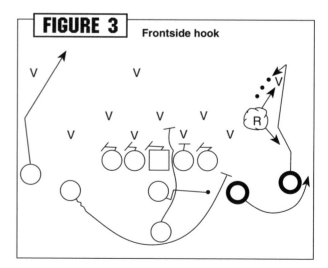

FIGURE 3 Frontside hook

end if the defense is supporting the run as it should and if your run game is effective. The key to the play is a 13 comeback to 11-yard hook, and the QB must make it look just like the option. He reads the rover for his release.

The backside hook is the next progression when the defense is overplaying the run and reacting very quickly (see Figure 4). You should end up with one-on-one coverage on the backside also, and the QB will read the drop off LB whether to go to the SE on a 15 comeback to 13-yard post hook or to the flare back. This gives you some misdirection to your offense and should slow the defense down so you can get more mileage out of your option.

These are the sequences of passes off the base option. Of course, there are many frontside and backside routes you can build off of. The main coaching point is that it all must look like the

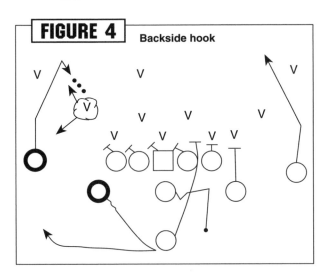

FIGURE 4 Backside hook

option running play, and the players must add a lot of "acting" and deception to their maneuvers. Also, you will probably want to consider misdirection running plays, because the defense will probably show the tendency to run with your motion from this set.

You can see that this is a complete package of the triple option from a double-slot or Flexbone set. The defense must also be ready to contend with and defend the pull-up and sprint-out pass game from this alignment. Therefore, you have the defense off-balance in normal situations and still have a good third-and-long and 2-minute offense formation.

—1984 Summer Manual. Coach DeBerry is head coach at the Air Force Academy.

The Double Wing-T Package
HAROLD "TUBBY" RAYMOND

The Delaware Wing-T has always been series or sequence football, threatening several points of attack as it flows toward a particular flank. This style of offense creates defensive conflicts and involves packages of plays.

Formations create blocking angles as well as tactically place eligible receivers and, of course, every formation has two flanks. Traditionally, our formations fell into two categories: those with tight end and wing (see Figure 1), and those with a slot (see Figure 2).

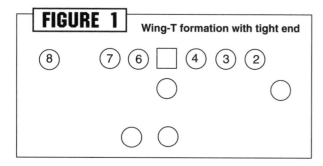

FIGURE 1 Wing-T formation with tight end

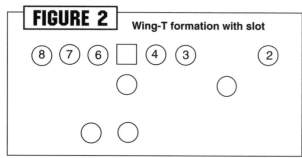

FIGURE 2 Wing-T formation with slot

Double-Wing Formation

An effective addition for us was the double-wing formation that has a strong running-game potential yet encourages the use of the pass (see Figure 3). This formation gives us a 4-back running attack from a 1-back formation. It has a wing at one flank and a wide slot at the other, giving us the advantages of our other two most effective formations.

Our game plan is to direct attack flow toward a selected flank or flanks. In the formulation of a plan, we select plays that have a good chance of driving the ball in areas that are defended by play-

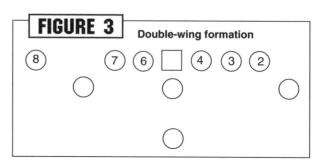

FIGURE 3 Double-wing formation

ers who have dual responsibilities or conflicting defensive assignments. For example, a flank that is supported by a defensive man who must also cover the flat, or an end who must seal and contain, may be particularly vulnerable. Plays that have a reasonable chance of making 4 yards are called primary plays and may become "short-listed" on our game plan. Short-listed plays that are related and flow toward a particular flank are called "play packages."

At one flank we have the traditional tight-end wing that provides excellent blocking angles on No. 3, while the two receivers at the wide slot on the other flank make it difficult for No. 4 to create a hard corner to the wing. We will attack from this formation in three ways: with short motion attacking either flank, with extended motion to either flank, or with no motion at all. Now let's examine the flank defense to the wing against a typical seven-man front (see Figure 4). Player 3

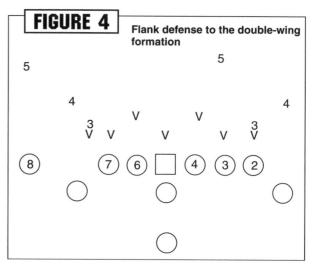

FIGURE 4 Flank defense to the double-wing formation

is outflanked by our wing, yet he must be ready to seal the end's shoulder, protect himself from being blocked down by the wing, and still contain the quarterback. Player 4 is off the line.

Double Wing-T Package

Using our "package theory," here is a typical series of plays to each flank, beginning to the wing. We'll run the two traditional plays to the wing: the power sweep and the buck sweep.

The power sweep forces the end to meet strength while pursuit from the defensive front is picked up with the tackle and guard "over blocking" and the end's consciousness of the scraping linebacker (see Figure 5).

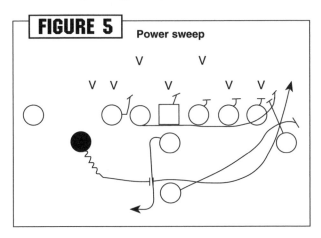

Blocking for the buck sweep forces both the defensive end and tackle to be aware of a block down on them while being threatened by companion trap plays (see Figure 6).

The next play in this wing package is the quick trap on the end. The pressure of the sweep to the wing makes the defensive end (3) vulnerable for this quick fullback trap with blocking related to

the buck sweep. Remember, the end is threatened by the block down from the wingback.

The tight end "reads down" (i.e., he will move toward the defensive tackle and if he is closing down with his tackle's down movement, the end will move up to block the backer). The tackle blocks down, moving into position to block the defensive tackle if he stunts down, the linebacker if he plugs, or the noseman if he charges. The guard pulls and traps the end inside out. The quarterback hands the ball off to the fullback slanting over the right tackle's outside foot (see Figure 7).

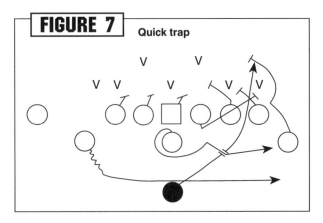

The next play in this package is the "down option." The tackle and end start to block down as blocking the trap, but the tight end quickly moves up to block the backer. The tackle blocks down again and the onside guard logs 3. The quarterback again reverse pivots and fakes the ball to the fullback, who will carry this fake and block the defensive tackle. The quarterback executes the option on 4 of keeping upfield or pitching to the left half (see Figure 8).

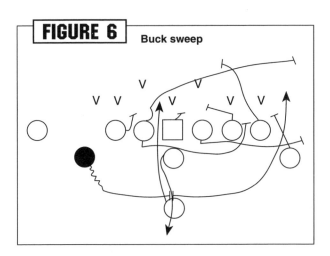

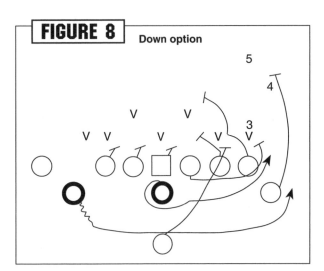

The pass from this option play has been equally effective as the run. The right half releases with width and looks over his outside shoulder. The end moves to block down, delays two counts, then releases into the deep flat at a 45-degree angle (see Figure 9).

This pass will be thrown from behind the right tackle at a depth of 3 to 6 yards, depending upon how long the quarterback is able to threaten the flank executing the run-pass option aspect of the play.

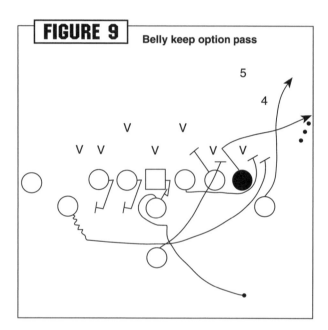

FIGURE 9   Belly keep option pass

Wide-Side Flank

Now let's look at the wide-side flank and a package of plays that flows to that flank. We like the option to this flank, as opposed to power sweep or blocked sweep, because we don't like the idea of our wingback having to block a tackle.

When running the trap option to this spread flank, the spread end's assignment is to crack on 4 if he is inverted, and if not, release outside and stalk No. 5. The wing's assignment begins with checking 4. If 4 rotates quickly and leaves the area that would allow the spread end to crack on him, the wing must block 4. If not, the wing will flare and stalk 5 (see Figure 10).

The fullback bends his path around the quarterback, fakes the trap aspect of the trap option, and keeps his hands over an imaginary ball. After the second deliberate step away from the center, the quarterback completes his pivot and runs directly at 3, executing pitch-keep option.

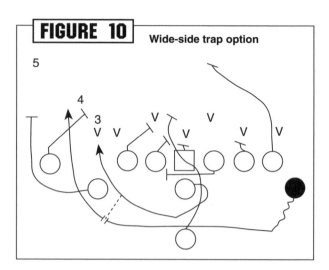

FIGURE 10   Wide-side trap option

Trap-Option Pass

The trap-option pass is the next play in the package. The protection is simple and the options work right off the basic play.

The spread end begins his crack path on 4, anticipates his support action against the option, then turns up field, being careful not to move into the coverage of the free safety. The slotback flares and immediately looks over his inside shoulder. The left half leaves in motion, develops a pitch relationship with the quarterback, and will either get a pitch or continue in the pattern as wide as the field will allow, with little depth.

The quarterback reverse pivots with two steps exactly as when executing the trap option, and allows his head and shoulders to complete the pivot so he can determine as quickly as possible what 4 is doing. If 4 reads the trap-option threat and begins to support, the spread end should be open and the quarterback will hit him quickly (see Figure 11). If the cornerback suspects a pass

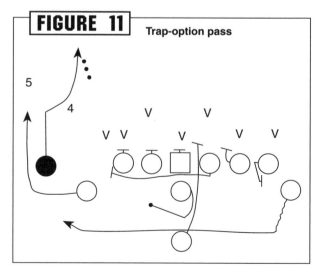

FIGURE 11   Trap-option pass

and covers the spread end, the flaring right half may be open. If both 4 and 5 drop with the release, the quarterback may execute the option of either pitching the ball or keeping it.

We've probably used the trap-option pass as much as the option itself, with a great deal of success. Once we are able to predict the defensive reaction to the trap option, the pass may become an attack all by itself.

The Trap Play

The final play in this package is, of course, the trap itself. When the defensive tackle becomes anxious to pursue the option or rush the passer and doesn't close down without tackle's movement or stunts outside, he becomes vulnerable to the trap.

Against even spacing, the tackle will lead down on the defensive tackle then move up to block the backer. Against odd spacing, he will take a lateral step inside, avoiding contact with the defensive tackle, then move up to block the backer. The guard will post even spacing or lead versus odd spacing. The center will block the area against even or post against odd. When posting the noseman, the center must be aware of the offside

backer in case he blitzes. The guard traps and the offside tackle pulls down to seal the front before blocking back on the defensive tackle.

The fullback now has position priority as the quarterback reverse pivots. The fullback dives for the right foot of the center, and the quarterback will move across the midline as he hands the ball off (see Figure 12).

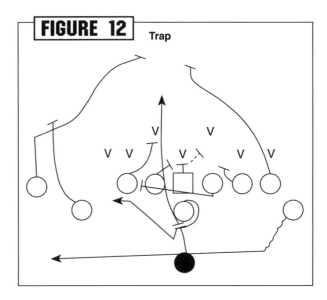

FIGURE 12 Trap

—1982 Summer Manual. Coach Raymond is head coach at the University of Delaware.

Controlling the Ball With the Pass

BILL WALSH

My philosophy has been to control the ball with the forward pass. To do that we have to have versatility—versatility in the action and types of passes thrown by the quarterback.

Dropback Passes

We like the dropback pass. We use a three-step drop pattern, but more often we will use a five-step drop pattern of timed patterns down the field. From there we go to a seven-step drop. When our quarterback takes a seven-step drop, he's allowing the receivers time to maneuver down the field. Therefore, we will use a three-step drop pattern when we are throwing a quickout or hitch or slant which, by and large, the defense is allowing you to complete by their alignment or by their coverage.

The five-step drop pattern for the quarterback calls for a disciplined pattern by the receiver. He runs that pattern the same way every time. He doesn't maneuver to beat the defensive back.

Too often in college football, either the quarterback is standing there waiting for the receiver, or the receiver has broken before the quarterback can throw the ball. These are the biggest flaws you will see in the forward pass. Now when the receiver breaks before the ball can be thrown, the defensive back can adjust to the receiver. Any time the quarterback holds the ball waiting for the receiver to break, the defensive back sees it and breaks on the receiver. So the time pattern is vital.

Play-Action Passes

You can't just dropback pass. You have to be able to keep the defense from zeroing in on your approach. That's why the play pass is vital. By and large, the play-action pass will score the touchdown. The dropback pass will control the ball.

For play-action passing, we have certain blocking fundamentals that we use. We will show different backfield actions with basically the same

offensive line blocking. We will go to the play pass as often as we can, especially as we get to the opponent's 25-yard line.

Action Pass

The third category of pass that most people use is what we call the action pass, where your quarterback moves outside. There are a couple of reasons for moving outside. One certainly is to avoid the inside pass rush. For a dropback passing team we'll sprint—or "waggle" as we call it—outside to avoid blitzers who approach straight up the field on us. The other advantage is to bring yourself closer to the potential receiver.

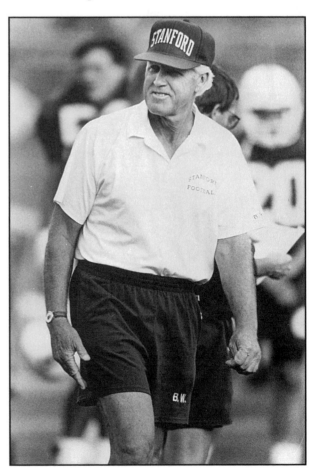

We'll get outside to throw the ball and get ourselves closer to the man we want to throw to. When you can get outside, the trajectory of the ball can be flatter because normally there isn't a man between you and the receiver.

The versatility also includes changing your formations. We continuously change receiver width and spacing. We seldom will line up our receiver with the same spacing on two or three plays in a row. If we want to throw the ball to the outside, we will reduce the split of the receiver. We need running room to the outside. We don't want the ball in the air very long. If we want to throw inside, we will extend the split of our receivers, so that there is more maneuvering room to the inside, and spread the defense. Our backs, as many teams know, will cheat to get where they have to be. We know that if we throw to backs, the first thing on their mind is how to release out of the backfield. We are quite willing to move the man to get the release and sometimes telegraph what we are doing. We are quite willing to do that with the idea that when we want to break a given tendency, we simply line them up there and run something else.

We will vary the split of the receivers according to the pattern and the coverage and, of course, to add versatility. The biggest problem you will have in the forward pass is when you have to throw the ball a number of times and, with a very limited inventory, you begin to throw the same pattern over and over. You get into trouble.

The argument that you will throw the interception has to be qualified with how much you know about the forward passing game versus the running game. In our last game, our opponent fumbled five times, and we threw no interceptions. That might have been the difference in the game.

Play Selection

One of the factors involved with our success years ago with the Cincinnati Bengals was that we would begin to set a game plan for the opening of the game. We continued that at Stanford. In a given game, say, for instance, against Southern California, we ran the first 12 plays we had decided on in order. Of course, we ran out of lists because the first 12 worked and none worked after that. But the point is we went 12 plays in order, right down the line. We went eight straight games scoring the first time we had the ball.

By the time we have completed 8 to 10 plays, we've forced the opponent to adjust to a number of things. We've kept him off balance with the type of thing we were doing, and we pretty much established in a given series what we would come to next.

That's a good approach to offensive football. It forces you to go into that game with a certain calmness. You know where you're going, rather than having to say, "What in the hell do we do now?" Occasionally planned plays don't work, but we keep going. We don't change; we don't worry about it. We try to create an effect on our opponent. The effect is that he feels he has to adjust. We present different looks and dilemmas. We run the ball right at him. We throw the ball over his head. Meanwhile, because we know what the play is, we readily see what their adjustments are. We try to get a line on their first down defenses, but we take it from there.

In Scoring Territory

I have seen many teams march the ball beautifully, but right around the 15-yard line, they are already warming up their placekicker, because right at that point defenses change, the field they can operate in changes, and suddenly their basic offense goes all to pieces.

My contention is that if we are on their 25, we're going for the end zone. Failing at that, we will kick a field goal. In an evenly matched game, I don't want to try to take the ball from their 25 to the goal line by trying to smash it through people, because three out of four times, you won't make it. Unless you are superior. Of course, if you are vastly superior it makes very little difference how you do it.

Why? First, every defensive coach in the country is going to his blitzes about right there. The pass coverage, by and large, will be man-to-man coverage. We know that if they don't blitz one down, they're going to blitz the next down. Automatically. They'll seldom blitz twice in a row, but they'll blitz every other down. If we go a series where there haven't been blitzes on the first two downs, here comes the safety blitz on the third down. So we are looking, at that point, to get into the end zone.

By the style of our football, we'll have somebody to get the ball to a little bit late—just as an outlet to get 4 or 5 yards, to try to keep it. But from the 25 to the 10, we're going for the end zone.

Midfield

Between our own 10-yard line and the opponent's 25, we operate our field offense. We know that on first down our ball-control passing is vital. By and large, on first-and-10 you'll get a 2-deep zone—zone-type defense. We can drop the ball off to a back late and still make 4 to 5 yards. Those 4 or 5 yards are as important to us as some other team making the same on an option play.

You often will see us run with the ball on second-and-10, because we want 5 yards. If you run a basic running play, you can get your 5.

At third-and-5, we are right back with a ball-control pass, dumping to a back, and we're making it. If we can make 30 first downs a game, we'll win.

Short Yardage

We have standard passes to throw against a goal-line defense. Too often people try to go in there and butt heads with good linebackers on the goal line. Too often they don't make it.

If we get inside that 5-yard line, half the time we are going to throw the ball. Now, if you're marching through somebody, you can just close your eyes and hand the ball off. But when it's very competitive, that goal-line pass is vital. So we have a series of those. We never call them anywhere else on the field.

When we are around their 35-yard line in a short-yardage situation, if we don't see somebody standing deep down the middle, we're probably going to go for the six points.

To make it on third-and-1 we will often throw to a back out of the backfield. Third-and-3 is the toughest of all to make. We have a certain list of runs and a certain list of passes. When we have a third-and-3, we don't grope. We go to it.

Ball-Control Passing

Don't isolate throwing the forward pass to a given down and distance. If you are going to throw the ball, you must be willing to throw on first down, not a token pass hoping for the best, but a pass that is designed to get you a certain amount of yardage.

In our ball-control passing, we will use the five-step drop pattern on first down, because we know, through the drilling of our quarterback, that we can get 4 or 5 dropping the ball off to a back, who is an outlet, or to a tight end. So we are quite willing to throw a ball-control pass on first down,

and then go to our seven-step drop maneuvering pattern on third down. As you can see, most of our offense is based on ball-control passes, no matter what the situation.

Figure 1 shows you a ball-control pass that Sid Gilman may have developed some time ago. It's one of the most effective forward passes we've used.

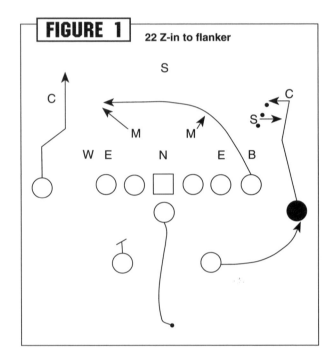

FIGURE 1   22 Z-in to flanker

22 Z-In

This is a five-step drop pattern. The quarterback takes five big steps and a hitch step and throws on time. The receiver splits 12 to 14 yards. The flanker releases inside for 5 to 6 yards and then bursts hard to the outside foot of the cornerback. What he wants to do is to get that cornerback on his heels. Then he'll turn in about three steps and catch the pass 12 yards deep.

The fullback runs what we call a scat pattern. He doesn't have any pickup, and he releases to the outside. He never catches the ball more than 2 yards past the line of scrimmage, most often right at the line of scrimmage. If the backer blitzes, he looks for the ball early.

Our tight end picks off the near end backer. He'll put his head past that man's shoulder, slow down, and make contact. He bounces off it and goes to the far guard position, turns and faces the quarterback, and watches his eyes because he's the last outlet.

The quarterback throws the ball related to the sky safety. If the safety gives ground, he'll throw to the fullback. If the safety flattens out, we'll throw in behind him, in this case to the flanker. If it's man-to-man, the flanker runs a man-to-man pattern trying to beat the corner. If it's man-to-man, the safety will often chase the tight end, and there will be a good throwing lane with the backer coming out on the fullback.

When we throw to the fullback (see Figure 2) the ball should arrive to him a foot in front of his number. If the fullback has to reach, he will take his eyes off the ball, slow down or break stride, and probably get nothing out of it.

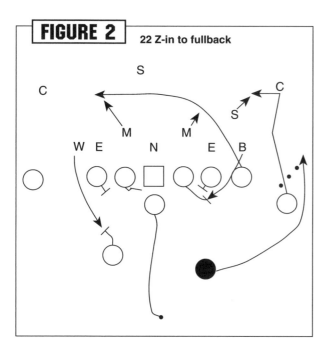

FIGURE 2   22 Z-in to fullback

When he catches it, he goes up the sideline. We tell our backs, "You want the sideline." The reason is that only one man can tackle you at a time, and he often underestimates a ball-carrier along the sideline. What we are after on 22 Z-in is a 7- to 9-yard gain to the fullback, or a 12-yard gain to the flanker. The fullback gets it about two out of three times.

If the two primary receivers are covered, our quarterback will come back and look at the tight end. As soon as the tight end sees the quarterback's eyes, he slides laterally for the pass (see Figure 3).

We have several other options off our 22 action, depending on the defense. We have a Z-in with fullback motion, a circle-out with our flanker, and a Y-out with the tight end. The key to the pass is the fullback. He should average 7 to 8 yards a catch. That's what we mean by ball-control passing.

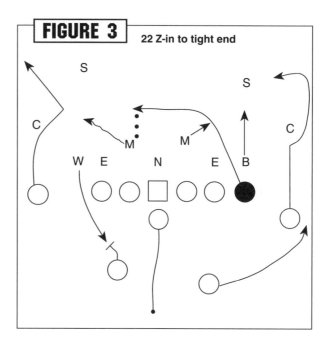

FIGURE 3   22 Z-in to tight end

Out Pattern

The out pattern is a timed pattern thrown from a five-step drop. On a timed pattern, a quarterback does not take a hitch step.

The receiver goes straight up the field as close to full speed as he can. At 10 yards he crosses over and breaks out. He catches the ball at 12 (see Figure 4). The SP doesn't care about the coverage, other than if they roll up, he runs a seam. He doesn't care where the defensive back is located, and he doesn't change his angle of release. He just runs the pattern.

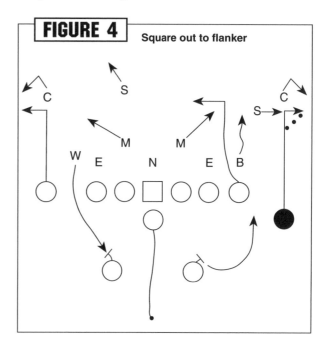

FIGURE 4   Square out to flanker

The quarterback decides prior to the snap and just after the snap whether he's going to throw him the ball or not. The quarterback takes five quick steps. Notice I said five big steps in the Z-in. Now that we're throwing out, the QB takes five *quick* steps. He can't lead the receiver with the pass because any time you lead a receiver who is running parallel to the ball, he'll never catch up to the ball.

Throw right at the man's hip. If you throw into his body, the defensive back doesn't have any way to get to it. What we are trying to get here is the defensive back giving ground this way and then losing lateral ground this way. That's on single coverage.

On this particular pattern both receivers do the same thing, but I would say most often the flanker gets it. The tight end takes an inside release, goes straight up the field, and runs a full speed crossing pattern, but never crosses the ball. The tight end on his basic crossing pattern is the one you go to on man-under defense. If a team is running man-under, that kind of an out is suicide. So if our quarterback sees inside-out coverage on wide receivers, reasonably close, his drop now goes right to the tight end; he's looking for the tight end to beat a man-under linebacker.

M Pattern

The backs play a key role. They check the backers on a blitz. After reading for the blitz, the back runs what we call an M pattern.

In the M pattern, the back moves 1 1/2 to 2 yards back from his blocking position. When he is 6 yards deep and 3 yards outside the offensive tackle, he turns upfield looking for the M pattern.

On the M pattern, the weak linebacker—some call him a defensive end—takes away the square out, we hold the ball, and pop it right off to the halfback (see Figure 5).

There's also a tight end option off the double square-out pattern. As you can see in Figure 6, when both middle linebackers cover backs to the outside, and blitz one man, this isolates our tight end on a backer. He has a good chance of beating the backer.

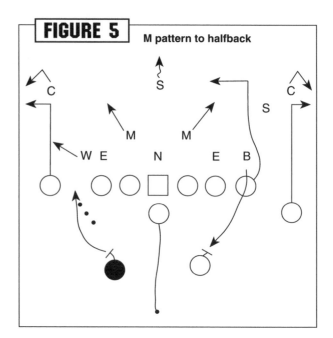

FIGURE 5 — M pattern to halfback

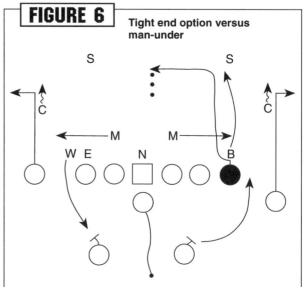

FIGURE 6 — Tight end option versus man-under

Hook Pattern

Now let's look at the seven-step drop pattern. This is one play that we've almost worn out.

On a seven-step drop pattern, our receivers will maneuver. We're going to run a blue left for us, a right, which is motion, and we're going to run a 79, which is weak flow pass protection. Now X is going to run a pattern on the weak side (see Figure 7).

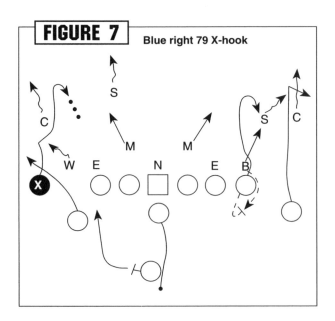

FIGURE 7 Blue right 79 X-hook

You vary the width of the receiver. He may be 1 yard split or he may be 12 yards split, depending on which linebacker we are trying to beat. X works up the field, gets past the man who has short coverage, and turns in. We tell him to get past the W and beat the M.

On this pattern we tell our receiver that he must go at least 12 yards and never more than 18 yards on the hook. Not because he can't get open, but because the quarterback can't wait that long to throw. A lot of it is predicated on pass rush. We say never less than 12, because we can't have a hook develop at 12 when our quarterback takes seven steps.

—1979 Proceedings. Coach Walsh was offensive consultant for the San Francisco 49ers.

A Simple and Flexible Passing Game
HERB MEYER

We've been an I-formation team since the mid-'60s, utilizing the pro, slot, twins, and power sets (see Figure 1, a–d). Philosophically, we are primarily a running team but feel that in order to move the ball consistently, we must: (a) have offensive line communication, (b) be able to trap, and (c) be able to throw the ball.

Being able to throw the ball doesn't mean just throwing it, but rather being prepared to do so whenever it best complements your running at

FIGURE 1B Slot right

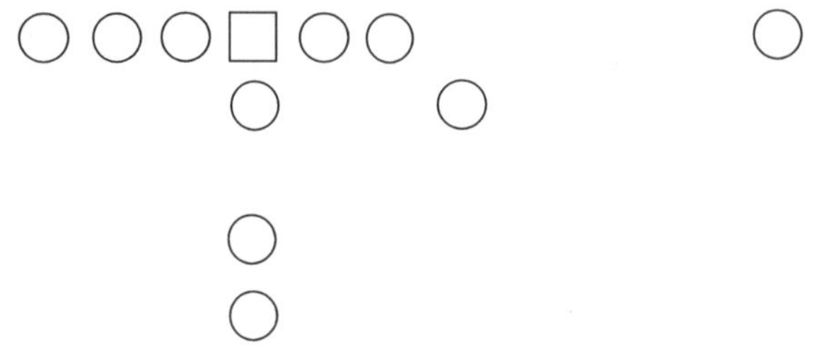

FIGURE 1A Pro right

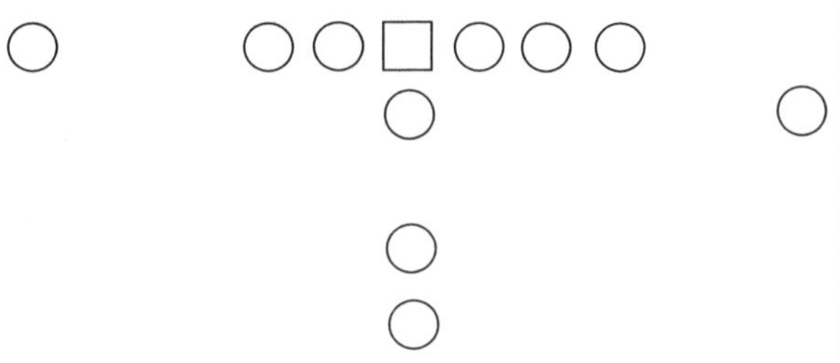

FIGURE 1C Twins right

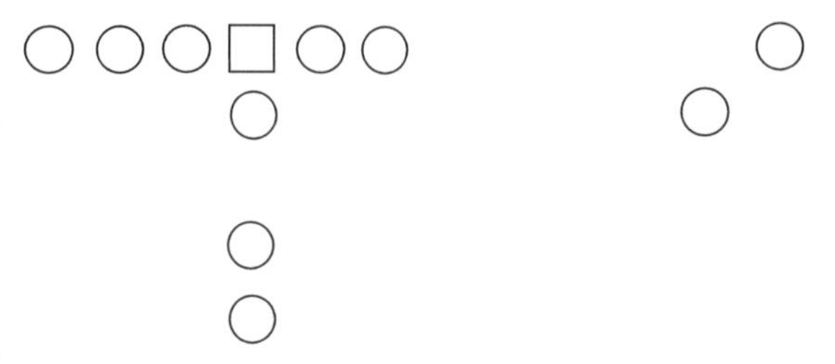

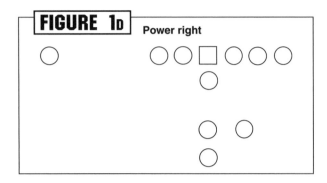

FIGURE 1D   Power right

tack. It also means being able to throw when you have to in the 2-minute situations and when you're trying to play catch-up.

Our emphasis on the passing game varied from year to year with the ability of our quarterback. We used all phases of the passing game—dropback, sprint-out, play-action, quick passes, and bootlegs—but in a haphazard fashion. As defenses became more sophisticated and put greater pressure on the running game, it became apparent that we'd have to do a better job of coordinating and integrating our passing attack.

To pick up some ideas, we spent two off-seasons contacting colleges that ran the I and had successful passing offenses. It was during this time that we first became acquainted with Paul Hackett, who was recruiting our area. Since then, he's had the greatest influence on our thinking as it applies to passing the football.

Spread Formation

Paul showed us the virtue of utilizing the spread set (see Figure 2) in the obvious passing situation and how it could facilitate both the quick passing game and the sprint-out pass. We adopted the quick-pass series from the spread—both sides running the same patterns off five-step cuts, with the quarterback using a three-step drop. Our outside receivers always line up with their outside foot back.

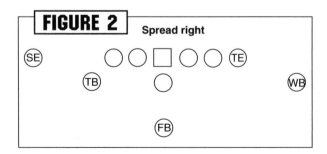

FIGURE 2   Spread right

The double look-in (see Figure 3) and the double quick-out (see Figure 4) are just two of the patterns we use. On both plays the outside receivers make their break on the fifth step. The quarterback must decide, with a pre-snap read, which side he will throw to; he then has a key to throw off of, to that side.

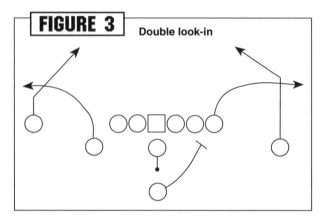

FIGURE 3   Double look-in

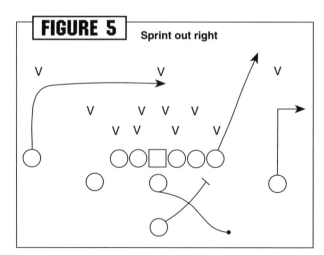

FIGURE 4   Double quick out

The spread also allowed us to audibilize our sprint out at the line to take advantage of defensive rotation (see Figure 5).

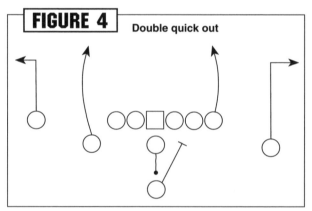

FIGURE 5   Sprint out right

The USC passing attack philosophy is to balance power running with "read passing." The Trojans *never* ask the quarterback to run with the ball. Since we'd incorporated various option plays with our basic I-formation running attack, we didn't feel we could spend the necessary time to perfect a pure "reading" pass game. However, with the balance of the spread formation, we could expand the quick-pass theory with a five-step, dropback game. Our primary pattern is shown in Figure 6.

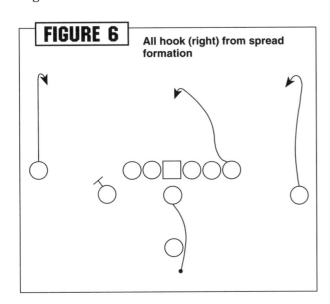

FIGURE 6 — All hook (right) from spread formation

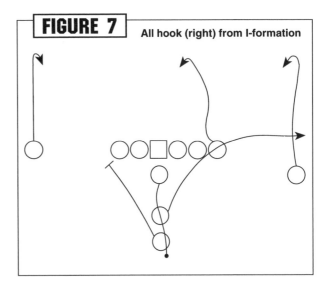

FIGURE 7 — All hook (right) from I-formation

When the quarterback determines the side we are going to throw to, the *inside* receiver to the other side stays in to block, always trying to protect the quarterback's backside. The tailback's assignment is the same (block or run his route) when he is in the I-formation, just as when he is in the wing position on the spread (see Figure 7). Any of the receivers can be called into an individual route off the basic pattern to take advantage of an individual defender or defensive weakness.

We also refined our basic sprint-out pattern to the frontside with an 8-yard out and seam and incorporated the "come open late" receiver on the backside with a 14-yard post-curl (see Figure 8). This allows us to sprint either way and still protect the quarterback's backside.

Against an overshift or four-man rush on the frontside, we can get an extra blocker with a "Max" call and pull the uncovered G or C to protect the backside (see Figure 9).

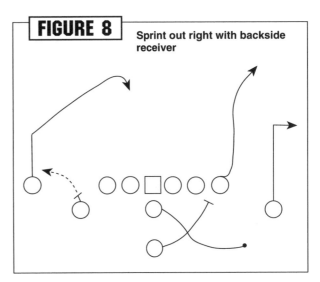

FIGURE 8 — Sprint out right with backside receiver

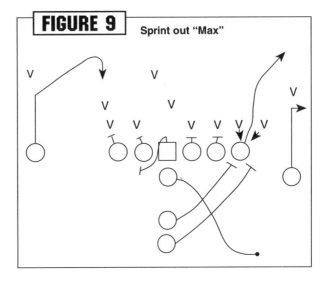

FIGURE 9 — Sprint out "Max"

By applying the same principle to dropback and play-action passes, we can determine the side of the play in advance (pre-snap read) so that the quarterback has only to read his key to determine which receiver to throw to. Our basic patterns that can be used with all actions are the sideline pattern (see Figure 10), the curl (see Figure 11), and the across (see Figure 12).

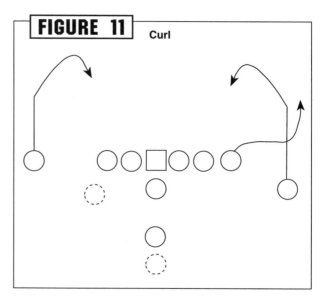

FIGURE 11 Curl

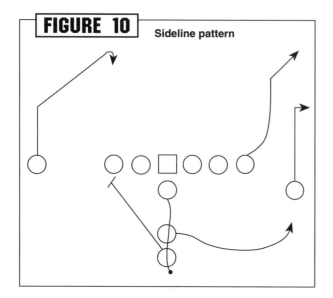

FIGURE 10 Sideline pattern

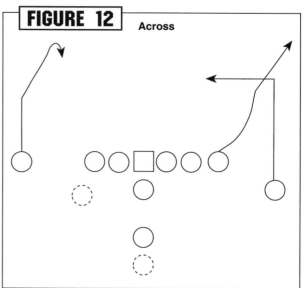

FIGURE 12 Across

—*1982 Proceedings. Coach Meyer is head coach at El Camino (CA) High School.*

Making Pass Pattern Adjustments
LaVELL EDWARDS

We are committed to the forward pass as our means of offensive football. Our passing attack is basically fivefold:

- **We try to protect the passer at all times.** Our efforts are to devise schemes that will protect the passer, leaving little to chance.
- **We want to control the football with the forward pass.** We emphasize throwing the ball downfield, but we also emphasize the short and intermediate passing game.
- **We run to set up the pass, and pass to set up the run.** We run the draw to slow down the hard upfield pass rush and run wide to take advantage of the soft corners, who are more concerned about pass coverage than about run support.

- **We look to take advantage of what the defense gives us.** We guard against being greedy and going for the long ball if it's not there, or forcing the ball into coverage. We try to execute, be patient, and attack the inherent weaknesses in any defensive scheme.
- **We keep it simple.** We show the defensive team as many different looks as we possibly can while still running the same routes and plays over and over again.

My focus here is on the specific adjustments we make on particular pass patterns. For the sake of clarity, let me define two terms for you. A *pass route* is the route run by an individual. A *pass pattern* is the total package of pass routes run by the various receivers.

The halfback in our offense must be a versatile athlete who can block, run, and catch the football. He must also be smart and very alert, as we give him a number of pattern adjustments. For example, Figure 1 shows our halfback read option from our basic formation. Note that he aligns as wide as possible, often directly behind the offensive tackle or at least splitting the inside leg of the tackle. We also have him in a two-point stance, as we do with our wide receivers. His width allows him to release better into the pass pattern and his stance allows him to see the linebackers and coverages a little better.

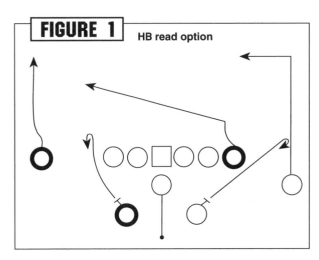

FIGURE 1 HB read option

Figure 1 illustrates how we attempt to vertically stretch a defense. The single wide receiver turns a fly with an outside release. The inside of the two receivers runs 6 to 8 yards upfield from an inside release, then plants and aims for a point 15 to 17 yards downfield in an area that, hopefully, has been vacated by the single receiver. The outside receiver on the two-receiver side runs a 20-yard in, a route that's crucial for us against man-to-man coverage. There is a large void area because most of the coverage is weak, and this route, if run properly, should be good for a 20-yard advantage in man-to-man coverage. The fullback runs an arrow to facilitate the 20-yard in to the outside receiver. The quarterback's progression is to the halfback, to the crossing route, and then to the clearing route.

Being the primary receiver, the halfback must be able to make the appropriate reads. If the defense is in a 3-4 alignment and both weak outside and inside linebackers drop in a strong invert coverage, then he finds an open area approximately 6 yards deep. Splitting the two linebackers, he turns and readies himself to catch the football (see Figure 2).

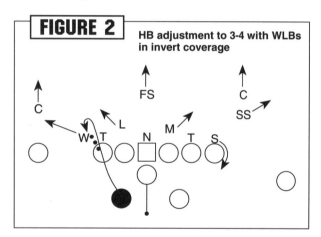

HB adjustment to 3-4 with WLBs in invert coverage

If the defense is in some type of man-to-man coverage, then the halfback releases hard, and utilizes pressure to get as close as he can to the defender. He is allowed to go either inside or outside, depending on the position of the defender.

Figure 3 shows the route of the halfback versus a man with a free safety coverage, with the weak outside linebacker on a blitz. If the inside

linebacker rushes, the only thing that changes is that the halfback must now run his route versus the weak outside linebacker, rather than the inside linebacker. This same adjustment applies in any man-to-man coverage, regardless if there are one or two safeties free (2-deep, 5-under man). As the figure illustrates, there is a lot of field to work with versus man coverage, as everyone has cleared out of the area.

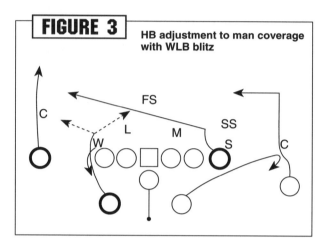

HB adjustment to man coverage with WLB blitz

Man blitz coverage presents the problem of pass protection if the defense decides to rush both weak outside and inside linebackers at the snap and chooses to cover the halfback with the free safety (see Figure 4). In this situation, the halfback breaks hard on a shallow flat, right along the line of scrimmage and, hopefully, the free safety has a long way to go to tackle him. If he misses, a big play will unfold. We will throw the ball immediately, utilizing the "hot" principle, as

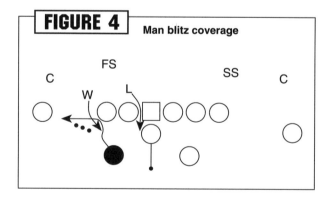

Man blitz coverage

the quarterback knows that there will be a defender unblocked and that the halfback will look immediately. He must deliver the ball before the defender reaches the halfback.

The defense may choose to take away the halfback by "squeezing" him on his route with both weak linebackers. In that case, the read then goes to the inside double receiver, who should find a hole in his intermediate route (see Figure 5).

We have presented several coverages to give you a feel for our adjustment philosophy. This pass pattern has been a good one for us and allows us a good pattern, regardless of the type of defense we anticipate or encounter.

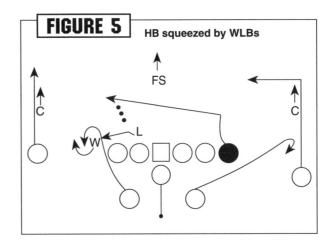

FIGURE 5   HB squeezed by WLBs

—1985 Proceedings. Coach Edwards is head coach at Brigham Young University.

The Three-Step Passing Game
JOHN MACKOVIC

A complete passing attack has the ability to throw the ball long and short, on first as well as third down, and to use the dropback, play-action, and even an occasional sprint or roll-type action. The three-step drop is part of a complete pass offense, whether the offense is primarily for dropback or sprint-out passing. In this article I'll present some of the fundamentals of how we teach the three-step passing game and what some of our strategies are for using it.

A three-step passing game is used most effectively on first and second downs when defenses are keyed to play the run as well as the pass. Although we're known as a passing offense, we also want to be able to run the ball effectively and keep defenses off-balance. This forces our opponent to play coverages that put them in better run support positions, but that may be vulnerable to the pass.

The three-step passing game is predicated on getting receivers against defensive backs in a one-on-one situation. If you can't run effectively, the defense will very likely roll its coverages and double cover the wide receivers, forcing all the throws to come back to the inside to tight ends and backs for less yardage and less success.

The 90 Series

We use the 90 Series to attack defenses by creating one-on-one situations between wide receivers and defensive backs. These passes are used exclusively in run situations where the defenses are committed to playing both run and pass. We'll also use it a limited amount of time in the 2-minute offense when we feel that we can take a quick completion to the outside and kill the clock.

We use a variety of formations over the length of the season, as teams look for down-and-distance tendencies in certain formations. We want to disguise our intentions as much as possible. Therefore, on any given day we may throw the 90 Series from as many as four or five formations or different looks than what a defense may have been prepared to see.

90 Series Protection

The 90 Series is basically a three-step drop series with quick routes and aggressive protection (see Figure 1). The backs are responsible for the end man on the line of scrimmage and must block aggressively before releasing into pattern.

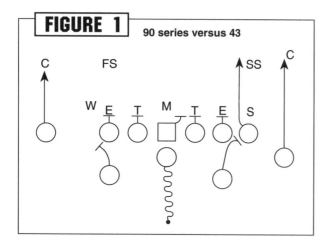

FIGURE 1   90 series versus 43

Three-Step Quarterback Drop

The QB should get separation from the center on his first step with the right foot, keeping body weight forward over the left foot, and his left shoulder pointed downfield or slightly open. He should shorten the second and third steps, and be prepared to pivot and throw as the third step hits the ground.

The elapsed time from the snap to pivot is normally 0.9 to 1.0 second, and the QB is 4 to 5 yards from the LOS when he throws.

Sample 90 Series Plays

We have a few plays in the 90 Series that have been especially successful. For our purposes we'll distinguish them by the primary pattern being run by the two outside receivers.

Hitch

This play works best when the corner is lined up deep or gives ground quickly on snap. It's more often open to the left, due to a slower read by the right corner. Select a formation that predicts a safety zone. In a slot formation, key the defender over the inside receiver (Y).

Ball must be thrown on time and with velocity. This is a no-lead pass, thrown away from defender. Use backs as outlets after checking outside receivers (see Figure 2).

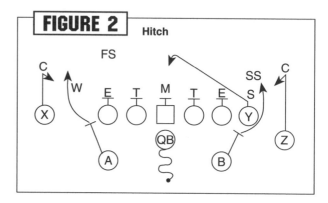

FIGURE 2   Hitch

QB—Pick a side and verify on snap. Five-yard drop.
X and Z—Hitch at 5.
Y—Release inside. Hook over ball at 5/6.
A and B—Aggressive protection.

Quick Out

Now let's look at a good first down and second-and-short play. Be alert on pre-snap read for single coverage. Try to select formations to create a safety zone. In slot formation, key the defender over Y. This is a no-lead pass, especially to the short side. The ball must be thrown on time and with velocity and accuracy. Keep the ball down and in front of the receiver. Do not force the ball; you can always throw it away (see Figure 3).

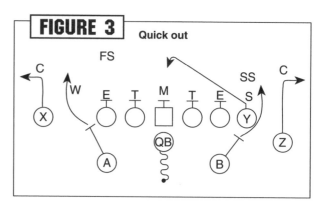

FIGURE 3   Quick out

QB—Pick a side and verify on snap. Five-yard drop.

X and Z—Out at 5. Fake versus kick.

Y—Inside release. Hook over ball at 5/6.

A and B—Aggressive protection.

Slant

On this play, the outside receivers make a fast release driving at their defender. They plant the outside foot on the third or fifth step, break inside at a 40-degree angle, and are alert for the ball all the way (see Figure 4).

The ball must be thrown between the seam in linebacker drops. Accuracy is the key, not velocity. This is a no-lead pass as corner will close quickly to the ball. Backs are outlets (shoot) when linebackers drop inside. Receiver splits are important: The wider the split, the more shallow the break. The closer the split, the deeper the break.

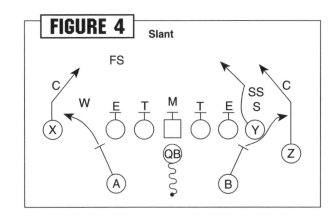

FIGURE 4 Slant

QB—Five-yard drop in +20 and versus man-to-man coverage. Seven-yard drop versus press.

X and Z—Slant at 5.

Y—Release inside. Alert for pop pass.

A and B—Aggressive protection.

—1990 Proceedings. Coach Mackovic was head coach at the University of Texas.

Airball
STEVE SPURRIER

The three most important factors for judging the success of a pass-oriented team are whether it can: (a) control the ball, (b) make first downs, and (c) stay on the field. We've had successful passing teams, seasons where we had the ball longer than our opponents while throwing over 45 times per game. We didn't buy the old theory that says if you throw over 35 times a game, you can't win. Brigham Young has been proving that theory wrong for many years.

Our practice time involves about 75% passing and 25% running. And still, at times I think we spend too much time on the running game. So in this article I'll focus 100% on our two-back sprint draw and one-back dropback passing games.

Sprint-Draw Passing Game

Our sprint-draw passing probably looks like just about everyone's, but I think one reason we've had so much success is that we throw to the tailback more often than other teams. We believe that

in any good passing attack, the backs should catch as many passes as the wide receivers.

We also release our wide receivers on an inside angle when running the post and middle route, which is different from most teams. Our preference for throwing against a 3-deep zone would be the wide-field curl (see Figure 1). We

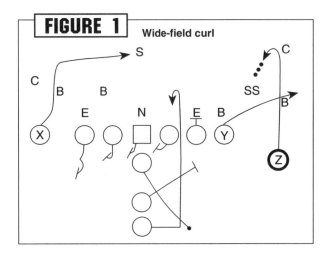

FIGURE 1 Wide-field curl

try to hit Z or Y, then back to TB. Z will catch the ball at about 16 yards.

Our preference for a 2-deep zone would be the short-field corner (see Figure 2). If the coverage takes away the WRs, we try to immediately find the TB and get rid of the ball. We'll hit X or Z at 20 to 25 yards.

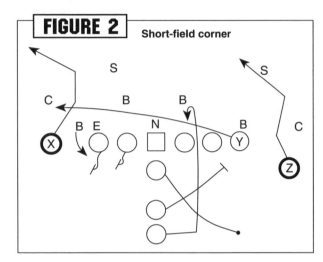

FIGURE 2 Short-field corner

We also have a "middle" route against a 3-deep zone (see Figure 3). We look for Z if no safety is deep, then X, then Y or TB. All four receivers are in view of the QB.

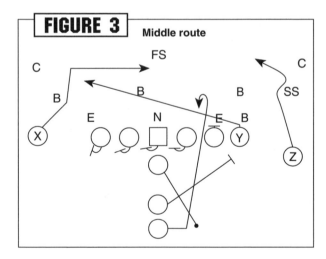

FIGURE 3 Middle route

Our protection scheme, and the results, have been so good over the years that we continue with the basic turn-back protection principles. When expecting a blitz, we like to get into a twin formation and throw Z a post or corner route (see Figure 4). This protection gives us a chance to block eight rushers.

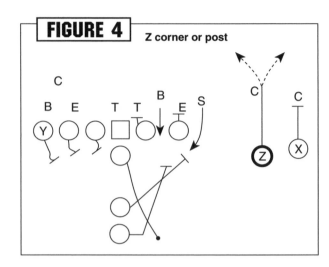

FIGURE 4 Z corner or post

One-Back Passing Game

In our one-back passing game, we use two protections. Our slide protection is designed for only four rushers but can protect three from each side. It is the same as sprint-draw protection to the offensive line. The one-back has a double read from the inside LB to the outside LB. This protection is designed to get four receivers out quickly with no blocking responsibilities.

Figures 5 and 6 show patterns against a 3-deep zone and a 2-deep zone, respectively. Again, we want to throw curls against 3-deep and corners against 2-deep.

If we get eight rushers when in a one-back formation, we go to the 3-deep pass, the offensive line blocks the inside gap area, the back goes weak, and Y also blocks inside (see Figure 7). We allow the wide rushers to come free, expecting the ball to already be thrown.

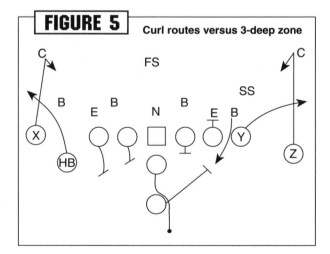

FIGURE 5 Curl routes versus 3-deep zone

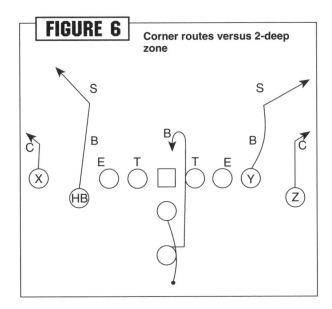

FIGURE 6   Corner routes versus 2-deep zone

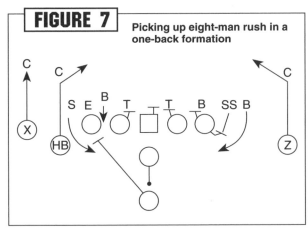

FIGURE 7   Picking up eight-man rush in a one-back formation

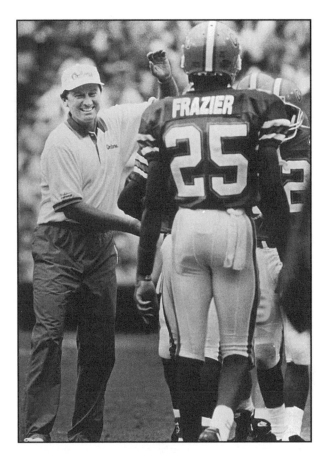

These are just a few of our pass protections and formations. We believe that to have a highly successful offense, it must appear to be very complicated. But it must also be simple for the coaches to teach, and easy for the players to learn.

—1989 Proceedings. Coach Spurrier is head coach at the University of Florida.

Spreading 'Em Around and Airing It Out

JIM WACKER

Why go to the "one-back, no-back" passing attack? The first reason is simply that it is a formation made for the passing game. The more you can spread out the defense, the easier it is to throw the ball. There are several reasons for this.

The first, and maybe the most important reason, is that it is easier to read blitz when you are in a one-back or no-back formation. If they have to cover four or five receivers on the line of scrimmage, that means the maximum that they can bring is either seven or six. If our quarterback does a good job of recognizing a blitz, we should minimize the number of sacks, and we have a chance of really putting a lot of points up on the board.

When they blitz you in the one-back, no-back, they turn the game into high stakes poker. As long as you have a good triggerman, you've got a good chance of making the scoreboard explode.

The second reason we like to spread the defense is because it opens up routes for your short, horizontal patterns. The simplest pattern in the world is to run four or five receivers, stop them all at 7 yards, and throw to the guy that looks open. You spread them out in the trips formation on the hash, with three wide receivers to the field and two into the short side. In the middle of the field you can go two and two, or three and two, but the defense must go out and cover them.

It's important that you throw any time you have an uncovered receiver, and we motion to get to the no-back offense a lot of times in order to take advantage of mistakes by the defense. If they make a mistake and we get an uncovered receiver, it's the shortest, quickest, easiest throw in football. We've had some of those turn into really big plays for us. The following are some examples of the short passing game from the one-back and no-back formations.

Blitz-Beating Routes

Figure 1 shows a pro-right formation with fly motion, which puts our B-back in motion towards the tight end. We then run five-step routes for a quick horizontal stretch and the quarterback throws to the guy that he thinks is going to be the most open. If they blitz, obviously, he can go into any one of the five receivers because it is a three-step route. We will run this same route with corner routes by the No. 2 receiver to one side and the No. 3 receiver to the other, and this now puts a vertical stretch on the defense as well.

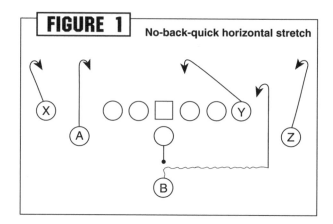

FIGURE 1 No-back-quick horizontal stretch

Figure 2 puts three receivers on stop routes and the two inside receivers on corner routes. It is excellent against cover 2 or one free, and you can now really burn the defense with a deep corner as long as the quarterback has time; of course, if he is feeling pressure, he will take it to one of the short stops underneath. Both of these routes are excellent against the blitz because the quarterback can unload the ball in a hurry.

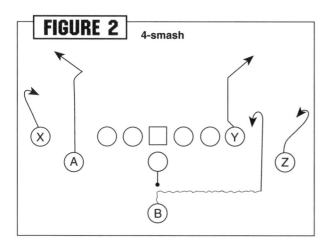

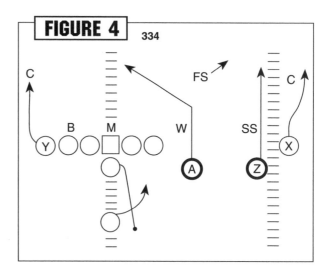

Low, High, and Take the Top Off

In spreading the defense you can put receivers "low, high, and take the top off the coverage." We structure a lot of our passing game around this particular principle. An example would be 84 Stretch, shown in Figure 3.

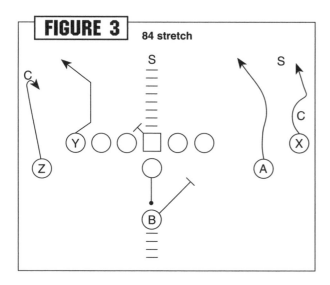

The low, high, and take the top off the coverage principle can be incorporated into a number of different formations and different patterns, and is especially effective when you are trying to attack zone coverage.

On our 334 pattern we will run two receivers down the hash marks and two receivers deep down the sideline, and basically key the free safety. If he plays in the deep middle, we should be able to hit the A-back underneath, as he is running a "jump route" down near the hash mark (see Figure 4).

If the free safety jumps the A-back, we will take a shot at our Z, who is running the far hash. If either corner overlaps, we will throw to one of the wide receivers on the outside. If they are playing a lot of man-to-man, we will again try to hit the A-back against "one free," but we will try to check out this pattern if they blitz. Another very effective complementary route is to run the B-back on either a B flat, a B option, or a B delay, depending on linebacker undercoverage.

Another version of the vertical stretch would be 334 Switch (see Figure 5). We again are running four verticals. If the playside tight end opens early, we throw him the ball. If he doesn't open, we can either throw to the flanker in the side pocket on the strong side or we can look for throwback. If we look for throwback, the X is running the hash mark and the slotback is running the

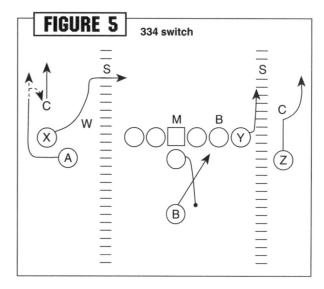

wheel down the sideline. Both of these are option routes.

If it is cover 3, the X-receiver will run deep down the hash and look for the ball and try to catch it in the seam between the free safety and the corner. If it is cover 2, he will set the route down at about 15 to 18 yards and look for a throwing window inside of the Will linebacker.

The A-back also runs an option. If it is man-to-man coverage, he will either take the top off the coverage, running hard up the sideline, or he will "set it down" on his wheel pattern. The 34-35 play-action really ties in well because it looks exactly like our base running play, which is a zone dive. The quarterback then simply reads the coverage and tries to find the open receiver.

Another way that we work low, high, and take the top off the coverage is with our curl and spear route (see Figure 6). This is a five-step pattern and the quarterback will now read the Will linebacker. If he cushions the curl, we will throw to the slotback on the spear. If he works through to cover the spear, we will throw to X on the curl.

The tight end will run a post pattern across the face of the free safety in order to keep him out of the curl area. If the free safety tries to rob the curl to X, we will throw the post to the tight end. We will also sometimes motion the B-back towards the tight end and then run him on a quick spear to uncover the strong side curl pattern. This would

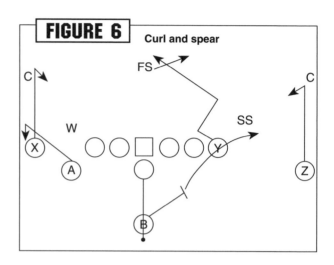

FIGURE 6   Curl and spear

put us in a no-back formation and the quarterback can read the same pattern to either side.

The low, high, and take the top off the coverage concept can be developed throughout the entire passing game. If you are using this concept against zone coverage, the receivers always work to find a throwing lane inside of the linebackers. If it is man-to-man coverage, the receivers turn the pattern into a runaway, which means they simply run their patterns across the field. Running away from the nearest defender who is covering them is the easiest pattern to hit against man coverage. This has been an easy rule for our receivers to remember.

—1992 Proceedings. Coach Wacker was head coach at the University of Minnesota.

Passing First and Passing Deep

JIM SWEENEY

It's always interesting for me to talk with coaches who are run-oriented in their thinking but, nevertheless, make statements leading you and themselves to believe that they are coaching a "balance" between the run and the pass.

I ask them a question which separates "runners" from "passers": "How often (percentage-wise) do you throw on first down?" Playing defense against a team that throws the ball one half or two thirds of the time on first down makes football an entirely different game.

Pass on First Down

Our game-plan philosophy is that we're going to pass on first down. We believe that our run will be better if the defense is thinking pass. Therefore, we package the play and "check with me" versus defenses which are strictly pass structured.

Our coaches in the press box are programmed to think pass on first down and to anticipate their next call as being second-and-10. Therefore, they're always thinking about throwing the ball. It's easy to throw a 7- or 8-yard pass completion on first down and then make a successful run call because every defensive coach now treats second-and-short as a long-yardage situation, and it becomes almost a gimme to run the ball. In studying game films in college and pro football and making the same observations in watching TV, it's our opinion that teams score with alarming regularity when the offense makes a big play (20-yard gain or more) somewhere in its drive to the goal line. Teams that try to grind it out on the ground, with no big plays, seem to score less often.

Our offensive philosophy as veer coaches for many years was based on the objective of attacking the vertical (uncovered) seams in the defense with as much velocity and quickness as possible. We now base our offense on getting the ball into the vertical seams upfield. Note the comparison of vertical seams in a veer offense versus a pass offense (see Figures 1 and 2).

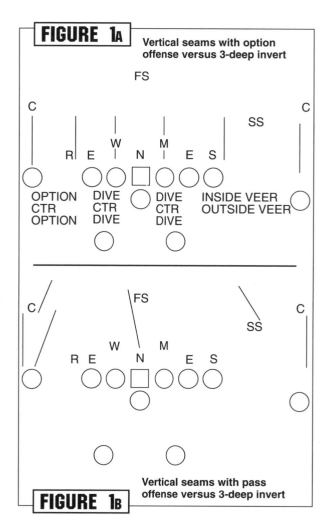

FIGURE 1A Vertical seams with option offense versus 3-deep invert

Vertical seams with pass offense versus 3-deep invert **FIGURE 1B**

We still are going to package the play against the defense—and we are going to spend as much practice time in picking up blitzing and dogging defenses as we used to spend in perfecting our veer tracks and ballhandling.

Pass Deep

Our offense is predicated on the deep pass, but almost always we are going to be able to throw the ball on two levels according to the drops of the backers and defensive backs. We are also going to put a lateral as well as a vertical stretch on

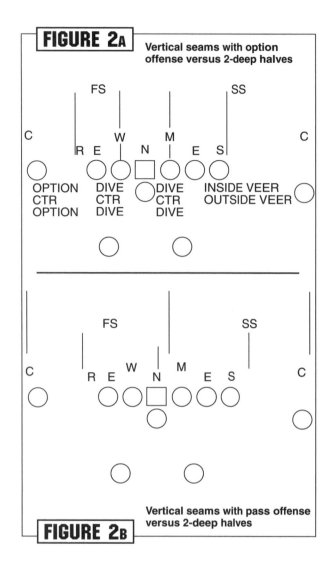

FIGURE 2A Vertical seams with option offense versus 2-deep halves

Vertical seams with pass offense versus 2-deep halves FIGURE 2B

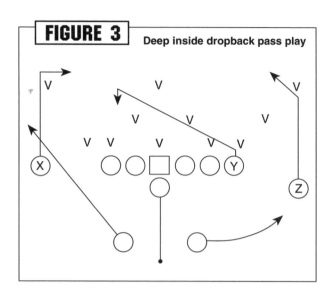

FIGURE 3 Deep inside dropback pass play

the defensive coverage (without backs), therefore dispersing your "cover" people over as great a field area as possible.

The first pass we'd like to perfect is one which we work weakside more often than not, but we always have the "z-alert" phase of the pass active if the pre-snap read indicates a high probability of completion (see Figure 3).

Our split end (X) runs a deep crossing route (16 to 18 yards). Our weakside setback runs a 6-yard-deep hook pattern in the vertical track of the split end. Our tight end makes an outside head-and-shoulder bobble, releases inside, and hooks up 7 yards deep in front of the weakside tackle. Our Z-back runs a "clearing" post route 12 yards deep and continues through the free safety area, keeping off the strong post side of the midfield.

The quarterback takes his pre-snap read and determines if the probability of the strongside post

pattern is high. If so, he programs himself to throw the ball in the seam to the flanker at the 12-yard breaking point on the fifth step of his drop.

If not, he works the pattern weak on a seven-step drop progression. He keys the weak inside backer to determine his depth. If the inside backer's drop has eliminated the crossing route by X, then the quarterback throws the ball to the tight end. We expect the tight end to get tackled and probably be short of the first down, but it is hard to gain 8 yards consistently on a run play.

If the tight end absorbs the backer coverage, the quarterback throws the ball to X. The split should get to a depth of at least 15 yards, accelerate out of the vertical route, and go slightly downfield. This last is of utmost importance as it keeps him from a direct collision point with the free safety whose attention has been attracted by the flanker, but who is now "clueing" the quarterback and breaking the ball.

We should also look at a pass play designed to go deep outside (see Figure 4). These stems (outside routes) look alike on release but break outside to keep the defense from zoning the formation, thereby forcing them to zone the field. Our X-end runs a post-corner pattern. Our flanker runs a post-corner pattern. Our tight end (Y) runs a deep down-the-middle route versus the 2-deep and a deep (17 yards) pull-up in front of the 3-deep safety or safety rotation.

Our back runs what we call a wide route. A wide route is a 5-yard upfield stem and a lateral break outward. We usually keep one of the backs in and prefer working the route weak versus reduced defenses and strong versus balanced defenses.

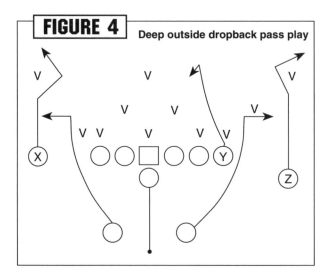

FIGURE 4   Deep outside dropback pass play

Versatility at Quarterback

When I was very young, I heard a great coach state that "Your quarterback doesn't have to be able to do everything—he just has to do one thing well." He was talking about the quarterback being a sprint-out or dropback or play-pass type thrower. We believe the opposite now. I would rather have a quarterback who can do a "little of each" very well.

We begin our passing attack by being positive about our methods of protection. We feel that we need different types in order to handle different problems. One of the best ways to keep the defense off-balance is to change the spot from which the passer throws.

We build our running attack with that thought in mind. We want to run the sweep play reasonably well so that we can run our "roll pass" action from it (see Figure 5).

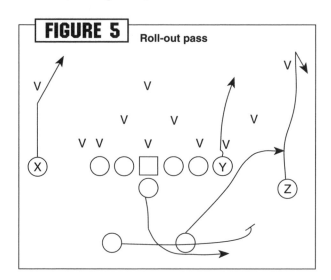

FIGURE 5   Roll-out pass

We also want to run two types of bootlegs from it, one of which is shown in Figure 6.

We play pass also from our sprint-draw run play. Figure 7 shows one of two patterns we run off this action.

We feel that our trap and weak side "under sweep" are two of our best running threats, so we want to be able to throw from that action also. The best run play a dropback pass team can have is the draw play.

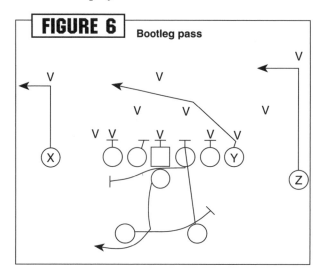

FIGURE 6   Bootleg pass

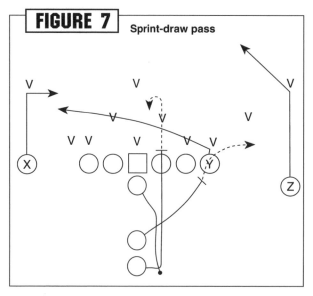

FIGURE 7   Sprint-draw pass

The best pattern we run from dropback pass action is this one which makes the "Mike" backer shorten his pass drop and allows us to hit the flanker with a high percentage of completions and for large gains (see Figure 8).

We have, as do all other dropback pass teams, many patterns which we favor in certain situations. We've discussed only the main concepts and

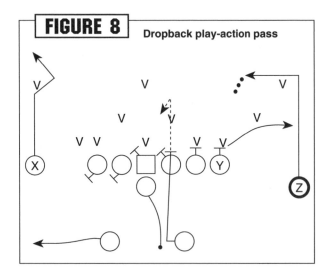

FIGURE 8 Dropback play-action pass

strategies of our passing attack. I've found it exciting and a rebirth, of sorts, to undergo the change of run coach to pass coach. This switch can stimulate your creativity and heighten the interest of players and fans.

—1983 Proceedings. Coach Sweeney was head coach at Fresno State University.

Identifying Fronts and Coverages
STEVE AXMAN

A young quarterback's introduction to the world of attacking defenses is often a rude awakening. He's sometimes overwhelmed by all the coach is asking him to learn: 2-deep, 3-deep, combo, blitz, man-under, drop end, rush end, gap control, nickel, brackets, and on and on.

With the name of today's defensive game being multiplicity and disguise of both front and coverage, a coach must find the right starting point from which to help a quarterback develop a basis of understanding of fronts, coverages, and their subsequent interrelation. There was a time when a coach could simply start with the concept of odd seven- and eight-man fronts and their related coverages. However, the increased usage of

nickel and even dime personnel has all but shattered those basic teaching constructs.

Where does one start? One starts by understanding that rarely does a front and a coverage design exist without an interrelation to one another. Fronts and coverages are almost always related, complementing one another to help produce a coordinated defensive package of deep coverage, curl/flat zone coverage, underneath coverage, perimeter support, and gap control fronts. As a result, an understanding of the interrelation of fronts to coverages and coverages to fronts can help produce what are fairly reliable indicators in the effort to attack defenses with run, option, and pass packages.

Defensive Fronts and Coverages

To understand the designs of the wide variety of fronts, it's important to know the concepts of gap control. In its most basic form, gap control defense relates to the assigning of seven front defenders to the seven gaps of a left and right pro offensive formation (see Figure 1).

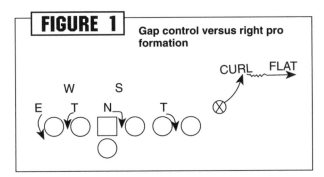

FIGURE 1 Gap control versus right pro formation

With few exceptions, gap control defense allows for one front defender (usually an outside linebacker) to be a flat or curl/flat zone defender to one side or the other. This is in addition to his perimeter support responsibilities. In the previous diagram, the overshifted, reduced front 5-2 alignment allows for the tight end side outside linebacker to be that curl/flat zone, perimeter support defender.

There are many varieties of coverages. Structurally, however, we define five basic families of coverage:

- 3-deep, 4-under zone
- 2-deep, 5-under zone
- man-free
- 2-deep, man-under
- blitz man (3- or 4-deep)

Three-deep zone, of which strong safety invert, or sky, is the most common, is a strong-oriented coverage (1 1/2 deep defenders strong and 1 1/2 defenders weak) that is usually easily recognizable. There is a free safety aligned in the middle of the formation as shown in Figure 2. (When the ball is on the hash, however, he may initially align on the hash in a 2-deep alignment to give a 2-deep look.)

There are two corners aligned deep, usually 7 yards plus. The most distinguishing 3-deep sky defender alignment is usually the inverted strong safety to the formation/field side.

The 3-deep strong-oriented coverage provides a curl/flat zone, perimeter support defender to the

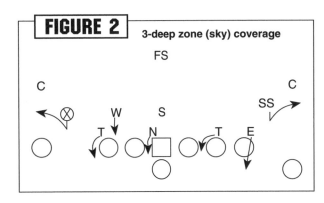

FIGURE 2 3-deep zone (sky) coverage

field/formation side in the form of the strong safety. (Field and/or formation strength is, of course, relative to the offense's formation.) Therefore, the front must provide a flat zone/support defender to the weakside of the formation.

To accomplish this, the front should also work (angle/slant) weak to provide a contain defender to allow for a drop outside linebacker. In this way, the coverage and perimeter support can be balanced to both sides.

Therefore, the 3-deep, strong-oriented coverage allows us to reliably predict that

- the weakside outside linebacker is the drop outside linebacker;
- the front will work weak in its gap control efforts to provide a contain defender weak (the weak DT);
- the defensive line's A gap defender, if there is one (the noseguard), will work weak to the weak A gap as in Figure 2; and
- the rush outside linebacker (E) will come from the formation/field side.

Three-Deep Zone Coverage Indicators

Besides the middle attitude alignment of the free safety and the often obvious inverted strong safety alignment, here are some other helpful indicators that the coverage is 3-deep zone (sky):

Weak Corner Off 7-Plus Yards: The weak corner is usually in more of an isolated, one-on-one attitude because he is away from the formation side. As a result, there is usually less effort by him to "disguise."

Weak Outside Linebacker Aligns Off LOS: The weak outside linebacker "cheats" his alignment to enable a better/quicker drop in his flat (curl) zone pass responsibilities (see Figure 3). Such a cheated alignment may happen late, just prior to the snap of the ball.

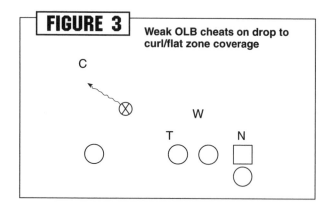

Weak OLB cheats on drop to curl/flat zone coverage

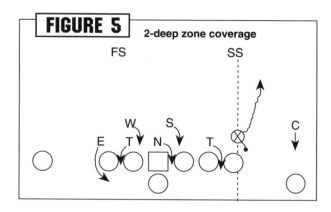

2-deep zone coverage

Defensive Linemen Shade Weak: An Okie noseguard aligns/shades weak to best control the weak A gap. The strongside Okie DT aligns head up or on an inside shade to best control the B gap. The weakside Okie DT is in a heavy contain alignment (see Figure 4).

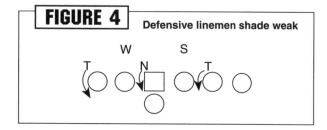

Defensive linemen shade weak

Two-Deep Zone Coverage Indicators

Two-deep zone, even though there are two balanced secondary defenders to each side, is treated as a weak-oriented coverage. Field and formation considerations force 2-deep coverages to get additional curl zone coverage from the strength/field side of the front, lest there be definite coverage weaknesses left open to exploit. And yet, it's a tilted umbrella coverage structure in that there are two short zone defenders covering the curl and flat zones under a half-field safety aligning near, or on, the hash to the formation/field side (see Figure 5).

The two safeties may do their best to disguise the 2-deep look. However, by the snap of the ball, they'll usually be aligned on the hashes. In 2-deep, the emphasis of the coverage structure is that the main perimeter support defender is weak, away from field/formation side. Therefore, the front must provide a curl zone defender to the strong/field side of the formation. To accomplish this, the front must also work strong to provide a contain defender to allow for such a drop type outside line-

backer so that the coverage and the perimeter support can be balanced to both sides.

It is the squatted weak corner defender that allows us to reliably predict that

- the strongside outside linebacker (O) is the drop linebacker;
- the front will probably work strong in its gap control efforts to provide a contain defender strong (the same DT);
- the defensive line's A gap defender, if there is one (the noseguard), will work strong to the strong A gap; and
- the rush outside linebacker will come from the weak short side.

Besides the squatted weak corner and the safeties aligned on the hashes, here are some other indicators that the coverage is a 2-deep zone:

- Reduced (Eagle) alignment weak
- Less than a reduced (Eagle) look
- Drop outside linebacker walks out on spread set

Two-Deep, Man-Under Coverage

Two-deep, man-under coverage requires a coverage structure designation of its own even though it so thoroughly derived from what may look like 2-deep zone. Two-deep zone is pure zone with a structure of 2-deep/halves coverage safeties and 5-under, short zone coverage defenders. Two-deep, man-under plays normal 2-deep/halves zone coverage safeties, but the 5-under coverage defenders are all manned to specific receivers as shown in Figure 6.

Two-deep, man-under is still treated as a weak-oriented coverage that is tilted strong. The main perimeter support defender is weak away from the field/formation side. The front must provide a man coverage defender to the field/formation

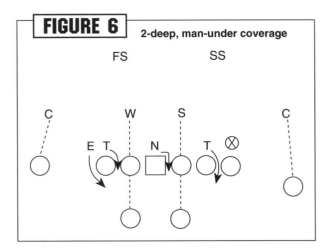

FIGURE 6 2-deep, man-under coverage

Man-Free Coverage

Man-free is a coverage that has many and varied uses. By design, it allows for the rush of five front defenders while manning on up to five receivers, with a free safety left to play centerfield. In its most common usage, the front will bring the two outside linebackers and man the inside linebackers on the backs (see Figure 8).

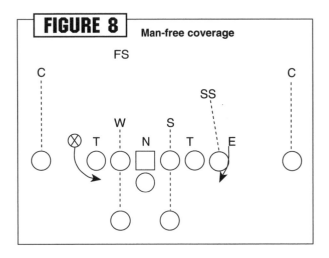

FIGURE 8 Man-free coverage

side (usually the strong side outside linebacker) to cover the tight end type receiver man. The front must work strong to provide such a drop, man outside linebacker so that the coverage can man up on all five potential receivers and so that the perimeter support can be balanced to both sides. In addition, 2-deep, man-under reliably allows us to predict that: (a) The front will probably work strong in its gap control efforts to provide a contain defender strong (the strong DT), the defensive line's A gap (the diagram's right), and (b) the rush outside linebacker will come from the weak/short side.

Reduced (Eagle) type fronts and drop outside linebackers aligned out on spread set receivers also relate to the similarities of 2-deep zone and 2-deep man-under and their related front structures. The following are some of the indicators that the coverage is 2-deep, man-under:

- **Inside-out corner alignments**—Showing man rather than head up to outside zone look. This may take the form of a tight man or bump coverage alignment (see Figure 7).
- **Strongside outside linebacker aligns on TE**—Showing man rather than a more normal zone alignment. The defender might align head up (see Figure 7); inside out; or in a tough, bump type alignment.

Versus man-free, we are thinking two rush outside linebackers. The A gap defender will probably work to strength away from the short corner, weakside rush of the weak outside linebacker and weakside defensive tackle. Man-free usually brings both outside linebackers to create the five-man front rush, due to the need for contain rush assignments since both corners are in a man coverage mode.

Man-free certainly has a much more varied use than what was mentioned above. Multiple fronts and motions will often tip the hand of man-free and expose its structure due to the main aspect of the coverage. Sometimes, varied formations will show that linebackers other than the onside linebackers are the rushing front defenders. For this reason, we must analyze the front as well as the coverage to determine such concepts as who is the A gap defender and to what side the A gap defender and the front are working. The following are some of the indicators that the coverage is man-free (all illustrated in Figure 9):

- **Free-safety midfield**—The free safety will usually try to play centerfield to back up all man coverage play. He may not initially align in the center of the field. However, on the snap of the ball, he will usually work there quickly.

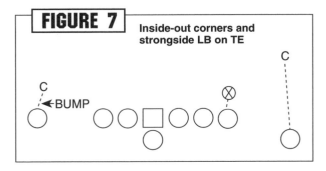

FIGURE 7 Inside-out corners and strongside LB on TE

- **Three-across man look**—Of the two corners and strong safety. The inside-out 7- to 8-yard deep configuration is often a giveaway.
- **Strong safety aligns on TE**—Along with the FS in centerfield, this is often man-free's biggest giveaway. The coverage can disguise 3-deep sky very well. However, it's hard to disguise an inverted sky strong safety look when his assignment is (inside-out) man.
- **Inside-outside corner alignments**—Showing man rather than a head-up to outside zone look.

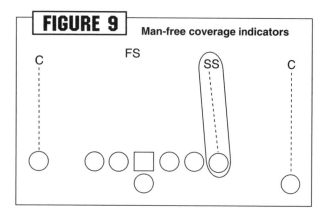

FIGURE 9 Man-free coverage indicators

Blitz Coverages

Blitz coverage is man-up coverage to cover for a blitz. Here comes pressure! The quarterback and receivers must recognize the blitz if it is to be handled and beaten. Blitz coverage has its own set of rules, as does the subsequent design of the blitz rush of the front and secondary. Our big concerns are no longer which way the front will work, who and where the A gap defender is, or who the drop and rush end/outside linebackers are. On a blitz, the defense is gambling—relying on surprise, disorder, and pressure to disrupt the offensive design it is facing.

We break down blitz coverage into two categories: four-across and 3-across blitz man in relation to the number of defensive backs being used to cover and/or blitz.

Four-Across Blitz Man Coverage. With 4-across blitz man, we're expecting up to a 7-man blitz rush from the defensive front. The following are some of the indicators that the coverage is 4-across blitz man:

- **Free safety aligned to cover first receiver out of backfield (the second receiver to the weak side)**—Even with disguise, the safety usually works to a 7- to 8-yard deep man alignment by the snap of the ball.
- **Four-across man alignment look**—Of the two corners and the two safeties.

Three-Across Blitz Man Coverage. With 3-across blitz man, we're expecting up to an 8-man blitz rush. The major concern is a fourth potential rusher to one side of the formation or the other from the secondary. This might entail a weak corner blitz, a free safety blitz, a strong safety blitz, or even a strong corner blitz. In addition to some of the normal man look indicators, the following are some of the indicators that the coverage is 3-across blitz:

- **Cheated alignments of the corners or the safeties**—To put them in blitz position.
- **Three-across man alignment look**—Of the non-blitzing defensive backs.
- **The cheating over of the free safety or strong safety**—To man cover for the blitzing corner or strong safety, as shown in Figure 10.

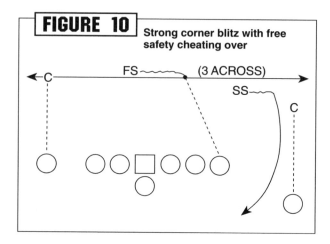

FIGURE 10 Strong corner blitz with free safety cheating over

This is only a beginning. It's a start—a foundation for the quarterback's understanding of the interrelation of front and coverage structure. Such an understanding is a must if a quarterback is to successfully attack a specific coverage and its related front, or a front and its related coverage.

—1989 Summer Manual. Coach Axman was head coach at the University of Northern Arizona

Key Indicators for Quarterbacks
RAY DORR

A football team, or any organization, can be successful only with proper leadership and direction. By the very nature of the position, the quarterback is thrust into a position of responsibility. The coach has a tremendous responsibility and opportunity to educate this pupil.

We place a premium on a quarterback understanding defensive football. We rely on his ability to recognize various defensive fronts and secondary alignments. During quarterback sessions, we discuss these basic defensive front alignments: seven-man, eight-man, and combination fronts. Examples of these alignments are shown in Figure 1, a through c.

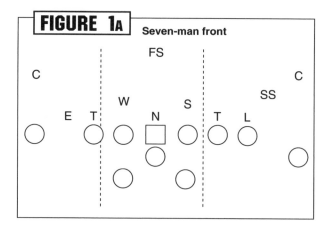

FIGURE 1A — Seven-man front

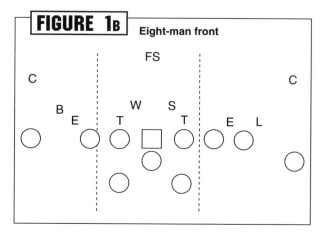

FIGURE 1B — Eight-man front

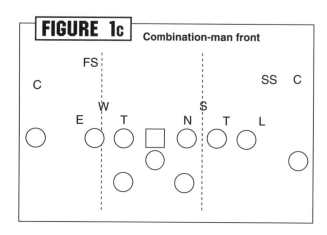

FIGURE 1c — Combination-man front

Once those three basic frontal alignments are understood, then the four gaps to the left and right of the center are assigned a letter name. Then different defenders are given numbers based on where they align against our offensive linemen. These numbers are referred to as *techniques*. In Figure 2 are the letters and technique numbers which help our quarterbacks understand gap control, contain principles, and which member of the defensive front might be involved in underneath coverage.

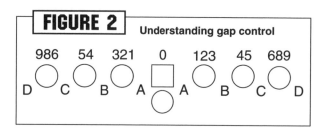

FIGURE 2 — Understanding gap control

Recognizing and being able to anticipate the responsibility of a particular defensive player's area is a major factor in our success. Secondary coverages are generally broken down into 1-, 2-, 3-, 4-, and no-deep defenders. We also find many secondaries playing forms of combination coverages, using 1-, 2-, and 3-deep zone principles and assigning man concepts to their underneath defenders.

Once a secondary alignment indicates how the deep zone is defended, it's essential to recognize the type of underneath coverage being employed: zone, man, or a combination of both. This can be done with a high degree of accuracy only after hours of film study, a very complete understanding of the route, and how releases affect defenders when they are playing man or zone principles. Figure 3 shows a field balance horizontal-vertical stretch chart and receiver distribution concept that helps identify defensive indicators.

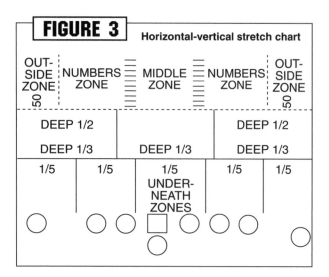

Keys and Reads

The starting point for identifying defensive secondaries begins with safety alignments. By the very nature of the 4-deep scheme, the strong and free safeties should give you both early keys and reads on movement. Another area of the defense we study is flat coverage responsibility. It's also beneficial to understand receiver distribution and how it affects the defense, either horizontally or vertically.

A quarterback will oftentimes be able to determine a defender's area of responsibility before the snap by initial alignment. This is referred to as a *key*. Even when he's not certain of the total coverage, a quarterback might eliminate some coverages or narrow them down to a couple of possibilities.

Early keys are difficult because of the constant positioning of secondary personnel before the snap. When this occurs, quarterbacks must *read*—meaning to evaluate or discover—the nature of defensive responsibilities through close observations of a particular defender on movement after the snap.

Our primary key is generally the strong safety positioning in the defensive secondary. We have also found it helpful to identify different free safety alignments in relationship to the field distribution balance chart. Finally, we look for an early indicator in alignment that could identify flat responsibilities.

Principles of Identifying Coverages

Early keys are possible when the defensive personnel are deployed into their areas of responsibility prior to the snap. In many cases, a defender virtually eliminates the possibility of moving to another area after the snap. These early indicators can be affected by formations and the use of offensive motions.

Strong Safety Indicators

Figure 4, a through c, shows strong safety indicators in the 7-man front, 4-deep secondary scheme. Figure 4a is referred to as a low safety. In Figure 4b, the quarterback would think strong safety *blitz* and simultaneously check for movement from the free safety. The strong safety could be positioned in any of these three alignments. If there is a *high* indicator look (see Figure 4c), the quarterback should then look closely at the field distribution balance from their free safety.

Free Safety Indicators

Many of these early indicators have been in direct relationship to strong flat responsibilities. The following series of diagrams will demonstrate free safety attitudes in relationship to field distribution balance.

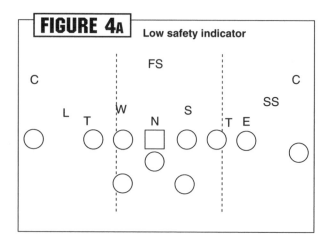

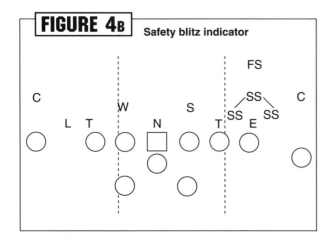

FIGURE 4B   Safety blitz indicator

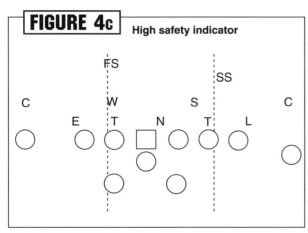

FIGURE 4C   High safety indicator

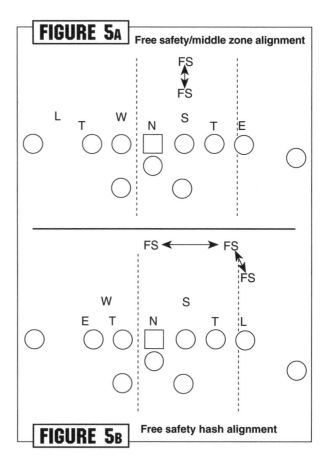

FIGURE 5A   Free safety/middle zone alignment

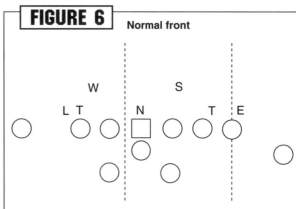

FIGURE 5B   Free safety hash alignment

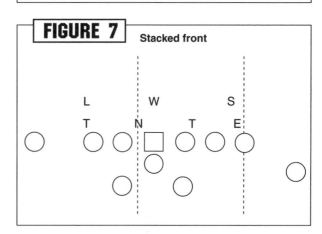

FIGURE 6   Normal front

FIGURE 7   Stacked front

The free safety will position himself in one of the five zones. These zones extend from the line of scrimmage to the opponent's end zone. The outside zones extend from a sideline to the numbers. Adjacent to the outside zones are number zones, which continue to the hash marks. Our middle zone is between the hash marks. Now, the quarterback must ask himself in what zone the free safety positioned himself and at what depth. In Figure 5a you'll see the free safety in the *middle* zone, occupied at different depths. If he positions himself high on either *hash*, as in Figure 5b, it becomes important to determine flat adjustments. Weak flat responsibilities are given a descriptive name. This name generally indicates how the defense is aligned in that area of the field.

Defensive Front Indicators

In Figure 6 is a *normal* defensive front. Normal is the starting point.

In Figure 7, you'll see that the front has changed to a *stacked* weakside flat alignment. Through closer observation, you will see all the linebackers have changed their attitude.

In Figure 8, you see the reduced *Eagle* look.

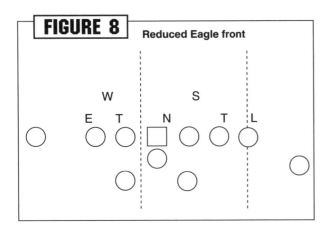

FIGURE 8 Reduced Eagle front

Putting It All Together

The quarterback is now armed with enough information to step out onto the playing field on Saturday and execute the master plan. Figure 9 shows all three different indicators at work. These indicators will paint a mental image in the quarterback's mind before the snap.

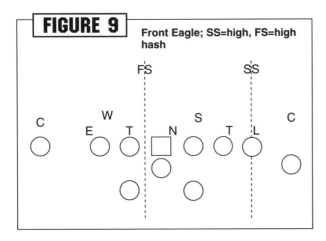

FIGURE 9 Front Eagle; SS=high, FS=high hash

If the play called was a corner pattern by the outside receivers with middle pressure (see Figure 10), this would be our quarterback's decision-making process:

1. Where does this pattern place the greatest amount of pressure on any indicator?
2. What indicator verifies the defensive image?
3. Is the early key holding true as I retreat into the pocket?

In this case the quarterback reads the alignment of either high safety to solidify attacking the outside zones.

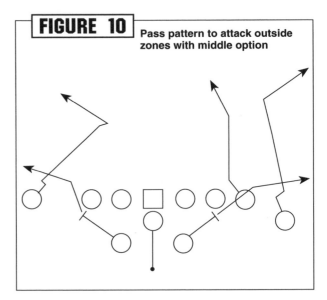

FIGURE 10 Pass pattern to attack outside zones with middle option

Teaching and coaching quarterbacks in an orderly fashion allows them to develop a rhythm and good judgment in their decision-making process. The great quarterbacks can mind-set an image and react to its change quickly.

—*1990 Summer Manual. Coach Dorr is assistant coach at Texas A & M University.*

Protecting the Passer
LARRY LITTLE

During my 14 years in the pros, I had the opportunity to play for some outstanding offensive line coaches: Joe Madro for 2 years with the San Diego Chargers, and the next 12 years for Ernie Hefferle, Monte Clark, and Jon Sandusky with the Miami Dolphins.

In the years that I've been head coach, I've had three outstanding quarterbacks and some excellent receivers, but their success could not have been accomplished without the fine protection that our offensive linemen provided. We try to instill a tremendous amount of personal pride in our linemen to protect the quarterback, not individually, but collectively, as a well-coordinated unit.

To anticipate and adjust to any type of defensive charge or maneuver—to do this with any type of efficiency—requires that linemen know every possible detail about their opponent. Offensive linemen should not be interested in physically punishing an opponent, only in keeping him off the quarterback.

Key Coaching Points in Pass Protection

These are the basic instructions I give to linemen for pass blocking.

- Set quickly into a good fundamental position with both feet in contact with the ground, body under control and in good balance. If the defensive player makes contact while you're still leaning back to set up, the defensive player has the advantage.
- Know where the quarterback is on each play. Know which side to favor as well as how deep you can retreat without interfering with the quarterback.
- Make an initial stand on or near the line of scrimmage.
- Unless it's an aggressive pass, let the rusher commit first. If you're overanxious and overaggressive, you'll get into trouble.

- Never cross over, since it is very easy to lose balance or be thrown off-balance. Slide your feet to stay in front of the defensive player just as a basketball player plays defense.

Teams protect the quarterback differently according to the kind of offense they run. Some teams run all play-action passes, trying to get the quarterback to roll right or left to break containment in order to have the option to run or pass, with the offensive lineman run blocking, trying to hook or wall the defensive lineman away from the direction the quarterback is rolling.

Some teams use only three-step drops by the quarterback, where the offensive lineman takes on the defensive rusher on the line of scrimmage. Other teams use regular dropback protection, where the offensive linemen set a pocket for the quarterback who takes a five- to seven-step drop.

Types of Pass Protection

We teach several pass protections: fire, fire cut, firm, and regular protection.

Fire Protection

Our fire protection is used for play-action passes, mostly for quick out passes where the quarterback takes very short drops. These are the blocking techniques we teach for it:

1. Fire aggressively into the middle of the defensive rusher, look eyes in, as if it's a running play.
2. Beat the defender to the punch, strike out quickly, hit up and through the defender using the hands to control him. Hit and maintain contact and keep him occupied with the hands to regain position and balance quickly to accept his new charge.
3. Don't overextend. Keep your head up— you're susceptible to being grabbed, pulled, and thrown off by the defensive rusher.
4. If you can't get away, use your hands to control the defender and prevent turning.

- *Center and guards*—Hands in the middle, fight to keep them there.
- *Tackles*—Favor outside slightly, never lose head inside.

Fire Cut Protection

This is a variation of fire protection. Here the blocker is looking to cut down the opponent.

1. Stay low right from stance, fire into groin to force the defender to keep his hands down.
2. Look into the middle of the man, keep head up, and stay after him while keeping the feet moving.
3. Throw block high enough and with enough force so defender can't jump over you. *Never just fall down in front of the defender.*
4. Anticipate slant charge either way, and be able to adjust and stay under control.

Firm Protection

Firm protection is used for quick dropback passes with the quarterback taking a three-step drop. Instructions are to take the defensive rusher on at the line of scrimmage, but not to fire out. By position:

Center and guards—Keep head up, set quickly with hands in front, stay squared (don't get turned), and don't retreat more than a yard because of the quarterback's short drop.

Tackles—Take one or two steps back on a slight angle to force the defender outside or upfield. Don't get beat inside. If the defender slants inside, use hands to drive him into the pile without retreating too deep.

Regular Protection Techniques

Regular protection is used to form a pocket for the quarterback when he takes a seven-step drop. This allows offensive linemen to retreat a little deeper. By position:

Center and guards—Responsible for formation of the pocket. Must stay parallel to the LOS while retreating. Use hands to keep the defensive rusher from grabbing or pulling and to keep from being turned.

Tackles—Take slight angles; never stay parallel to the line of scrimmage. Force the defensive rusher outside or upfield. Stay in front of rusher, use hands to control, and slide feet to maintain balance.

In conclusion, offensive linemen should remember that their feet are just as important as their hands. They must keep their feet moving, but must never retreat too deep into the quarterback's face. The quarterback must have room to throw the football and step up into the pocket.

—1989 Summer Manual. Coach Little is head coach at North Carolina Central University.

Blocking the Blitz

JACK BICKNELL WITH MIKE MASER AND VINCE MARTINO

The key to a successful passing game is protecting the passer. We emphasize this phase of our offensive scheme with time allotment in practice and with the assignment of our coaching staff.

When we sit down as a staff to talk protection schemes, the first thing we talk about is blitz pick-up. We have never had a practice, whether it be in spring or fall, without a 10-minute blitz pick-up period.

The key to success in pass protection is assignment communication; that's why we settle on our starters as soon as possible and don't change very much. By working together, your linemen learn to communicate with one another. If we have an inexperienced lineman, we try to have experienced players on either side of him.

We have two basic maximum pass protection schemes, play-action and straight dropback. As in all maximum pass protection schemes, we want to solidify the back side of the formation at all times, which means trying to get at least four men concentrating on the side away from the pattern concentration. This is built into the scheme itself from day one. We believe in teaching the protection thoroughly and modifying it slightly, and only when necessary.

Play-Action Pass Protection

Our play-action pass protection is derived from our sprint-draw action. It is based on a man scheme with zone principles built in. Figures 1 and 2 show this protection versus seven- and eight-man fronts.

The man part of the protection scheme involves the frontside tackle, fullback, and tailback. The other people have man attack points, but zone principles take over if the defense changes its gap responsibilities. The backside principle is emphasized from the frontside guard. If the gap that is assigned is not filled, then a 45-degree drop to the backside is now taken. The key here is control and the angle of drop. We want to take on the defender as far away from the quarterback as possible so he doesn't "feel" the pressure.

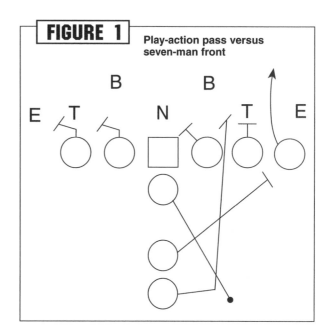

FIGURE 1 Play-action pass versus seven-man front

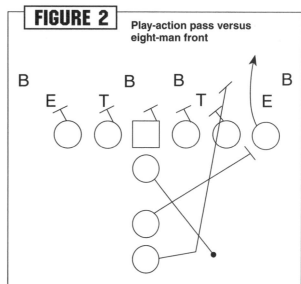

FIGURE 2 Play-action pass versus eight-man front

Secondary stunts are the responsibility of the backs, and an alert call is made to the quarterback, either before or after the snap, to alert him that a secondary stunt is coming and the fake will be disregarded. The alert call does not change the protection up front in any way.

Dropback Pass Protection

Our dropback pass protection is a man scheme. It's directed from a call in the huddle and incorporates the same three frontside principles and four backside principles that our play-action pass employs. This scheme is shown against seven- and eight-man fronts in Figures 3 and 4, respectively.

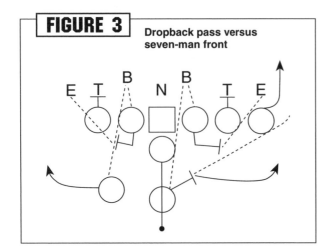

FIGURE 3 Dropback pass versus seven-man front

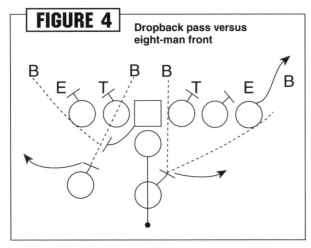

FIGURE 4 Dropback pass versus eight-man front

Versus both the seven-man or eight-man fronts, we try to incorporate the check release principle for our backs. Against the seven-man front, they are tied up with the guard on checking linebackers to ends. Against the eight-man look, the tailback is tied up to the center in the same relationship, while the fullback has a true double check sequence to the frontside of the play. We don't double-team the nose because we don't want our tailback or fullback blocking an end-of-line rusher in a normal situation, when they could get out and be a safety valve receiver. We help out the center with either guard after his double check gives him no one to block.

The big similarity between the play-action and dropback protections is that it takes both backs and the line to protect in a maximum scheme. The backs must be aware that when we use these protections, they are blockers first and pass receivers only when their rules and checks are fully covered.

Hot Protection

Our philosophy is to *spread them out* on defense and not to squeeze in and maximum protect. We do not want the *defense* to *dictate* to us where we need to audible a lot.

Here is one of our most used hot protections. This hot protection is a directional read to the open end called Lucy/Ricky. The quarterback must read the defenders to the frontside for hot. For example, if our tight end is to the left, we would use Ricky protection (see Figure 5).

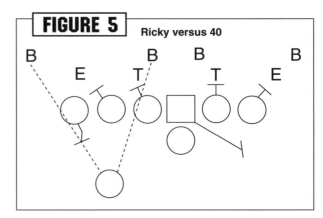

FIGURE 5 Ricky versus 40

We would use Lucy if the tight end is to the right (see Figure 6).

Two tights would give us the ability to go either direction. One of our linemen is double-checking. If both defenders rush, it's hot.

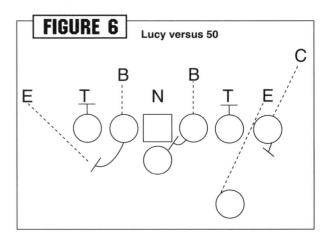

FIGURE 6 Lucy versus 50

We also need to have some line calls in case the inside linebacker's alignment causes the back a problem. Two such cases are diagrammed in Figures 7 and 8.

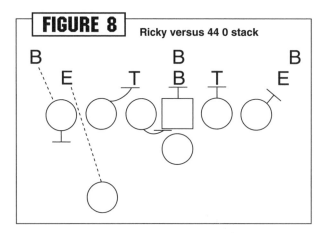

FIGURE 8 Ricky versus 44 0 stack

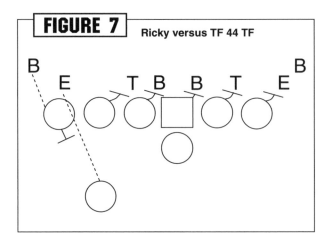

FIGURE 7 Ricky versus TF 44 TF

Shifting the back up closer to the LOS or shifting to the shotgun are other options for the tough linebacker alignment. This is an excellent protection for the quarterback and allows us to run our offense without a lot of audibles.

—1987 Proceedings. Coach Bicknell is head coach of the Barcelona (Spain) Dragons in the World League of American Football. Coach Martino was his assistant at Boston College. Coach Maser is assistant coach for the Jacksonville Jaguars.

||||||||||||||||||||||||||||||||||||||||

Mixing the Run and the Pass
DAVID RADER

||||||||||||||||| |||||||||||||||||||

We've attempted to combine a good solid ground game with a polished, pressuring air game. We, like most teams, would like to have a good and effective mix. Following are a few ideas for mixing the run and pass.

Play and Play-Action

To combine a running play with a pass of the same action, we will try to make every aspect of the two identical up to the point of ball fake or hand-off. As shown in Figure 1, a and b, we want the pass and run to seem identical.

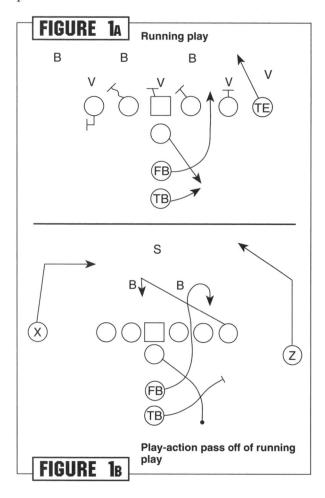

We want the tight end and interior linemen to take the same steps for run and play-action. We try to stay "big on big," and keep the tight end on the same path whether we're facing a 50 or an Eagle defense. The interior will show pass and, of course, remain that way with the play-action. On the run, they will try to influence the defender to continue with his pass rush. When the defender lets up, the blocker must apply pressure and continue at least until the ball carrier passes through. We repeatedly stress that the run and pass plays must be identical.

Our most successful route is the Cadillac pattern (shown in Figure 1b), which was and still is so very good for Florida State. The individual routes stay consistent versus 2-deep or 3-deep zones. The split end stays with the 16-yard in cut, the flanker with the deep post, and the tight end with an 8-yard stop.

The fullback will run a 6-yard hook as a dump. The quarterback will set up at his seven-step drop depth after making the play fake. His progression is flanker, split end, tight end, and fullback. The quarterback will see the safety and linebackers for keys.

Dropback Pass and Draw

The dropback passing game has been good for us, but we always are looking for ways to improve our dropback game. One of the ways is to slow the rush. Giving the quarterback as much room and time as possible should allow more passes to be completed. Even with the liberalized blocking rules, pass protection is a most difficult assignment.

The use of a delay or draw play can be an effective way to slow the pass rush. In addition, the draw play complements the dropback game by attacking along the line of scrimmage. With the draw being part of the dropback offense, the entire field can be threatened. The dropback pass can attack short and long, left and right. The draw can attack right at the line of scrimmage. One of our most successful draw plays has been the lead draw. The assignments are the same as for a weakside isolation play (see Figure 2).

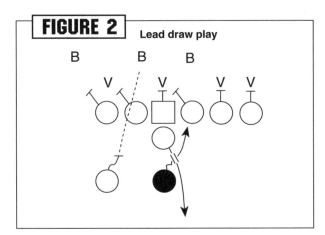

FIGURE 2 | Lead draw play

The interior line and tight end pass set, and allow the rushers to charge in their rush lanes without losing contact or control. The offside guard can "help" on the nose, but must not be too early or too late on coming out for the linebacker (a count of about 1,002). Timing is critical to the play's success.

In the backfield, the quarterback, halfback, and fullback must be good actors. We stress that a pass is being faked, and the defense must be sold on it. So before the ball is handed off, all three must show pass. The two backs set in a pass blocking fashion with their eyes upfield and on their draw read. They shuffle slightly to build momentum and position themselves to carry out their assignments.

The quarterback drops back with his eyes on a safety or linebacker for his first two steps away from center. On the third step, he drops his eyes and hands and makes the handoff with the fullback. On his fourth step, his eyes go back upfield with his hands in pass carrying position, and he continues to his seventh (setup) step.

The backs have the same read. The first read is the nose. Sometimes, both backs will run to the same side of the nose (or weak side 2 if no nose), but that's not often the case.

A coaching point: Remember this is a draw, so don't get in a hurry. However, the halfback needs to be a little quicker in reaching his assignment. While the fullback breaks past the nose and the line of scrimmage, he must see the block of the halfback. The halfback should "throw" through the weakside linebacker's outer thigh. By mak-

ing the block, the halfback allows the fullback to break outside and away from the defenders inside.

A pattern that we have used with the draw action is shown in Figure 3. The interior linemen will have the same assignments as they do on the draw. On the pass, they will have to be more aggressive since this is a five-step drop pass. The initial set can be similar to the draw but not as "soft."

We want to throw the ball to the weakside just as we tried to run the draw weakside. The plan is to influence the inside and outside linebackers to the weakside. If the draw and pass look identical, then the linebackers could have trouble in distinguishing the difference. Again, the backs must be good actors.

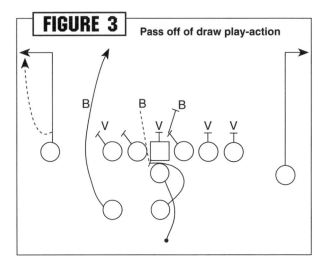

FIGURE 3 | Pass off of draw play-action

The routes and quarterback read are simple. The split end runs a 12-yard out back to 10. He adjusts to a fade versus 2-deep zone. The halfback sprints for the near hash and aims for a point at about 15 yards to cross the hash or to come in front of the safety. He must be quick. He is looking to receive the ball behind the linebackers and in front of the safeties.

The quarterback takes the same steps as the draw. He makes a draw fake on his third step. If, versus 3-deep, the split end is to his back side, he must quickly turn his eyes to the weakside, outside linebacker. If the pass is to the quarterback's front side, he must make sure he looks upfield on his first two steps and not at the receiver.

The ball should be delivered away from the outside linebacker and just before the receiver goes out of bounds. If on the hash mark, the quarterback must have confidence that the split end will come open from behind the outside linebacker.

The quarterback has the same steps versus 2-deep. The throw to the halfback requires more touch than the out cut. The ball must be delivered on the fifth step and over or between the inside linebackers. If thrown short, the ball is picked; if thrown long, the halfback is laid out. The ball must be well thrown.

Play Selection

It's been said that familiarity breeds contempt, and it's been said that variety is the spice of life. Both of these sayings hold true in play selection. We want to use plays that are continuously good for us, but at the same time we don't want a defense to be real familiar with our offense. Variety in selection helps us to keep a defense off-balance.

During the season, we make a conscious effort to keep up with our run/pass ration in several areas. Some of those areas are field position, down and distance, game totals, and personnel. It is important that we have feeling for how a defense perceives us.

Therefore, we must often run when we should pass and vice versa. The play-action pass and the draw are nice complements to that thinking. They can be kind of a "crossover" type play.

Each year we "rediscover" that better personnel makes better plays or better defenses. Needless to say, it's important to have the best position players, and it's also important to have the players in their best positions.

In mixing the run and pass, an offense must use their best players to execute or to decoy. So, a good mix would also include mixing personnel as runners, receivers, blockers, and decoys.

—1990 Summer Manual. Coach Rader is head coach at the University of Tulsa.

Keeping the Defense Honest
GARY MOELLER

In order to have a good offense, you must make the defense play honest. Take advantage of all the opportunities that are given the offense. Use the whole field; use every down as well as every player in the formation. Set the tempo of the game and play at your pace.

We always want to be able to run the football, because the team who can rush the ball has a greater chance of success. But, in order to run the ball, we must make the defense play honest. If they don't defend the whole formation, then we must use the pass to keep them honest because we no longer employ the option. We want to control the ball and the clock by using both the run and the pass.

I like to attack and not allow the defense to set the tempo and dictate the nature of the game. We must stay away from the *negative* play and not turn the ball over because, as we all know, the number one stat in predicting victory is the turnover margin. The second most important stat

is rushing the football. I don't care how you approach the game, pass first or run first, you must find a way to rush the football.

We employ three types of running schemes and three types of passing schemes. We base block, lead block, and gap block. In the passing game, we like hard play-action where we block the running play, use turn-back protection with our fake draw series, and pocket pass. What I'd like to show you is how we use the pass in order to make our running game more productive.

Base Blocking Plays

In Figure 1, you'll see one of our base off-tackle plays against an Eagle defense. Although this is a base-blocking scheme play, we use some lead principles.

In this setup we, hopefully, have a mismatch with our tackle blocking a smaller defender (if he can stay with him). The first thing we'd like to do

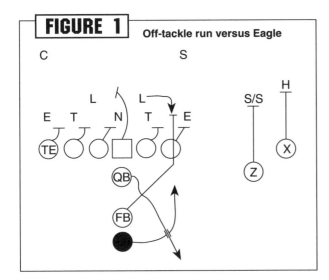

FIGURE 1 — Off-tackle run versus Eagle

would in turn-back protection (sprint draw series).

Along with the fire-out blocking by the lineman, our backs must do a great job imitating the off-tackle play. The fullback will search for the linebacker in the same areas as the running play and will encourage the linebacker to meet him in the LOS. As the linebacker attacks our fullback, he is ready to chop the linebacker to the ground. The running back has one assignment, and that's to "get tackled."

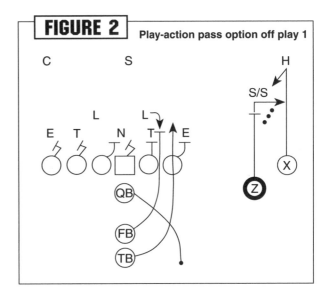

FIGURE 2 — Play-action pass option off play 1

is have our tackle lead his man and force him to widen or get hooked so we increase the running area. Our guard might be at a disadvantage size-wise, and therefore our tackle must get a great block.

Like the tackle, we want our guard to reach the outside of the defender over him. The guard will usually get stuffed if he attempts to drive straight into this man, since the defender can use all of his force. By reaching his outside, you force the defender to move laterally so you can take away some of his strength.

The FB must find the LB through either A-B-C gaps, and like the guard and tackle, he should lead his man to the outside, which will also add stretch to the play. We seal off the back side with the backside guard and center combo blocking the nose to the backside LB. The tackle and the TE use normal cut-off. The cut-off is the most important part of all the blocking. You must eliminate the pursuit with your blocking. The ball-carrier must option run the block of the tackle first and the guard second and hit the crease quickly. Our wide receiver must be able to block the perimeter players (every player on every play) effectively or he won't play. Our quarterback opens at 4:30 or 7:30 (fronts out) and gets the ball to our running back as deep as possible.

In Figure 2, you will see what appears to be the same basic off-tackle play, but it's not; it's a pass. Make X and Z look like twins.

The line must simulate the same kind of blocking as it did in the running play, with a little less aggressiveness. The linemen should allow the fake of our backs to assist them with their blocking. Backside blockers will start for their cut-off blocks and then turn back somewhat as they

Our receivers must run excellent routes, attempting to simulate the run as much as possible. The split end (X) will take a proper split (if the ball is on the hash mark, he should be 2 yards outside the other hash mark) and run a curl route at 15 yards deep and bring it back to 12 yards. He should continue to move towards the quarterback. The inside receiver, our flanker (Z), should take an alignment off the ball, splitting the distance between our offensive tackle and X. He should attack the defender over him as though he will block him, again simulating the running play. He'll actually break down into a blocking position (quickly), avoid contact, and sprint directly to the outside, looking for the ball over his outside shoulder. In our scheme, he is the first choice of the quarterback. Our quarterback makes a good fake, settles back three steps off the fake, and throws the ball to the open receiver.

The flat curl is one of the oldest routes in football and is easy to execute if we can isolate one defender. The strong safety will be on an island as long as we can control the linebackers with the fake. We've now eliminated the strong safety's help. The flat curl has always been a good route, but it becomes an excellent route versus one-on-one coverage if you can control the linebackers. We want to force the defense to commit more than just two defenders to our two receivers.

Gap Blocking Plays

We've always run gap blocking scheme plays. Many teams have taken this play away by bouncing the ball outside with their end. The defensive end, when the fullback comes to block him, crosses the fullback's face, forcing the ball-carrier to the outside. The inside linebacker scrapes wide and it becomes very difficult to get a blocker on him (see Figure 3).

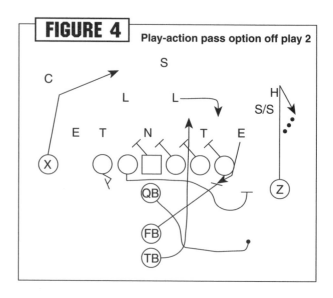

FIGURE 4 Play-action pass option off play 2

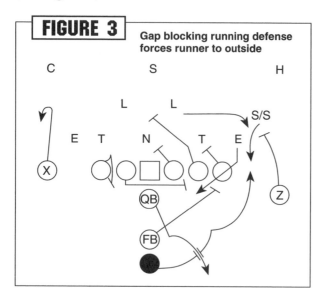

FIGURE 3 Gap blocking running defense forces runner to outside

start for depth to clear the fullback's block. He'll now look outside for the strong safety. If the SS isn't coming, then the guard should look back to the inside for the linebacker or any other inside pursuit. The guard mustn't go downfield unless he gets a "go" call from the QB, indicating the QB is running the ball.

A defensive end shouldn't be allowed to play like this; I refer to this as cheating. Make your opponent play honest and force him to keep the end outside to contain the QB. Figure 4 shows how to force the defensive end to be honest.

The key to this play, like any good play pass, is that it simulates the running play as much as possible. The linemen will execute the running blocking techniques with two exceptions: They must be a little more under control, and, of course, they can't go downfield.

The fullback should take the same (kick-out) course at the end, and not go upfield and tip the play. His block may be the most important block in the play. Many times the block won't be necessary because the end, using a bounce technique, will take himself out of the play.

The pulling guard should take his run course until he reaches the playside B Gap, then he'll

The tailback must get tackled; if he doesn't, he could drag in the flat late as an outlet man. Sell him on getting tackled, not on being a receiver.

The flanker (Z) should run a 20- to 25-yard come-back route. The depth depends on the speed and timing of your players. He should keep coming back for the ball until he catches it or until he knows the QB is going to run. If it's a run, the flanker must set a block. On the pass, he must beat the deep defender. The underneath coverage will be controlled by the fake and the QB.

The QB should make a great fake, make it look like the run, and then continue to roll to the outside, looking for his flanker. If the flanker is covered, then the QB should run the ball. If the QB gets to the outside, the flat defender (strong safety) is in a bind. If he comes up, the QB should throw over his head; if he stays back, the QB should run the ball.

—1992 Proceedings. Coach Moeller is an assistant coach with the Detroit Lions.

The Air Option Offense
HOMER RICE

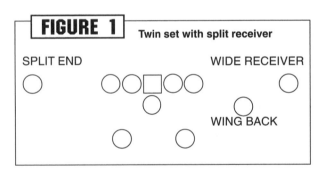

Our offensive football philosophy is to develop the best of both worlds—a running game that attacks the defense and can control the ball when needed, and a passing game that exploits a wide-open attack that can also be utilized in catch-up tactics if needed. We achieve this blend with the triple option as our running game and the pocket pass as our passing game. Since we keep the ball in the air via the option pitch and/or the passing game with a variety of option keys, someone called our offense the "air option."

If a coach can perfect this combination, then he will dissect defenses to his advantage, becoming highly successful with his offensive unit. Naturally, talent is needed to execute any offense. In the air option, the quarterback must be an average runner with above-average ability as a passer.

In teaching football, we strive to make the assignments as simple as possible in order to work primarily on technique. The basic elements must be adhered to before we can add any flair. Our total thinking is simplicity with sound basic techniques.

Basic Formation

Our basic formation is the twin set with a split receiver (see Figure 1).

FIGURE 1 Twin set with split receiver

SPLIT END — WIDE RECEIVER — WING BACK

The spacing is highly important. Between the offensive linemen we split one yard or wider. Be certain you understand what a yard is—measure it. Most people do not adhere to this principle. We want our offensive linemen off the ball as much as the rule allows. This ties into our timing for both the running and passing game. It also aids in picking up stunts and allows the offensive linemen to block an inside gap charge without difficulty. The two running backs align directly behind the guards 4 yards deep.

Our wide receivers set one third of the field from the ball, but are restricted by a boundary rule—never align any closer than 8 yards from the sideline. This is important in our passing game. The inside receiver or wingback sets 5 yards inside the wide receiver in the twin alignment.

Our team reports to the line of scrimmage in a prestance (the receivers are down ready to sprint off the line) because we snap the ball on a quick sound for our pocket passing game on many occasions.

After the quick sound we use a numbering system (26 to 29). If the numbers are live, that represents our audible calls. Going down, we then snap the ball on the first, second, third, or fourth sound. I believe the cadence should be an important phase of your operation. By varying the sounds and rhythm, you can keep the defensive charge from ever overpowering you. We number all our plays into double digits to simplify our audible and play calling. The formation, spacing, numbering, and cadence initiate the beginning of an exciting offense.

The Run

We never execute the triple until we get it exactly as we want it. Therefore, it is necessary to use our "check-with-me" audible system. We must first determine direction. This is determined by the alignment of the free safety. If he lines up as shown in Figure 2, we direct our attack toward the formation side.

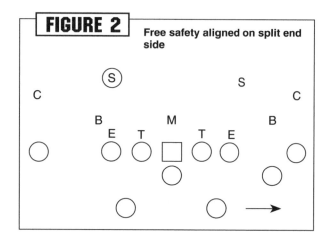

FIGURE 2 Free safety aligned on split end side

The nature of our wide-spaced formation permits our quarterback to easily identify the alignment of the free safety. Should the safety set up on the opposite side, then we direct our plan away from formation toward the split end.

When the free safety sets in the middle—as shown in Figure 3—we can go either way. If the ball is on the hash mark, we favor going to the formation. When the ball moves toward the middle of the field, we favor the split end side.

Once we determine direction, we then ask our quarterback to decide upon calling either the

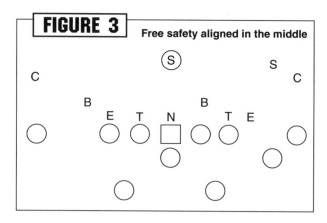

FIGURE 3 Free safety aligned in the middle

triple or a designated pass to complement our intentions. Should the direction indicate formation side, we must count the defenders in the area. When the defense aligns three people in the twin area, we will call the triple (see Figure 4).

When only two defenders deploy into the twin area, we then call and execute a complementary pass (see Figure 5).

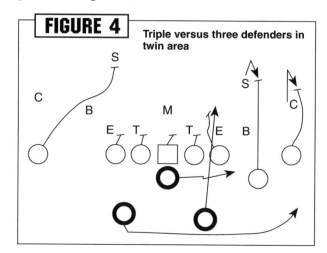

FIGURE 4 Triple versus three defenders in twin area

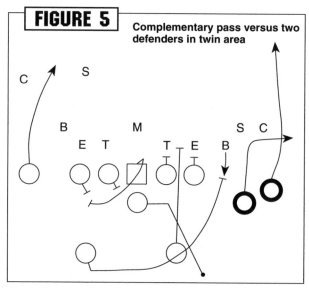

FIGURE 5 Complementary pass versus two defenders in twin area

The "check-with-me" is a simple operation. The quarterback calls only the formation in the huddle and takes the team to the line. They do not have a play until he calls it on the line of scrimmage. This keeps everyone concentrating on the defensive alignment. Should the direction take us to the split end side, the quarterback will call the triple when two defenders play our split end. If only one defender covers our end, we will immediately call and execute a pass.

Our blocking scheme for the triple allows us to block areas rather than people. Versus an even front, we approach the handoff area with our center pivoting into the strong gap. Our strong guard blocks through the defender's outside leg and the strong tackle comes down on the linebacker. The quarterback handles the next defender with his "read."

Should the "read" take the handoff, then the quarterback steps around the collision and sprints to the inside shoulder of the outside rush for the pitch or keep (see Figure 6).

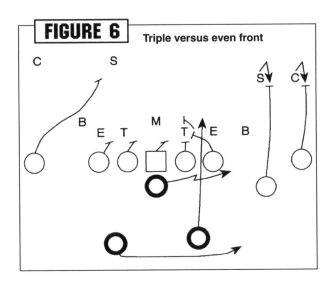

FIGURE 6 — Triple versus even front

The blocking scheme versus an odd front is similar to the even except that our tackle does not block down. The center and quick guard lead on the noseguard. The strong guard pivots toward the defensive tackle, with our strong tackle driving through the outside leg of the defensive tackle. If the defensive tackle steps out, our tackle will block him; our strong guard then picks up the linebacker. The ball will be handed off to the running back (see Figure 7).

Should the tackle close, the strong guard picks him up with our tackle on the linebacker. The quarterback read will take the ball outside for the option (see Figure 8).

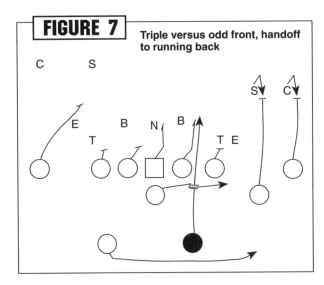

FIGURE 7 — Triple versus odd front, handoff to running back

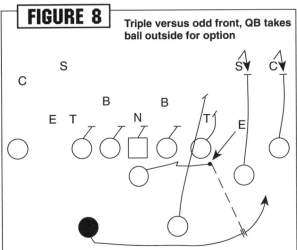

FIGURE 8 — Triple versus odd front, QB takes ball outside for option

Establishing the triple necessitates our spending 75% of our practice time on the running game and all the intricacies involved. We divide our practice time 50-50: 50% in passing and 50% in running. We don't add many supplementary running plays to our offense. This keeps us less complicated. When you become diversified, you are spreading the offense too thin.

The Pass

The passing plan unfolds from the dropback or pocket concept. Again we work for simplicity. By injecting only a few pass routes, we can teach technique and execution. By reading coverages correctly and adding flexibility on the many ways to get the ball to the receivers, we create an awesome passing game.

The entire passing game success depends on timing. It starts with the quarterback. He must learn to set up just short of 10 yards deep in 1.7 seconds. He accomplishes this by sprinting back in seven steps. By dropping his right foot back on the snap, he is able to sprint back the required seven steps on time. This takes a lot of dedicated work by your quarterback.

The receivers learn three basic routes, although we become more sophisticated with several combinations later on. It is imperative that they learn the step counts to perform the basic technique.

The three basic routes stem from the release (four steps), the controlled area (three steps), and the stick (three steps). The two wide receivers run the same route called in the huddle, either the post, bend, or circle (see Figure 9). The quarterback starts his release on the seventh step, throwing to the receiver before the receiver turns his head. This enables the receiver to catch the ball, put it under his arm, and turn and run before the defender can hit.

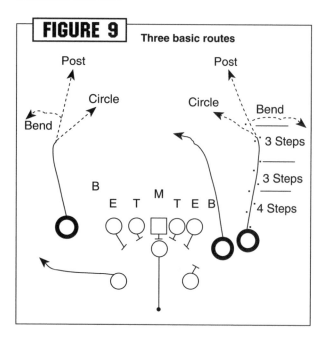

FIGURE 9 Three basic routes

The key to the passing game is timing, protection, and reading the coverage. We again utilize the alignment of the free safety, as indicated in Figures 2 and 3, to determine direction. Should our direction be the split end side, then it's a simple matter to drop back and hit our split receiver. This will change only in the event that the outside linebacker drops deep enough into the

throwing lane. Should this occur, the quarterback dumps the ball out to the halfback. The halfback can release since the linebacker is his blocking assignment if he rushes (see Figure 10).

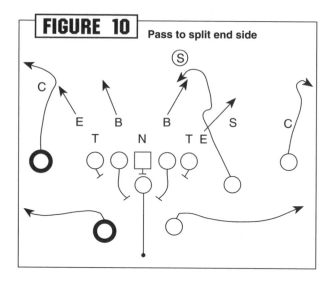

FIGURE 10 Pass to split end side

Should the free safety align in spot No. 1, then we direct our pass to the formation side. Now the quarterback must read the strong safety on the way back in the pocket to set because we have two receivers on the formation side and we cannot always determine the coverage. Should the strong safety stay with our inside receiver (wingback), we will go to the wide receiver (because this indicates man coverage) unless the outside linebacker drops deep into the throwing lane. If he does so, we can dump the ball to the halfback on that side.

When the strong safety performs any other action—roll, invert, drop—we stay with the inside receiver (wingback) because this registers zone coverages. We're better off if we allow the wingback to work on the inside linebacker into open areas (see Figure 11).

Once you're able to establish the basic plan with its techniques, you can lock in on one side or the other with a variety of combinations. We work on the vulnerable areas (shown in Figure 12) versus 2-deep coverages with five or six defenders underneath.

The coaching of the triple-pocket combination is a stimulating experience. Your players will be excited about playing it, and it's a lot of fun to coach.

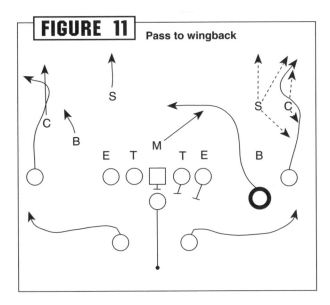

FIGURE 11   Pass to wingback

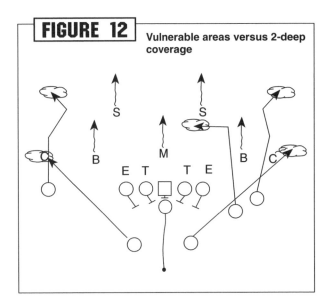

FIGURE 12   Vulnerable areas versus 2-deep coverage

—1979 Proceedings. Coach Rice was director of athletics at Georgia Tech.

Attacking the 46 Defense
HOMER SMITH

Many teams have had trouble with Buddy Ryan's Double Eagle defense. Offensive coaches everywhere have tried to develop game plans that will beat it.

We use a lettering system to identify each player in the defense, as shown in Figure 1. A strong safety type athlete often plays in the K position.

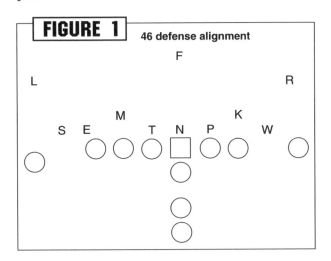

FIGURE 1   46 defense alignment

The defense has three prominent features:

- When both backs in a 2-back offense start to one side, it's difficult for the backside tackle to block the backside linebacker (see Figure 2a). It's almost as difficult for the backside guard and backside tackle to execute a scoop block on the defenders playing over them (see Figure 2b).
- In protecting a passer, it's difficult for the offensive guards not to take the man over them and for the center not to be left to block a noseguard by himself. Furthermore, it is extremely difficult for a center to block a noseguard who can rush on either side of him. A pass-protection block is made relatively easy when a blocker can deny a defender a route to the inside, invite him to the outside, and then ride him to the outside knowing that the quarterback can step forward.

A center cannot deny a noseguard one route in the same way, and a dropback passer cannot step forward to help the center when

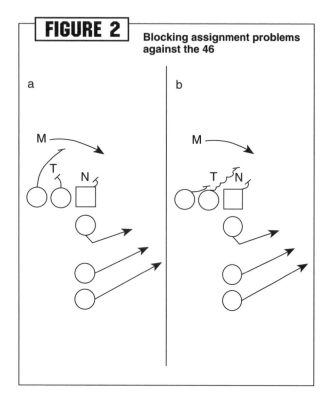

FIGURE 2   Blocking assignment problems against the 46

a

b

By featuring a constant naked *bootleg threat*, it might be possible to pull the outside split end side defender upfield with a naked fake and get a cut back play outside of the backside tackle and guard. The blocking for both fullback and tailback plays with bootleg threats is shown in Figure 3.

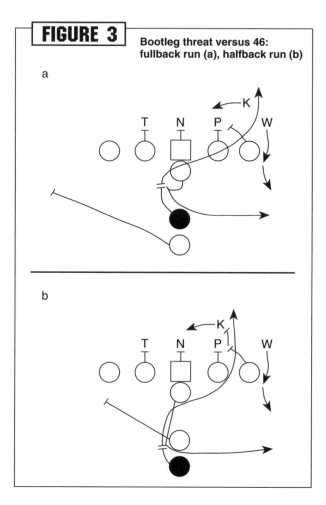

FIGURE 3   Bootleg threat versus 46: fullback run (a), halfback run (b)

a

b

the defender does get past him. In other words, there is no outside rush route to invite a rusher into if you are a center and your passer is dropping back.

• The W, K, M, E, and S are all linebacker-type athletes. Working together, the M, E, and S can make it difficult for pass blockers, because most of the time just one of them rushes. It's difficult to assign one blocker to this group when any one of the three may be the rusher.

It's also difficult to double-read when three rushers are working together. A double-read by an offensive lineman and a back on a defensive lineman and a linebacker normally tells both offensive players to watch the linebacker; the lineman can block the defensive lineman when the linebacker drops into the pass defense. Obviously, this is difficult to do when three defenders are taking turns being rushers and droppers.

Running Versus the 46

As mentioned, plays that have both backs going to the same side usually encounter an unblocked backside linebacker. Scoop blocks are required to get full-flow plays started. Scoops are possible when defenders are playing into gaps.

The *sprint-draw* play works well when the fullback can block to the side of the initial fake, and the tailback can run all the way back to the other side on a backwards scoop block. Figure 4 shows the backside tackle and guard attempting to entice defenders upfield to the outside, while the center and onside guard and tackle execute the backwards scoop block to get the tailback a running lane over the center. This is "uphill" football, but there does not seem to be another good way to execute a sprint draw against the defense.

The standard *counter sweep*, with a guard and tackle leading a tailback away from the direction of an initial fake, is not a good play because it is difficult to get a block on the backside linebacker.

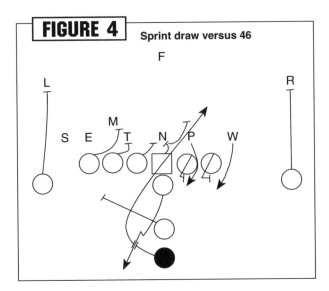

FIGURE 4 — Sprint draw versus 46

The play that would get everyone blocked would be an *off-tackle with counter action*. Figure 5 shows the tailback and fullback starting to one side, then curling back to the other side. The idea is that the initial action of the play would make it possible for the backside offensive tackle to block the backside linebacker.

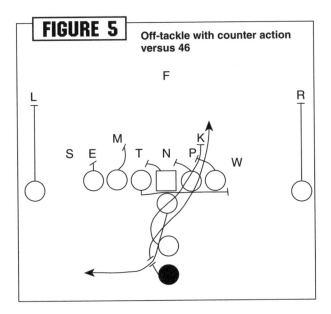

FIGURE 5 — Off-tackle with counter action versus 46

This is an unconventional play, but it should "nail" the defense. Getting enough counter action to give the backside tackle a "downhill" block on the backside linebacker is everything in running against the Double Eagle.

Veer option coaches would say that the counter dive and counter option should work well. The idea is that the counter action should give the backside tackle a chance to get the linebacker. The problem is in running the basic veer option to set up the counter option. The presence of the strong safety on the line of scrimmage makes the basic option very difficult, as shown in Figure 6.

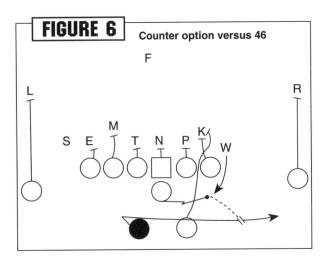

FIGURE 6 — Counter option versus 46

Conventional *trap* plays have the trapper moving in the direction of the fake. If the onside linebacker would take the fake of a trap option, the play could work. The problem is that the trap option is not practical because of the presence of the strong safety on the LOS. A backward trap play is a possibility, however (see Figure 7). Imagine the outside lineman on the split end side going unblocked with a trap play away from the fake by the quarterback and tailback.

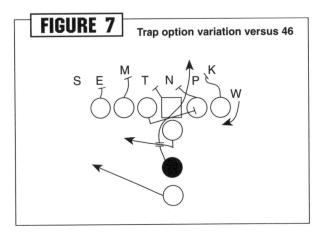

FIGURE 7 — Trap option variation versus 46

It should be possible for the backside tackle to get the backside linebacker who has two backs faking in his direction. The problem, though, is to get a viable option play to go with the fullback trap.

Pass Protecting Versus the 46

Basically, five defenders rush a dropback passer. The problem is that it's difficult to get the five linemen on the five rushers. If the center is going to have help on the middle guard, one of the tackles has to be assigned to a linebacker or to the inside. This means that one of the receivers must be assigned to one of the outside rushers, leaving the defense with six pass defenders against four receivers.

One of the ways to protect a dropback passer is to assign one tackle to a linebacker and tell him to help to the inside if the linebacker does not come (see Figure 8). This gets four linemen on three most of the time. A back is left on the two outside defenders on the tight end side, and the ball must be thrown "hot" if both of them rush.

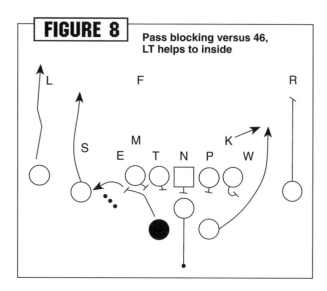

FIGURE 8 Pass blocking versus 46, LT helps to inside

You can never have great success with the forward pass using this protection. The pass defender/receiver ratio is not good, and the tight end who must be the "hot" receiver can be covered by the remaining linebacker.

Double-reading must be employed if possible. The problem is to do it with two pass blockers against three defenders. If the tight end splits so that one defender has to go with him, a double-read can be executed.

Although it's not easy, the tackle can block the linebacker if he rushes, and he can block the outside defender if the linebacker doesn't rush. By double-reading, the offense makes it difficult for the defense to tie up one of the receivers with just one of two linebackers (e.g., K or W). Figure 9 shows K rushing, W dropping, and the backfield receiver releasing.

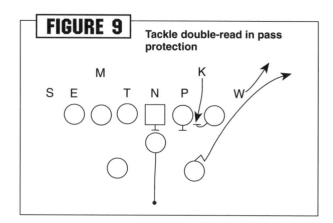

FIGURE 9 Tackle double-read in pass protection

If K had dropped and W had rushed, the tackle would have blocked W. At best, however, dropback passing has proved to be very difficult against this defense.

Figure 10 shows a strong formation in which both backs can participate in a double-read on the three potential rushers—the M, E, and S—even though the passer moves. The fullback can block M but adjust to block E if M doesn't rush. The tailback can block E but adjust to S if M doesn't rush. Either back can proceed into the pattern if his secondary target doesn't rush. Although this protection does nothing to get five receivers into a pattern, it does get blocking angles on T, N, and P.

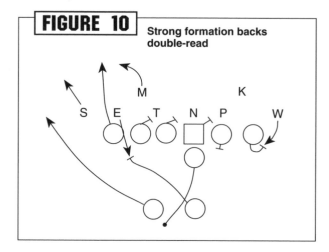

FIGURE 10 Strong formation backs double-read

The principle in this protection can be used with play-action passes. In Figure 11 all eight of the potential rushers are accounted for. The tight end releases if either E or S drops. The fullback is assigned to the end, and the tailback to the linebacker. One of the backs will almost always have to take a rusher.

The only way to get five receivers out against this defense is to do what the run-and-shoot

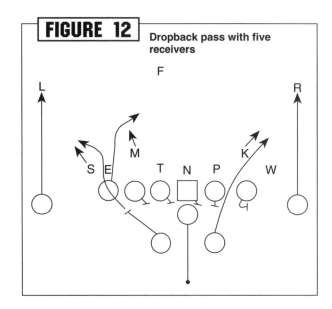

FIGURE 11 I-formation play-action pass protection

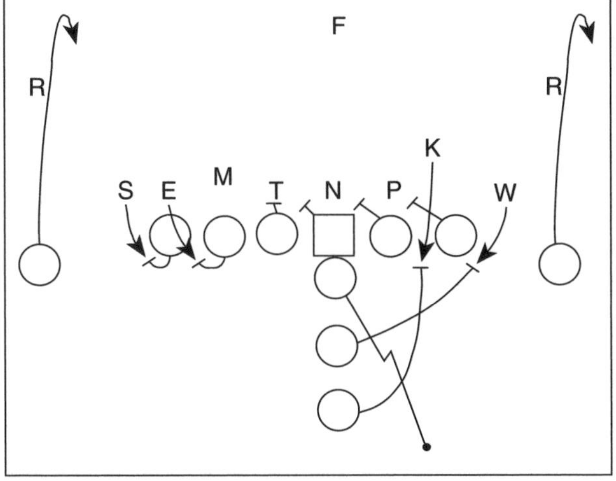

FIGURE 12 Dropback pass with five receivers

advocates, and that is to throw an onside screen pass to the back, who must always block one of the five rushers. Making the screen receiver a viable threat puts five receivers into six defensive backs and makes the advantage of pass defenders just over 17%. Figure 12 shows a dropback pass from a formation with a tight end split. If the tailback is in a double-read on the right side, and if the fullback is a viable screen threat on the left, the defense must defend against five receivers.

Mouse Davis, the leading advocate of the run-and-shoot, has perfected a way to get a blocker on any defender covering a screen receiver man-for-man. The screen is very important in getting the ratio between pass defenders and receivers back to where it favors the offense.

Conclusion

A bigger problem than finding plays for the basic form of this Double Eagle defense is finding plays for the variations of it. The creator of the defense uses the basic look as a base from which to launch all kinds of forays into other designs.

Throughout football history, defensive coaches have tried to position their players so that blocking is more difficult than shedding blockers. The 46 defense has shut down offenses that had comparable talent and plenty of time to practice. Most offensive coaches can defeat defenses as long as they have the chalk, but this defense seems to hold its own on the chalkboard without a defensive coach in the room.

—1986 Summer Manual. Coach Smith is offensive coordinator at the University of Arizona.

Passing on Third Down

POKEY ALLEN

The week before each game we devise a "ready" sheet to deal with every situation that will confront us during the course of the game. On Monday night we begin to consider our preliminary game plan. We evaluate what plays we're going to run in each situation and what formations we're going to use on each play. By Wednesday night we finalize our game plan and put the plays in the order in which they will be called.

This planning process helps eliminate the spur of the moment decisions that can often be inconsistent with our game plan. It also enhances our ability to get the play in quickly, alleviating delay of game penalties, and allowing the quarterback to audible if necessary. Decisions pertaining to play-calling are made more rationally during the week rather than on game day under what can often be emotional circumstances.

This article describes some of the thinking that goes into determining how we handle various third down situations in a given game. We'll focus on pass plays, but note that we don't *just* pass or *just* run in these or any other situations.

Third-and-Short

This is a 70 to 80% running situation for us so it's natural that when we decide to throw the ball, it should be off some form of play-action. As a general rule, defenses are more pressure-oriented in this situation, so in many cases we're looking to move our quarterback from his conventional dropback point. The bootleg off counter action is one of our favorites.

We have several variations of this play from a multitude of formations and situations, but our objective is to get the Willie LB to freeze or chase the pulling tackle. This, hopefully, allows clearance for the fullback's path to the flat, and allows the quarterback an opportunity to break contain (see Figure 1).

The crossing guard action can often distort LB reads and impede their ability to retreat effi-

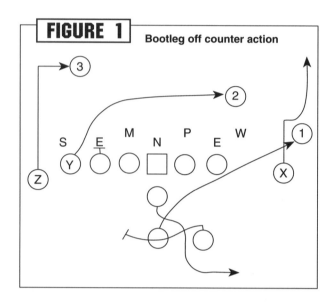

FIGURE 1 Bootleg off counter action

ciently from their respective responsibility. This, coupled with the crossing action of the backs, is very difficult for the LBs to deal with in man-to-man situations.

Third-and-Medium

This situation can also be a "pressure" down for many defenses. If we're going to dropback pass, our mentality is to protect and throw quickly. Our hot receiver package is a large part of our passing game, and we believe it can be implemented in this situation if necessary. We've had success with the tight end choice route (see Figure 2).

The tight end has an inside hot release and will option to drop the first LB inside. The fullback has a free release into the flat. The split end runs a 10-yard speed out and will run a fade versus any roll coverage. The quarterback will take a five-step drop and will "sight adjust" with the tight end.

If he feels the lane is squeezed by any two defenders (i.e., Mike and Sam, strong safety and free safety) he will dump the ball to the fullback. If, on the pre-snap read, the quarterback sees the

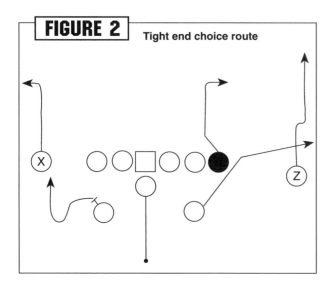

FIGURE 2 Tight end choice route

free safety cheating toward the tight end, he knows there's a strong possibility that he has single coverage on the split end and can go to him on the out.

Third-and-Long

We have a multitude of things we do in this situation, but the personality of the defense will generally dictate which plays we prioritize. Against pressure teams or teams who don't like to roll or press with their cornerbacks, we'll run the double square out (see Figure 3). Double means both the split end and flanker run mirrored routes. The speed out is a 10-yard, out-breaking cut designed to be thrown on time.

It's critical that the receiver maintains his speed coming out of his break. We use what we term a "speed cut." We want to eliminate planting the inside foot and thus slowing the receiver down. A good speed cut will help the quarterback time the throw and give the defender virtually no time to close on the throw.

The quarterback will take five quick steps and throw on time with the target area being the hip of the receiver. We don't want him to lead the receiver because if the ball is thrown on time the

receiver won't have gathered enough speed to run and get it.

Both wide receivers run 10-yard square outs. The tight end runs a choice route at 8 to 10 yards. The halfback checks and runs an option route opposite the drop off the first LB inside. The fullback checks and runs a medium route.

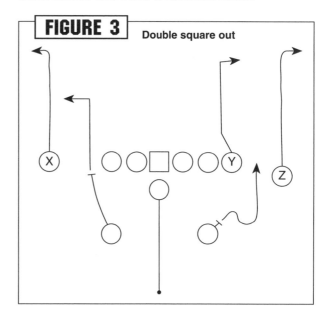

FIGURE 3 Double square out

On a pre-snap read, the quarterback reads the best located safety. By this, we mean the safety in the worst position to help on the square out. As he drops, the quarterback reads the side he has chosen. If he chooses the X-side, he will read the throwing lane through the Willie Backer. If the Willie Backer is in the throwing lane, he should look to the halfback.

It is the responsibility of the halfback to beat the inside LB, preferably on an outside cut. If he chooses the Z-side, he should read the throwing lane through the flat defender (i.e., strong safety or Sam linebacker). If this defender is in the throwing lane, the quarterback should look to the tight end. It's the tight end's responsibility to beat the first inside LB, again, preferably on the outside cut. If both lanes are squeezed, the ball should be dumped to the fullback.

—*1988 Summer Manual. Coach Allen was head coach at Boise State University.*

Passing in the Frigid Zone
TIM MURPHY

The general topic I'm going to address is how to make the most out of your passing game in an extreme northern climate. And the specific aspect that I'll focus on is our pass game philosophy inside the 10-yard line.

Though personnel and climate contribute to an offensive or defensive philosophy, a philosophy must have deep enough roots so that talent level and the elements will not dictate a change to something you don't feel comfortable with.

"Turf" teams have a little harder time acclimatizing to grass and changing conditions than the other way around.

We made a point to practice in all types of weather and field conditions (rain, snow, mud) so that our kids would feel comfortable and confident with changing playing conditions. Our acclimatization to inclement weather helps develop a greater degree of mental toughness. While this is not a novel approach, our climate gave us more diversified opportunities to practice in "rough" weather.

We felt that we needed to have four types of passes in our game plan to be successful inside the 10-yard line:

- Play-action pass
- Screen pass
- Dropback pass
- Sprint-out pass

Since these were all common elements of our upfield offense, we did not need to deviate from our overall philosophy in this area of the field. We did use motion and movement to a greater degree inside the 10 to create indecision and advantages versus man coverage.

Play-Action Pass

The first play we will discuss is a play-action pass off a sprint-draw action, which is a fairly common play for us around the 10-yard line. We call this the Zip Pro Right Tight Lee Throwback (see Figure 1).

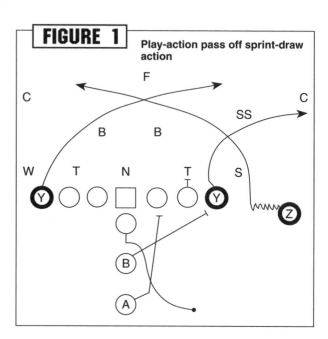

FIGURE 1 Play-action pass off sprint-draw action

This play is drawn up versus a 3-4 front with cover 3 behind it. We start with "zip" motion by our Z, who releases over the top of the FSLB. The frontside Y blocks "softly" down on the 5 technique for one count and releases to the frontside flat. The backside Y releases over the top of the BSLB and aims for the corner. Based on the play-action, the two Ys should easily climb over top of the LBs and attempt to stretch the strong corner. The Z will stay on the run versus man coverage and settle down versus zone. The play-action fake and the crossing action puts the defense in a bind in terms of play recognition and getting bumped off. This is an excellent first-and-goal play from the 7-yard line.

Screen Pass

Category 2 is a screen pass option. This particular screen is a glorified running play, but because we will consistently throw the ball in this area of the field, people must honor the action and it has been successful for us (see Figure 2).

Tin Pro Right Up Swing Screen Left is a screen pass to the FB that is good against cover 3 and

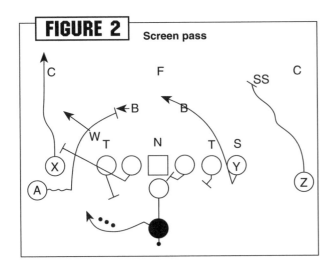

FIGURE 2 Screen pass

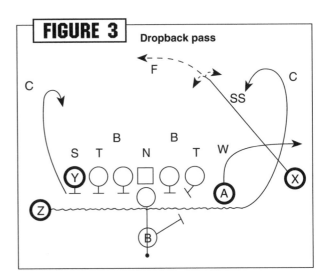

FIGURE 3 Dropback pass

great against any weakside coverage with the weak end coming. We will motion inside with our A-back to put him in the best possible position to pin the inside LB. The X will run a fade and breakdown and block the corner when he recognizes the dump. The playside tackle will chop the 5 technique at 5 yards, eliminating him from pursuit. The playside guard will show pass for one count and kick-out the first defender. The center will funnel the nose backside and lead the fullback up the natural seam between the kickout and pinned LB. This screen gives us a finesse run from many formations in an area of the field where it can be tough to run the ball.

Dropback Pass

From our dropback category, we will show one of our basic trips routes that we like to use in this area of the field, where vertical stretch is not available. Z Twins Right Up Flood 241 Choice is a five-step route where the QB will attempt to find the open man by reading the strong safety and strongside inside LB area (see Figure 3).

The X will run a choice route pushing upfield to the strongside hook area, curling in or out versus zone coverage. Versus man, he will continue across the field on the run.

The Z will run a curl route at 13 yards looking for the open area. The A-back will run a flat route at 5 yards looking for the ball right away versus man coverage. The Y will block outside backer and curl over original position. The QB will look A to Z to X versus cover 3 and A to X in man coverage. If used as an up-the-field route, QB's read will be X to A versus man coverage.

Sprint-Out Pass

Our last category is our sprint/roll category, and we will utilize extensive motion and movement to put ourselves in the most advantageous position (see Figure 4).

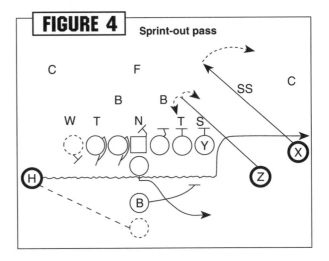

FIGURE 4 Sprint-out pass

Explode Over Trips Right Spring Right 221 utilizes an unbalanced formation right disguised by motion and movement. Our goal is to get our H-back uncovered into the frontside flat. The X will start inside to create congestion and indecision in the zone areas and will break sharply to the corner of the end zone to stretch the frontside defender. The Z will run a choice route in the frontside hook area turning inside or outside. The H-back will motion across formation to a position to give him a clean release to the flat. The QB will read H to Z to X, expecting the H to be open versus man and the X to be open versus zone.

—1989 Summer Manual. Coach Murphy is head coach at Harvard University.

Hang Loose, One of Us Is Fixin' to Score

BOBBY BOWDEN

I'm not one of those head coaches who can sit back and wait for my team to win with great defense and kicking. Some of the great coaches of the past have done it that way, but my nervous system won't allow it.

Therefore, on offense we're coming after you from every possible angle. We'll throw from our 1-yard line, run a reverse anytime from any yard line, and toss a screen pass from our end zone. We're going to do anything and everything to keep from punting. I hate to punt!

This philosophy sounds exciting, and it is; but there's a catch. If it backfires, our opponent will probably get some easy points out of it.

Do you remember the story Jerry Clower tells when he and his cousin were out hunting, and his cousin climbed a big oak tree to get a wildcat they had treed? Jerry's cousin and the wildcat got wrapped around each other high up in the tree, and it was hard to tell who was who. Jerry's cousin called down to Jerry, "Shoot the wildcat

dead," because he was getting eaten up. Jerry said he was afraid to shoot because he thought he might hit his cousin instead of the cat. His cousin shouted, "Shoot anyway 'cause one of us needs some relief." That's the way our offense works— either our team or the opponent is fixing to score and get some relief!

Strategy From the Minus 1

Every week of the season we go to our minus 1-yard line and practice coming out of there. The worst we must do by the time it's fourth down is to have the ball on our minus 5-yard line so our punter can stand back 14 yards to punt. But we don't want to punt, so here's our strategy.

First Down

The situation is this: our ball, first-and-10 on our minus 1-yard line, and we don't want to punt. On first down, the defense will be looking for a run, knowing we want to get off the goal line. Therefore, I'm going to throw.

To throw is not a gamble if it's calculated and perfected. For instance, I'm not going to throw across the middle or into the flats. The odds of a deflection are too great. Instead, we'll throw passes that have low risk of interception, or, if one is intercepted, will serve as a long punt and give our opponent possession deep down the field. This reduces our choices to three primary deep routes: take off, post, or corner (see Figure 1).

The worst possible result from any one of these routes should be an incomplete pass or deep interception 40 yards downfield. (Your receiver should be able to tackle the defensive back at the spot of the interception.) Compare that with having to punt backed up inside the 10-yard line. On a punt, the opponent may rush 10 players and block it, make you shank it, or hurry your punter into hitting a quick line drive that can be returned. Their chance of taking over inside the 40-yard line is high, even if you have a good kicking

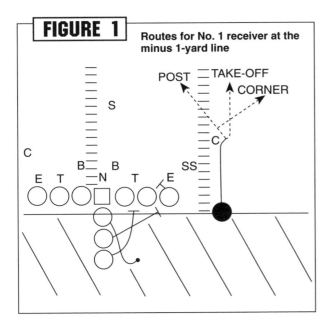

FIGURE 1 Routes for No. 1 receiver at the minus 1-yard line

game. Therefore, is throwing the bomb from your end zone on first down really a high-percent risk when you know the alternatives? If you complete the pass or get an interference call, you're off the hook!

Rules for Throwing From the Minus 1

- Line up with two tight ends to give high run capability.
- Make a good fake to the running back to freeze the opponent's rush and secondary coverage.
- Use both tight ends and running backs to block for maximum pass protection.

- Throw to the deep receiver only, and if he's open, hit him.
- No scrambling or dumping off to secondary receivers by the quarterback. He must hit the deep receiver or throw the ball away.

Second Down

If you didn't complete the pass and it wasn't picked off, it's second down and you're still on your minus 1-yard line. The defensive coordinator is saying, "That fool just passed from his end zone, what'll he try next? Should I blitz him? Double him? Play normal?" As offensive coach, I'd expect that defensive coordinator to loosen up some, and that's when I plan to get the ball out to at least the minus 5-yard with my best bread-and-butter running play.

Third Down

Now it's third-and-5 or -6, and my next call is based on how bad we need to get out of there. For example, if we're ahead by four or more points, I'd call a conservative play that has a chance to get the first down but little chance of a turnover or negative yards. A good example would be a trap or draw. If it's third-and-5 or -6 yards to go from the minus 5 or 6 and we need to move the ball downfield, I'd use any play that would get the first down and worry little about consequences of a turnover.

Whatever play we choose, it'll be one we've rehearsed over and over specifically for this situation. Therefore, if we don't make it, I don't have a guilty conscience because I know we've prepared our best.

—1986 Proceedings. Coach Bowden is head coach at Florida State University.

Fast-Break, 2-Minute Offense

PHILLIP FULMER

Whenever you speak of 2-minute offense, football coaches naturally feel a sense of anxiety or urgency, because many games are won and lost with this aspect of the game. There are other times that you may go into the "hurry-up" offense, but they're not the same as the possession where you must score to win with the clock winding down.

It's under this kind of pressure that both the coaching staff and the players develop a sense of confidence, if they have rehearsed the situation many times in practice. To prepare for it, you need a clear set of guidelines that have been planned out far in advance, not on the sideline as the final seconds tick away.

Different Versions of the 2-Minute Offense

One of the first and most useful ideas we came up with was to have three different tempos for our 2-minute offense. The various situations we faced during the course of a season demanded different reactions from our offensive personnel and coaches. We gave the various situations names so that there would be no problems with communication.

One of those tempos we called our *hurry hustle* offense. This is used primarily when there is plenty of time to score given our field position and/or the number of time-outs, or in a situation where we're down by more than one score and time is getting short.

In this offense, we continue to huddle after every play, but we move as quickly as possible to the huddle and then back to the line of scrimmage after the play is called. We utilize the same basic principles as we would in a desperation situation, such as getting out of bounds whenever possible and the quarterback laying the ball towards the boundary if the throw down the field isn't available.

The second tempo is named *situation huddle*. This is used mainly before the half when we have poor field position. We start with a safe call such

as a draw or screen, and if we make a good gain, we go into our 2-minute offense. If the screen or draw is unsuccessful, then we can elect to let the clock run and go to the locker room with the score as it stands.

The third tempo we named simply *2-minute*. This is the part of the game where a score is needed and little time remains. It may be a touchdown or a field goal that you need or want, and it may be before the half or at the end of the game, but a score is needed.

When we get into this tempo offense, it is very often "do-or-die" time, and that's the reason we spend so much time and effort studying and practicing this aspect of the game. It's something that you hope you never have to use, but when you do, you'd better be able to execute.

Two-Minute Situations

Nothing breeds poise and confidence in a team or a staff like quality practice time. I'd like to share the various situations we try to cover during our player meetings, practices, or scrimmages. I personally run the drill by creating various situations, marking the ball as ready for play, dictating the down and distance, etc. We put our offense in the following situations:

- Penalty on the offense or defense
- Before half and must have TD
- End of game and must have a TD
- Various number of time-outs
- Injury to offense or defense
- QB sack
- Long gain that does not get out of bounds
- Last play of game—Big Ben Play
- Last play of game from plus 25-yard line to the plus 4-yard line
- Intentionally grounding the ball to stop the clock
- Playing to set up a FG, getting the ball to the middle of the field
- Desperation FG with no way to stop the clock

Two-Minute Rules

Certain rules and principles are essential to success in a 2-minute drill. Number one, everyone must know the situation, not just the quarterback. The coaches should communicate on the sideline to our entire offense: whether we need a TD or if we will settle for a FG, exactly how much time is left, how many time-outs we have, and which of the three tempos we are going to execute. Also, the QB will remind everyone of the situation again on the field before we break the huddle for the first play.

Second, everyone must know it's time to hurry and do things quickly. For this reason, we go on a quick snap count to try and save every second on the clock. We also want to get in and out of the huddle and up to the new line of scrimmage as soon as we can. We can't run around trying to get organized. We must execute, be as efficient as possible, and waste no plays or time on the clock.

Third, receivers should get all the yards they can after making a catch but still be conscious of the sideline. This may sound elementary, but it's surprising how often you see players run immediately out of bounds. To help our players know exactly when to try to get out of bounds and when to just get north and south up the field, we teach what we call the *numbers rule*. If they catch the ball on or outside the numbers, they should get all they can and get out of bounds. Conversely, if they catch the ball inside the numbers, they should get upfield and make yards, and not worry about the boundary.

A fourth principle is to never take a sack. Sacks not only cost you valuable yards, but the time that elapses while the team gets lined up and ready for the next play is usually much greater than normal. Also, when you're going backwards instead of forwards, it requires more time for the WRs to get back and aligned correctly.

The QB should try to get rid of the ball if at all possible, but if a sack does occur, we always consider taking a time-out immediately. After a sack, you're usually faced with a bad down-and-distance, so the time-out gives you time to get your thoughts together and decide on the next play.

Another key principle is to take just what the defense gives up. Our motto in these situations is "be needy, not greedy," and this has to be the prevailing thought of the quarterback. The QB's decision-making process must remain the same or, if anything, become even more conservative than normal. At this point in the game, an interception or turnover usually means you lose the game.

If the defense has dropped deep to take away our primary receivers, then the lay-offs should be even more open and become better gains. When we lay the ball off, we prefer for the QB to work into the short side of the field. We've found that we have much more success getting the completion and then getting out of bounds and stopping the clock when the throw is to the short side of the field.

The QB must also decide when to take the short gain and when to just throw the ball out of bounds to stop the clock. In a normal 2-minute situation, our goal is to gain 7 yards on each play. Of course, we always want the bigger gain, but we don't want to force it and increase our chance of a turnover. If we're going to gain only 2 or 3 yards, then we either need to get the ball out of bounds or make a first down so the clock stops, at least temporarily. A gain of only a few yards is not worth the time we lose off the clock.

We try to use time-outs very discriminatingly, usually taking them only after sacks or short

gains when we don't make a first down or get out of bounds. Rarely will we take a time-out after making a first down unless we have more available than the situation dictates we'll need. We'd rather stop the clock with the QB intentionally throwing the ball into the ground, sacrificing the down to save the time-out. When we do this, the QB calls the code word for this play and everyone knows to get set. The QB calls for the ball as soon as everyone is set and the official marks the ball as ready for play. The line merely steps inside while everyone else stays in his stance until the whistle blows the play dead.

On-the-Field Procedures

Now, let's look at a few of the procedures we use and how we execute our 2-minute offense:

1. We identify which of the three tempos we want or need to employ, and then we alert everyone on the offensive team that we are going into that mode of offense. We also inform everyone exactly what our goal for the series may be, whether we need a TD or if we can settle for a FG.

2. Before the QB takes the field, we review that week's 2-minute plan and confirm with him how many time-outs we have and how many plays we should be able to run in the time remaining. We remind him what the best plays should be for that week, and what to expect from our opponent. We try to start a 2-minute drill with a play that's good versus a wide variety of coverages, which for us may be a curl route, a screen, or a draw. Whatever play you select, it should be one that your players know extremely well, execute well, and one that has answers for whatever look you may get. Success on the first play is critical not only just for the yards gained, but for the psychological boost it gives the team.

3. After the first play, we are into our 2-minute offense, and the coaches continue to call the plays from the sideline. We don't let our QB call his own plays during the regular course of the game, and we aren't going to expect him to do so when the game is on the line. The QB will immediately look to the sideline once the previous play is completed. Because of this, there is no real reason for us to call two plays in the huddle at one time. The signals are short and quick, usually only one or two movements of a hand, and the QB starts relaying the play to the rest of the offense as the ball is being spotted and the offense is getting aligned for the next play. Routes are usually communicated to the receivers first, then the protections are directed for the line and running backs.

In addition, we have found that we can change the personnel that we have in the game by having them right up there beside us and sending them in as soon as the previous play ends. This has been beneficial for us because we can go from four WRs to two RBs and back to five WRs without the defense having time to adjust its personnel.

Screens, draws, and the FB trap have been very effective plays for us the last few years, especially on second and short down and distances. By calling these plays during the last 2 minutes, we have an excellent chance to at least pick up the first down. These plays also keep the defense off-balance and slow down the pass rush.

—1994 Proceedings. Coach Fulmer is head coach at the University of Tennessee.

II

Pass Plays for the Final Drive
JACK ELWAY

IIIIIIIIIIIIIIIIIIIIIIIIII IIIIIIIIIIIIIIIIIIIIIIII

The final offensive possession is an opportunity to win the game. We've all been in such situations, and we've experienced great victories as well as gut-wrenching defeats. These situations always heighten the victory and seem to intensify the emptiness of a loss.

The situation we've been presented with looks like this: 30 seconds remaining, one time-out, first-and-goal from the 9-yard line. We need a touchdown to win—no problem!?

Getting into this situation is one thing; preparing to capitalize on the situation is the task at hand. Our preparation for this situation includes the following plan: identification of our "clutch" series, practice time devoted to such situations, and execution of our clutch series.

The offensive staff will select three or four plays that we can "hang our hat on." These are plays that, regardless of the defense, we execute to the highest degree of proficiency. We also prepare for what we expect a defense to present. One change we have seen in defensive football in these situations has been the use of more zone coverage than the heretofore man or blitz coverage. We will not discount the possibility of the combination defenses that will be used to make us earn a touchdown.

The last 30 minutes of Thursday's practice is always set aside for specific 2-minute situations. The practice time allows our offense to develop a sense of poise, purpose, and execution of the task at hand. We want to establish a tempo for 2-minute situations. Our players are instructed to get to the line of scrimmage as quickly as possible. Our skill players (WR, TE, RB, QB) are instructed on methods to conserve time and to stop the clock without the use of time-outs. Our QBs will hear constantly from us that their best decision may be throwing to row 17. The QB's recognition of a "no chance" play allows our offense to remain in control by avoiding a sack, a turnover, or loss of time.

We will give our QB two plays to call in the huddle with respective snap counts for each. Since there was no mention of where the ball has been

marked, we will take the liberty of placing it in the middle of the field. Let's get started!

84 Y Delay

The first play attempted will be an 84 Y delay, FB read, run from a doubles right formation. This play is drawn up versus a 3-4 front with cover 3 behind it (see Figure 1).

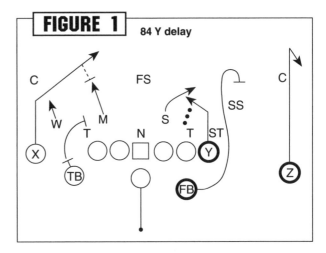

FIGURE 1   84 Y delay

The fullback is given a "free release" through the inside leg of the strong safety. He'll force the defensive coverage and specifically expand the strongside linebacker (S) by widening him to the top of his zone drop. We'll place our fullback (FB) at one yard deep into the end zone and as wide as the strong safety's (SS) original alignment. His function is to attract two defenders, S and SS. Our flanker will run his comeback route by driving the corner 17 yards into the end zone and coming back to 15 yards.

The tight end (Y) will "slow-block" by inviting the strongside defensive tackle (ST) upfield. Y will key the drop of S and occupy the area S has vacated. Y must be aggressive while slow-blocking and he cannot get held by the ST. Our tailback (TB) will check release off the weakside linebacker (W) and mirror the drop of the middle linebacker (M). He has an opportunity to occupy or block M, and we will have a successful play.

Our QB will take his five-step drop and key S. We have created a two-on-one situation with our FB and Y. Our objective is to make S wrong and look to our TE. There have been instances where we have found our flanker, but that has been the result of a great effort by our triggerman. This is our most successful play and we want our TE to gain a minimum of 5. By accomplishing this we have kept the football in the middle of the field, and we can get back to the line of scrimmage for play No. 2.

93 X

The situation is second-and-goal on the 4-yard line with 22 seconds to go. We anticipate the defense to run the same front and cover as the first due to their inability to huddle, substitute, or signal in a defense (see Figure 2).

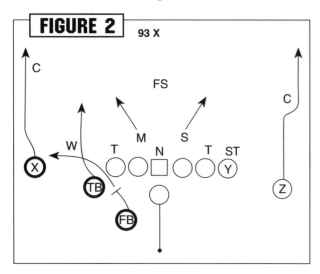

Doubles right 93 X is a fade by our split end (X). He will drive through the outside shoulder and fade to the back cone of the end zone. Our TB will release through the inside leg of W, and his route must widen W. By accomplishing this, we place the burden on M to get to the TB.

Our FB will slip release to the flat. This is a technique that enables him to prevent a potential pass rush from an area outside of our tackle. He then slips into the flat. Our QB will first check the corner. The alignment of W will change his focus to making W wrong. If he widens and hangs with TB, we dump to the FB. If W widens to the flat, our TB is prime. We complete to our FB who is unable to get out of bounds. Our final time-out is used with 12 seconds remaining on the 2-yard line, left hash mark.

338 Flood Pass

Our sideline conversation will include our next two plays. We also anticipate a defensive change so our third selection is a play we feel has a chance versus any defense where we need 2 yards. Our QB is reminded not to force the issue, and if it's not going to happen, to get rid of it so we'll have another opportunity. The play chosen is a 338 flood pass (see Figure 3).

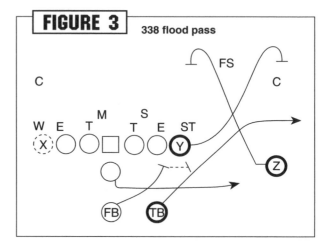

We'll bring X to a tight position weak. Our backs align in a near set. This play requires our flanker to motion pre-snap to an area 5 yards outside the alignment of Y. On snap, he will occupy the area S has vacated at a depth of 8 yards. Y will outside release and occupy a space 5 yards outside his original alignment and get to a depth of 7 yards into the end zone.

Our TB will sprint to the front cone. He must gain enough width and depth that a simultaneous hit and reception would break the plane of the end zone. Our FB must pin the defender responsible for "contain." If that defender widens to a point where a pin is not feasible, then he will keep him from gaining ground upfield. We want this block as close to the line of scrimmage as possible. Our QB must force the issue by getting outside, keying the block of our FB. He now looks to the TB and throws or runs to the front cone or out of bounds.

In the event he throws off-balance, leaning out of bounds, and somehow completes the pass to the flanker, try not to look stunned. Be composed and be the first to let your booster club know that you practice this amazing feat every Thursday.

— 1987 Summer Manual. Coach Elway is director of pro scouting for the Denver Broncos.

Team Defense

Emphasis on Defense

Setting Up a Successful Defense

DICK TOMEY WITH LARRY MACDUFF, RICH ELLERSON, AND JOHNNIE LYNN

We believe in playing defense with great effort and enthusiasm. We want a group of athletes that excel in the areas of hitting and effort. The height of a player isn't necessarily as important as his ability to run and his desire to get to the ball.

In order to develop an outstanding defense, you must do the following:

- Recruit players that can run and have the physical capabilities that fit your system.
- Establish pride in defense. Create expectations of stopping people, holding them to a minimum number of points and yards.
- Be willing to help your defense with the strategies you employ on offense and in the kicking game.
- Have a strong running game or a short passing game that will allow you to consume time when necessary to help the defense.
- Have a defensive plan and scheme that is sound, is based on stopping the run, and has enough coverage variety to both pressure the quarterback and stop the underneath throws on early downs.

Our defense uses one front that takes away cutbacks, forces the ball to the perimeter, and has very simple coverdown responsibilities against the variety of formations we see. Our coverage package is a 3-deep coverage and a man-free coverage.

Defensive Line

We construct our defensive front with four defensive linemen (two tackles and two ends), and a whip linebacker. Generally speaking, these positions will cancel all the inside running lanes, C gap to C gap, and rush the passer, with the possible exception of whip, who may be involved in the coverage if pass shows (see Figure 1).

We play with our inside foot back and place a great deal of emphasis on our initial footwork. We play our people left-right whenever possible

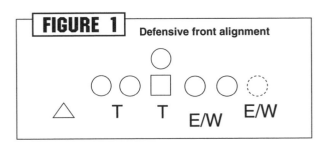

FIGURE 1 Defensive front alignment

to maximize the number of reps in a given stance. However, we balance this with the understanding that a position's job description, physical requirements, and opportunities will change dramatically depending on which way we set the front. What follows is a summary of alignments and responsibilities for our front five.

Stud or Callside End

Align one yard outside tackle or head up to TE. Cross the LOS on the snap of the ball. Defend the C gap versus the run as defined by the hip of the tackle. Spill the ball-carrier deep and wide. Rush the edge versus the pass. As the front is often set to the wide side, deny the QB the use of the field. Attack! Make your mistakes on their side of the LOS and make them full speed. There's some built-in margin for error at this position.

Call-Side Tackle

Align with feet outside the guard's stance, regardless of how tight the splits are. Cross the LOS on the snap of the ball. Defend the B gap versus the run, as defined by the hip of the guard. Rush the passer! Make your mistakes on their side of the LOS and make them full speed. Again, there's some margin for error at this position.

Nose or Backside Tackle

Align on the center with a slight shade away from the callside. Stepping with the inside foot, attack the middle of the center, win the LOS, and cancel both A gaps, one with his body and one with yours.

Keep the center from getting to the LB level at all cost. Versus pass, rush opposite the callside and expect to be double-teamed.

Flex

This position can be played by the whip or end. Align with a slight inside shade on the defensive tackle and flex 24" to 36" off the LOS. Defend the B gap versus the run, as defined by the hip of the guard. From this alignment, we can use our normal aggressive footwork and still expect a great run reaction. If pass shows, our end will fight for contain, or if whip is in the flex, he'll react according to the coverage called.

Backside Seven

Can be played by either the whip or end. Align and defend the run exactly like stud, but we will sacrifice some aggressiveness to insure correctness. Versus pass, the end will rush contain and whip will react according to coverage.

We allow our callside people to play "on the edge" every snap and expect our backside people to give us the margin for error that kind of play requires by being exactly correct. By challenging the gaps, using consistent footwork, and removing some fear of the mistake, we truly achieve the attack mentality our defense is known for.

A great deal has been made of our flex alignment. Interestingly, this system of gap cancellation has its roots in the Canadian Football League where everybody must align a yard off the ball. The question thus became who to move up. Getting up on the ball helps our pass rush and creates the threat of quick penetration. Playing off the ball helps us react appropriately to a wider range of blocking combinations and facilitates change-up in assignments from a single alignment.

Linebackers

Our inside linebackers are normally not tied to a gap in the tackle box; rather, they are expected to run the alley which our front five has forced the ball to bounce into. This requires them to align with a great deal of variety, depending on the threat posed by any given formation.

The linebackers align, along with the secondary, according to strength call that typically indicates the wide set of the field. Our rover, or strong inside linebacker, will align relative to the third eligible while Mike, our weak inside linebacker, will align with the second eligible on the weak side, counting outside in. Our linebackers (along with the strong safety) will, therefore, be the principal adjusters to any shifts or motion. This freedom of alignment facilitates man coverage, keeps us in proximity to changing reference points for zone coverage, and is consistent with our run responsibility.

Versus a balanced 2-back set, our base alignment is 5 yards deep outside shade of the guard (see Figure 2).

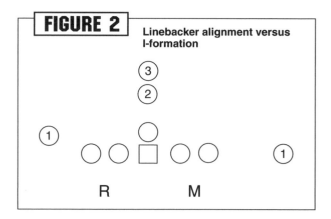

FIGURE 2 Linebacker alignment versus I-formation

If we are aligned versus a single back behind the QB, we deepen to 6 yards, with our near foot on the ball. When aligned on a TE, note that we assume a position (4 x 4) that allows us to force the run (see Figure 3).

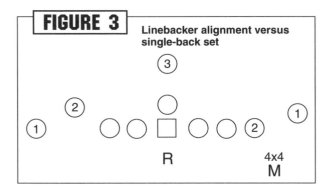

FIGURE 3 Linebacker alignment versus single-back set

When aligned on a TE to the weak side, we have the option of exchanging gaps with the end helping deny the QB the field (see Figure 4).

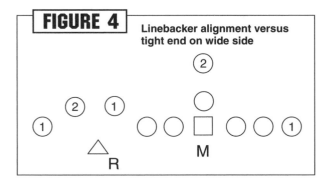

FIGURE 4 Linebacker alignment versus tight end on wide side

Our alignment rules are the same, regardless of the coverage called, and often our blitzes will adjust right along with changing formations. As a result, it's very difficult to get a pre-snap read on our intentions.

A key feature of our system is that because our linebackers aren't expected to step up and plug inside running lanes versus offensive linemen, we can sacrifice physical stature for speed when recruiting. The net result is that we have more people on the field who run exceptionally well, are effective blitzers, can man cover people, and can make plays in the open field. This minimizes the opportunities an offense normally has when they get a linebacker opposite a running back or receiver.

Secondary

Our secondary aligns along the same guidelines as the linebackers. The strong safety makes the direction call that determines what we'll treat as strength and then aligns relative to the second receiver, much as the Mike does on the weakside. Corners align with number one, and we can play them left-right or field and boundary. The free

safety will generally cheat his alignment into the strong B gap when the ball is on the hash or will split the difference between the widest eligibles when the ball is in the middle (see Figure 5).

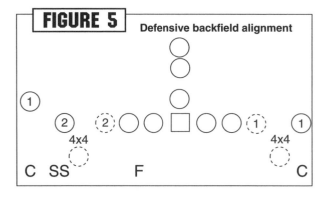

FIGURE 5 Defensive backfield alignment

A major part of our secondary package is our man-to-man coverage. In our man-to-man coverage, we show the same look as we do on every snap. The strong safety, being responsible for covering No. 2 strong, aligns 4 yards outside and 4 yards back from the tight end, or if the No. 2 receiver is a slot, he aligns in a leverage position between the end man on the line of scrimmage and No. 2.

On the snap, the strong safety maintains his inside relationship, knowing that he has help over the top. The free safety is aligned 10 to 12 yards off the ball in the strong B gap, and is responsible for deep middle help. The field corner and boundary corner line up on No. 1 strong and No. 1 weak, respectively. The field corner aligns 8 yards off the ball with an inside attitude on his receiver.

On the snap, the field corner maintains his inside attitude on the receiver by using a weave technique to stay square on the inside shoulder. The boundary corner aligns 8 yards off the ball with an outside attitude on his receiver. On the snap, the boundary corner weaves with the outside shoulder, knowing that he has deep middle help.

When we feel that we're capable of pressing the receivers, we use our basic press bump-and-run rules:

1. Crowd the line of scrimmage with eyes inside to check alignment.
2. Key receiver's chest with hands up and ready to punch (quick hands).
3. Pound receiver on top half of numbers, and turn and run with him. Punch his frame so he can't get his shoulders upfield.

—1994 Proceedings. Coach Tomey is head coach at the University of Arizona. Coaches Ellerson and Lynn are his assistants. Coach MacDuff is an assistant coach for the New York Giants.

A Fundamental Approach to Defense

BARRY ALVAREZ with DAN McCARNEY

I have a very strong belief in fundamentals. That is an area that is too often overlooked, particularly once the season starts and coaches are more concerned with game planning. After each game, our defensive coaches rate our players on these fundamentals:

- Squaring their shoulders.
- Keeping the playside arm and leg free.
- Maintaining a base. Don't cross over.
- Using cross faces. Again, don't cross over.
- Keeping their pads over the toes. Deliver, don't catch.
- Hitting with their hands and shoulder pads, never exposing the fleshy part of their bodies.
- Staying in a football position.

We have established a philosophy of controlling the passing game. We'll give up completions, but we stress not allowing the receiver to run after he catches the ball and, obviously, we don't want the ball thrown behind us.

First, however, we must stop the run and must commit as many people as possible to do so. The following is our philosophy versus the run:

- ***Eliminate the big play.*** Stretch the ball east and west, eliminating the cutback. Use proper pursuit angles. Take all the ball to reduce blocking angles.
- ***Disrupt the offensive rhythm.*** Play multiple fronts. Stem the front (pre-snap) and rock the front (on the snap).

- ***Eliminate mental errors.*** Stay simple and stay sound.
- ***Be physical.***
- ***Play conservatively.*** Play down-and-distance percentages and tendencies. Use two-man slants. Zone and man-free in secondary. Employ pressure as surprise.
- ***Take all the ball to reduce blocking angles.***
- ***Give players a three-way go.***

A Dozen Things to Stress on Defense

- Play with great emotion and enthusiasm each time you step on the field.
- Develop big play personality.
- Out-hustle the opponent and be stronger each snap as the game wears on.
- Believe in yourself and your buddy lined up next to you.
- Believe that you and your teammates are the toughest group on the field.
- Believe you can win and expect to win.
- Play together.
- Refuse to stay blocked, even though you'll get blocked from many angles.
- Develop a variety of techniques; have more than one way to defeat a block.
- Believe that you are going to make the tackle on every play.
- Don't use lack of physical skills as an excuse.
- Show great character. Overcome adversity, injury, and heartache to win.

—1994 Proceedings. Coach Alvarez is head coach at the University of Wisconsin. Coach McCarney is head coach at Iowa State University.

Switching From the 50 to the 43 Defense

GRANT TEAFF

Our defensive philosophy complements our offensive approach. We first must be able to run the ball and defend the run, and then work toward a balance with our passing game and defending the pass.

Defensively, we stress teaching responsibilities and principles. We believe in a base defense that is suitable to our personnel, that is balanced in relation to the offensive set, that is based upon gap control up front, and that is flexible and simple to execute. We challenge each team member with basic responsibilities on every play. When breakdowns occur, they're recognized quickly and adjustments are made.

Our base defense evolved from an Odd or 50 look with multiple schemes to an Even or 43 look. When we first went to the 43 look, we played only the two defensive tackles down. The defensive ends were linebacker types who stood up in front of tight ends. We've put our defensive ends down in front of the tight end now, although they occasionally slide down over the offensive tackles and play like a defensive tackle in an odd front.

Basic Responsibilities in 50 and 43 Defenses

In the 50 or Odd defense (see Figure 1) our responsibilities were broken down in the following manner:

Middle Unit (Nose and LBs)—Must control four gaps (A and B). Nose has both A gaps. Onside LB has B gap. Backside LB helps Nose with A gaps when ball is away. Backside LB must protect his B gap on counter flow and onside LB must help Nose with A gaps.

Outside Unit (Ts and Es)—Tackles must control respective C gaps outside in versus base block. Ball away, cross face of offensive tackle to control B gap on cutback. Ends control tight end from head-up position and contain QB (on option or pass) ball away trail for bootlegs and

reverse. Drop end is responsible for pitch on option and pass defense versus pass. On options, the one not responsible for contain should support alley (inside-out pursuit) to the ball.

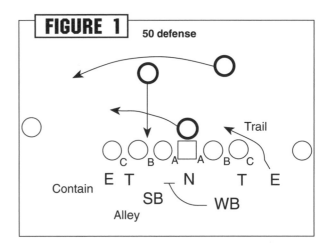

Our basic responsibilities in the 43 (see Figure 2) are as follows:

Middle Unit (Mike and Ts)—Must control four gaps (A and B). Mike has both B gaps either on quick flow or counter flow (dive threat). Both Ts must control respective A gap.

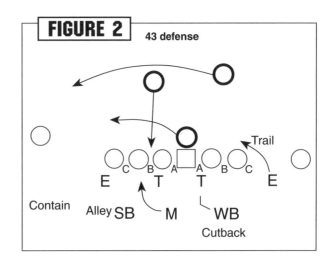

Outside Unit (Es and CB)—Must control C gap and contain QB. When ball is away, end generally has trail responsibility. The end or LB responsible for C gap must squeeze B gap outside in when ball is inside. On option, the one not responsible for contain should inside-out pursuit (alley) to the ball.

Seven Principles of Defense

Regardless of whether we are basic odd (50) or even (43), the following principles apply.

1. *Primary support*—Outside-in support on wide play. Take on lead blocker on sweeps and options. Normally responsible for the pitch.

2. *Force*—Widest man in defense by alignment. Never let ball-carrier outside of you. Responsible for the one out pass. Secondary support outside in.

3. *Contain*—QB on option and sprint-out or roll-out pass. Squeeze from outside in the off-tackle hole on play inside. Inside-out support on wire play.

4. *Trail*—Responsible for bootlegs, reverses, and wide cutbacks when ball starts away.

5. *Cutback*—Responsible for cutback when ball starts away—don't overrun.

6. *Gap responsibility and pursuit*—Front seven given gap responsibility and down the line of scrimmage pursuit.

7. *Option responsibility*—
   Linemen—If ball is faked or given inside of you, squeeze from outside in, but don't lose your outside position on base block. If offensive blocker opposite you blocks down, close down and play ball-carrier outside in. Keep pads square and get a piece of offensive blocker. If you are aligned head-up or inside of offensive blocker, don't let blocker off LOS on inside release. Always be in position to pursue inside out if ball goes wide.

   Linebackers—Read QB and pitchback for option. Keep position and don't step upfield. Base block, outside-in squeeze, out or down block, read mesh or shuffle out if everything in front of you clogs up. Don't overrun QB. Give alley support versus pitch.

   Secondary—The basic rule is we want one more defender on the perimeter than the offense has blockers. This is our premise regardless of the alignment of the front seven.

43 Versus Zone Option

The college 43 has some advantages over the odd alignment versus the split-veer attack and the blocking schemes that are popular. One of the trends in the veer attack is the zone option. This play has fused the inside and outside veer plays. It puts a great deal of pressure on the nose and defensive tackle in the odd alignment.

The QB reads the defensive tackle. If tackle stays outside, QB will give to dive back hitting inside leg of offensive tackle. If QB thinks he can beat the defensive tackle to the outside, he will fake the dive back and option off the next offensive man to show. The play is designed to create a running lane for the dive back, or tie up the defensive nose, LB, and tackle on the dive so the QB can option off the end.

The tight end and flanker are lead blockers, and the pitch back or QB, depending upon what the defensive end does, will have a one-on-one situation on the corner. The offensive line is zone, area blocking to the side of play to cut off inside-out squeeze by the defense, as well as widen the defensive tackle to create an inside running lane, or tie tackle up on dive back and get a one-on-one situation on the corner (see Figure 3).

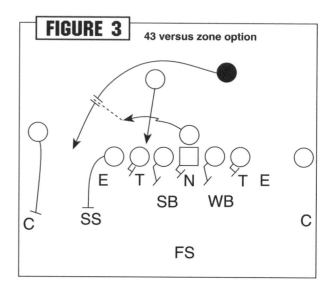

FIGURE 3   43 versus zone option

The 43 makes it more difficult for the offensive lineman to area block and cut off the inside-out squeeze by the defense, thus closing down the running lane of the dive back. The wide alignment of defensive end and the off-the-line play of the outside LB makes it hard on the QB and pitch back to get a one-on-one situation on perimeter. The dive back's angle gives Mike a quick read to the off-tackle hole. The alignment of defensive tackles makes it difficult for the center and onside guard to execute the zone block (see Figure 4).

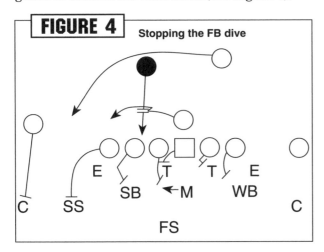

FIGURE 4 Stopping the FB dive

43 Versus Trap Option

Another popular play is the trap option from split backs. In the odd alignments, this play puts a great deal of pressure on the onside LB and tackles. The trap play, a companion to the option, forces the defensive tackle to close inside hard to stop the trap. This allows the offside offensive guard to seal off inside-out pursuit, and gives the QB and pitch back a one-on-one situation on the corner (see Figure 5).

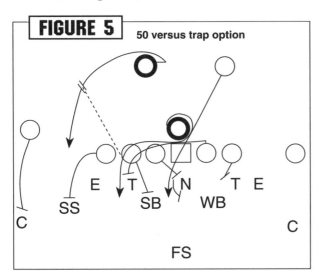

FIGURE 5 50 versus trap option

The trap option does not put the same pressure on the defensive end and LB in the 43, because by alignment the trap play must hit further inside than it does in the odd alignment. Again, the outside LB off the LOS has a better opportunity to read the inside fake and play off the pulling guard, making it hard for QB and pitch back to get the desired one-on-one situation on the corner (see Figure 6).

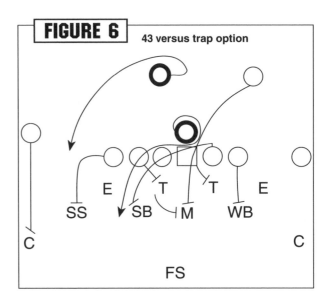

FIGURE 6 43 versus trap option

43 Versus Outside Veer

Another play that the veer teams like is the outside veer or load option, with the onside guard pulling to lead and block alley support. We feel that covering the offensive guards and penetrating with our defensive tackles makes it difficult to pull the guards on the loaded play and cut off our defensive tackles with the center or offensive tackles on reach or down block (see Figure 7).

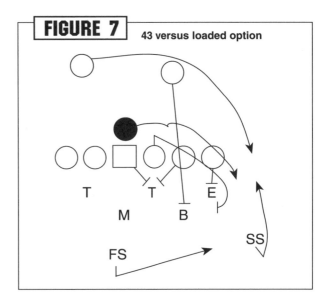

FIGURE 7 43 versus loaded option

43 Versus the Pass

It's always been our philosophy that a good pass rush is the foundation of effective pass defense. In our basic defensive scheme, we believe that a four-man rush with four men covering underneath and 3-deep coverage is the optimum ratio and distribution.

In our basic 43 alignment we have the tackles and ends always rushing and the three LBs playing pass defense. We are aligned in a balanced rush and these four get a great deal of repetition in pass-rushing techniques. Because of the type of athlete we recruit for defensive end, we often beat offensive tackles on the pass rush with speed and quickness. By moving the ends down and the OLBs outside, we can use games with the four-man rush that are very effective versus the drop-back pass. We teach three basic games to our front four rushers (see Figure 8).

Our basic underneath coverage with LBs is man or combination man. This is easy to teach and very effective versus draws, screens, delays, and dumps to the backs. We also play some combination man and zone as well as zone drops with our LBs. This is a good change-up in long-yardage situations to take away deep (17- to 19-yard) intermediate zones.

The third phase of an effective pass defense is, of course, the secondary. Through the years, we have used a number of coverages and change-ups. It's always been our philosophy that we must prevent the long or touchdown pass. Because of this, we usually zone 3-deep rotating with four secondary backs. We have evolved into a nonrotating free safety with man-to-man coverage on single receivers.

On the two-receiver side, our corner will play man in a zone. In other words he will play man on the wide receiver unless the second receiver on his side threatens the deep outside. Our strong safety will work underneath the wide receiver on the two-receiver side. By staying in this basic coverage 85% of the time, we spend a good deal of workout time on one-on-one coverage with the wide receivers. This has given our defensive corners a great deal of confidence in covering one-on-one. Our free safety has been primarily a centerfielder breaking on the ball. Due to the amount of man coverage we play, the basic balanced four-man rush from the 43 alignment has applied pressure on the QB to reduce the time he has to hold

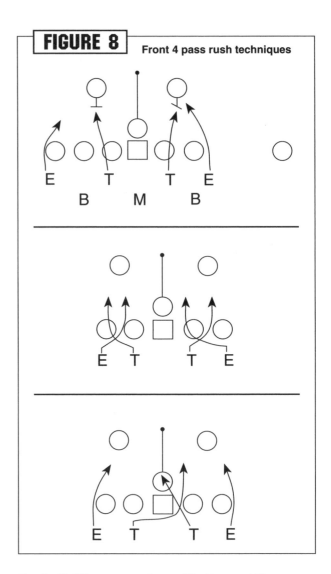

FIGURE 8   Front 4 pass rush techniques

the ball. We were not as effective putting pressure on the QB with the four-man rush in the odd alignment.

We have also found it easier to organize and coordinate our unit drills for both run and pass using the 43 instead of the 50. Regardless of the alignment, we believe in using a base defense concept that is most adaptable to your personnel, and that is based upon teaching responsibilities and sound principles.

—1980 Summer Manual. Coach Teaff is executive director of the AFCA.

Using a Multiple Attack Defense
PAUL TIDWELL

We have an aggressive "go-get-'em," attacking philosophy on defense. We teach, stress, and coach this attitude to our players. We want them to have a defensive mentality to go find the football.

Our defensive game plan is simple. First, we try to take away the bread and butter of our opponent. What are their five best running plays? What are their five best passing plays? What do we need to do to stop these?

Second, we want to disrupt their flow, frustrate them. By coaching an aggressive attack defense we'll create confusion, turnovers, momentum, and emotion that will work to our advantage. X's and O's are very important, and we do coach a sound fundamental package, but more than that we want a swarming, emotional defense that has all 11 players making an effort to get to the ball.

Third, we want an offense that can put points on the board. If our defense is creating turnovers and establishing good field position for the offense, we want to cash in.

Following are a few practice procedures used by our staff to stress our aggressive play:

- Perform a defensive team pursuit drill daily.
- Work each position on some type of tackling drill daily.
- Include a five-minute block called our "turnover period."
- During our pass skelly and team periods, have the defense pursue (sprint) to where the ball ends up, huddle, break, and then jog back to LOS. This can function as part of their conditioning, if done properly.

Defensive Packages

We basically have three fronts with reductions and adjustments off each one: an Eagle front, the 50 front, and the 4-6. Our defense is gap control, attacking as we read. Figure 1 shows an example of our gap responsibilities versus a run to the strongside.

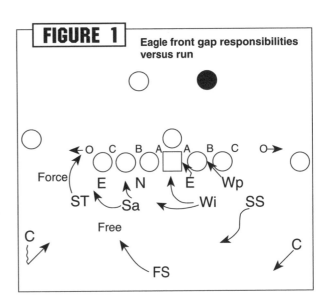

FIGURE 1 Eagle front gap responsibilities versus run

Eagle Defense

In our Eagle front, we're able to line up and run a variety of coverages: zone, man/man, and man/zone combinations and also a variety of twists, stunts, and blitzes. Figure 2 shows an example of attacking type coverage.

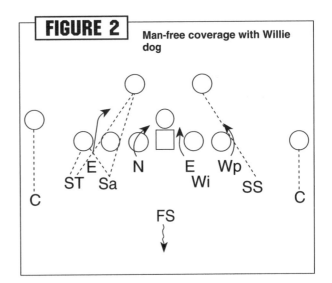

FIGURE 2 Man-free coverage with Willie dog

An adjustment off this is to drop the Willie backer in underneath coverage (dog the circle) as a free defender. He reads TE, backs out, quick slants, and looks to take away the intermediate routes (see Figure 3a). In Figure 3b you see how this defense reacts to an I-formation or brown formation where both backs release out the same side. We'll double read this with our inside backers and switch responsibilities. With both backs out the weakside, Willie backer now becomes a man defender. Sam backer is free.

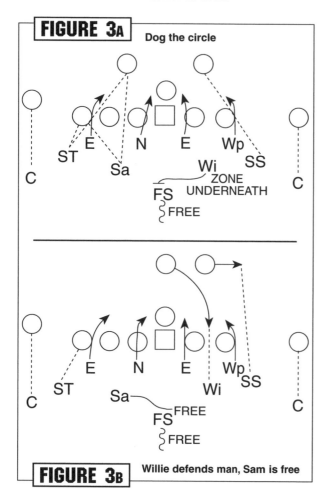

FIGURE 3A Dog the circle

FIGURE 3B Willie defends man, Sam is free

Figure 4 shows a more aggressive scheme that can be called for short-yardage situations or for a passing down where pressure is desired.

50 Defense

Our 50 front also allows us a wide variety of different options and coverages with only minor adjustments. We still have the capability to reduce, zone, man/man, man/zone combo, and use our up-front games. We're still gap control and our defense is on the offensive. Figure 5 shows

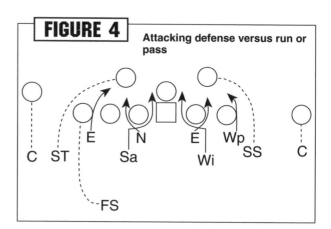

FIGURE 4 Attacking defense versus run or pass

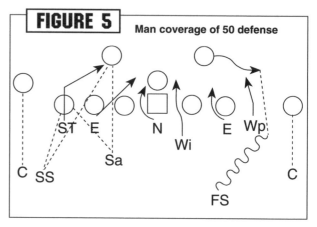

FIGURE 5 Man coverage of 50 defense

an example of our 50 defense and a man/man coverage.

Teams that run trips, doubles, and spread formations with single back or no-back offenses will try to get mismatches (LBs on receivers). With a few personnel changes and adjustments to our safety position, we're still able to get pressure up front. Figure 6 shows a double-wing with a single back. In our 50 front, we've reduced down, taken Willie out, and put a nickel back in. We can run this with a man free or straight man/man (as in Figure 6) freeing the Sam backer to blitz by putting the free safety on the fullback.

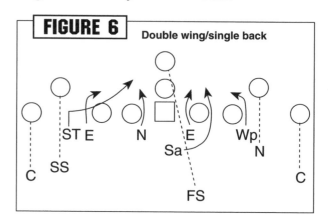

FIGURE 6 Double wing/single back

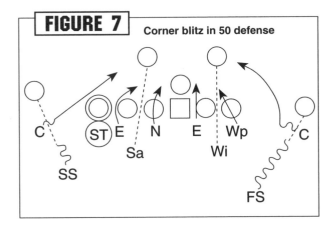

FIGURE 7 — Corner blitz in 50 defense

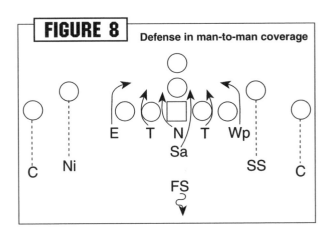

FIGURE 8 — Defense in man-to-man coverage

A secondary blitz that's used against certain teams and in certain situations is a corner blitz (see Figure 7). It is run out of a CV-2 man under look or a CV-2 zone look. This blitz has been successful every time we've used it. The two safeties will cheat over and cover the X and Z man-to-man. The two corners will also cheat up and slightly in to give them a greater advantage, but still not give away the blitz.

4-6 Defense

Our third front is a simplified 4-6 that is primarily used against a predominantly passing team or in passing situations (see Figure 8). We'll close up to the RBs with our strong safety if they stay in to block, looking for delays and screens.

Our purpose on defense is to create different looks, bring different players, attack one play out of a 4-6, then line up in an Eagle, show blitz again, but then drop back in a 3-deep or 2-deep zone. We want to confuse the pre-snap reads as much as possible and make blocking schemes as difficult as possible.

Our rules and adjustments on defense are simple and allow us to keep the personnel we want in the game without a lot of substitution. These defenses also allow us to run nickel and dime packages as well as our zone coverage.

—1990 Proceedings. Coach Tidwell was head coach at Snow College (UT).

||||||||||||||||||||||||||||||||||||||||||||||||

The Wrecking Crew Defense

R.C. SLOCUM with BOB DAVIE

||||||||||||||||||||||||||| |||||||||||||||||||||||||

Our players have nicknamed our defensive unit the "Wrecking Crew." That's because our philosophy is not one of "bend but don't break," but rather "seek out and destroy." We never want to line up and try to react to all of the different plays, formations, and motions that offenses can run. Instead, we'd rather dictate to them, make them limit their offense, and challenge them to adjust to our various types of pressures.

Every offensive coach has different blocking schemes, hot receivers, and blitz adjust type routes which they can, on the chalkboard, use to counter anything you can do as a defensive coach. We want to see if they can do those things on the field.

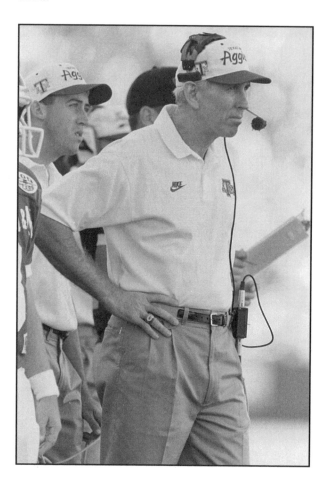

A Dozen Keys to Defense

Here are 12 things that lead to success on the defensive side of the ball.

1. **Believe that big defense wins big games.** Timing, weather conditions, etc., can really affect your offense, but if you have a sound defensive philosophy, it is reasonable to expect the defense to show up week after week and play steady consistent defense. You always have to coach your defensive team that they are the ones that win ballgames.

2. **Set high standards.** Know what good defense is. Before you can be good, you must have high standards for your defense and not be satisfied until you reach them.

3. **Get all players to play hard.** No matter what his ability level, every player that you put on the field can give all-out effort and chase the football.

4. **Develop an unselfish attitude.** You can't have stars on your defense and be successful. You're only as good as your weakest link. Your coverage is only as good as your pass rush, and your pass rush is only as good as your coverage.

5. **Use multiple fronts and minimum technique.** We would like to present the offense a number of different looks but, at the same time, keep our teaching to a minimum.

6. **Dictate offense with a pressure package.** We do this for several reasons:
   - *It limits opponents' offense.* Offensive coaches get concerned that they can't block all of your fronts or pick up all of your blitzes, so they reduce the number of plays for the game plan.
   - *A pressure package on defense helps your offense.* By working against each other, your offense becomes accustomed to pressure, tight man coverages, etc.

• *It's fun for the players.* It allows players to have some personality and to use the abilities that they have to make big plays.

7. *Maintain poise.* Bad things will happen! You must prepare your defensive team that in the course of the ballgame it is not unusual for an offense to turn the ball over. At this time, the defense has the best opportunity to prove their character. We often say, "It's not the bad things that happen to you that are important, but how you react to those things."

8. *Don't overload players mentally.* Be sure that all of your adjustments and checks are simple enough that your players can execute them on the field.

9. *Treat players as individuals and with respect.*

10. *Have fun.* Look forward to the big game. The bigger the game, the bigger the challenge, the more your players should look forward to it.

11. *Utilize individual talents—situation players.* It's important to take the talent you have and to try to use it effectively in a game situation. For example, a corner may not know the entire defense, but he might be able to go in and play man-to-man coverage.

12. *Be flexible in the game plan.* In reality, your game plan is a preliminary game plan. It is based upon what your opponent has done in the games prior to your game. Be ready during the course of your game to evaluate their plan and adjust yours if necessary.

Pressure Defensive Packages

In talking about our pressure defense, many people think of our blitz and straight man coverage package. We feel comfortable using all-out blitzes and blitz coverage, but probably don't use it as much as people might think. We're always looking for ways to pressure offenses and mix our coverages, taking the pressure off our secondary, but keeping it on opposing offenses.

We attempt to pressure offenses using a four-man rush and playing zone coverage behind it. In our four-man pressure package with zone coverage, we apply pressure through OLB stunts, line stunts, and ILB stunts.

Our base defensive package is a 3-4-4 alignment for three reasons:

• We like our fourth rusher to be a speed rusher (OLB), pitting a smaller, quicker rusher versus a big offensive tackle.
• It's easier to find four quality LB type players as opposed to four down linemen.
• It's flexible. We're able to play all 4-3 fronts, and yet drop eight in coverage, if needed.

Setting the Front

We like to be multiple, but try to keep terminology simple and easy to understand. We always tell the front where to align first. We think it's critical that the front gets aligned quickly and properly.

The front will align to the strength of offense's running formation (TE side), based on a strong call by the inside LB. The first digit of the call tells end to the strong call where to align; the second digit tells end away from call where to align. Our noseguard will slide automatically and shade to the 5 technique (see Figure 1).

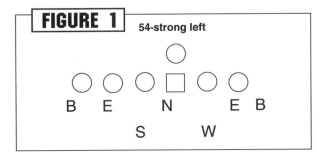

FIGURE 1 54-strong left

B E N E B
S W

In 44, with both ends playing a 4 technique, there are several things we can do with the nose. The base is to play him heads or in a 0 technique (see Figure 2).

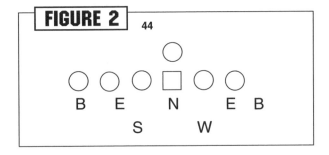

FIGURE 2 44

B E N E B
S W

If we wanted to play a reduced defense to the split end side, we'd simply change the second digit putting the end in a 3 technique (see Figure 3). The OLB would know automatically to squeeze down to a 5 if the end is kicked down.

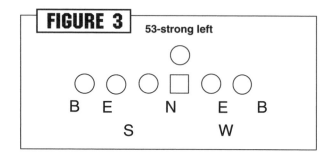

FIGURE 3 53-strong left

B E N E B
S   W

Setting the Coverage

Now that we have the front set, the secondary gets aligned based on the coverages called. In our package, the numbered coverages are zone and the colored are man.

To assure us of getting a fourth rusher and locking him into the open end side, we'll call two coverage calls in the huddle. If we choose to have the fourth rusher weak, we'll play the first digit versus a pro formation and second digit versus slot or twins. A base coverage for us would be cover 1/3. We'll play cover 1 to a pro set (see Figure 4).

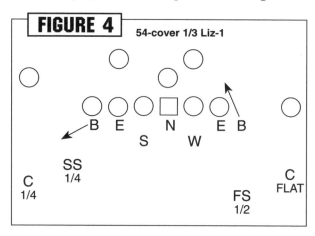

FIGURE 4 54-cover 1/3 Liz-1

B E N E B
S   W
SS 1/4
C 1/4
C FLAT
FS 1/2

If we get a twin or slot set, we will play a zone to the twins allowing the OLB on that side to rush (see Figure 5).

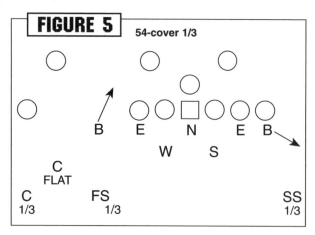

FIGURE 5 54-cover 1/3

B E N E B
W S
C FLAT
C 1/3   FS 1/3   SS 1/3

Any motion creating change of formation will be handled by the secondary and will change the coverage. The front and rusher will stay locked in (see Figure 6).

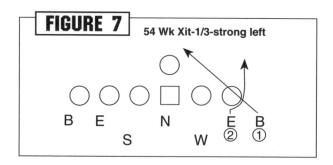

FIGURE 6 Liz 3 to Rip 1

B E W N S E B
C   SS
C
FS

Applying Pressure

Once we have our four-man rush in place and know where our fourth rusher is coming from, it's simple to incorporate pressure out of our base zone coverage concepts. One of our favorites is called Wk Xit (see Figure 7). In this pressure stunt, the OLB is free to come under all blockers and the defensive end is responsible for all contain situations.

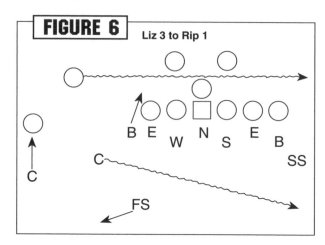

FIGURE 7 54 Wk Xit-1/3-strong left

B E N E B
S   W ② ①

Since we're in our four-man rush package, by double-digiting our coverage it's simple to incorporate line stunts that are good for run and pass. We've had a lot of success with a twist stunt involving the nose and end. By calling "53 Twist," we're telling our end (tackle in man front) to go first (see Figure 8). The end will run inside on snap using a dip technique. The nose will read the center's block and will twist unless he gets reach blocked. The change-up of 53 Twist is 53 Nest. Because nest begins with N, it's telling the nose to go first in the weak A and the end to now read.

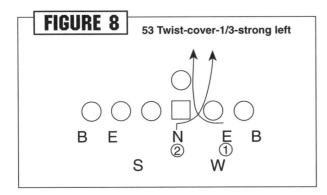

FIGURE 8 | 53 Twist-cover-1/3-strong left

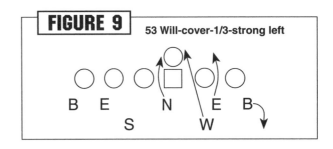

FIGURE 9 | 53 Will-cover-1/3-strong left

The next four-man pressure we use out of our base package is to plug one of our ILBs. If we choose to plug Will, we'll simply call out his name, as in 53 Will-cover 1/3, shown in Figure 9. The

OLB to Will's side replaces him on his pass drop (unless sprint-out pass).

We put a premium on keeping it simple and having all of our terminology and packages tied together. But also realize that *what* you play is not as important as *how* you play it. That's what makes the difference between winning or losing.

—1993 Proceedings. Coach Slocum is head coach at Texas A&M University. Coach Davie is defensive coordinator at the University of Notre Dame.

The Eagle Defense
BILL DOOLEY

We're a 50 shade defense, but there are some subtle differences in how we play the 50 shade package as compared to most programs. First, we always play our strong safety on the Eagle side. Second, we align the Eagle look where we want it.

We feel that with these two concepts integrated into our scheme, we can better deploy our personnel and achieve the defensive look we want against our opponents. With these concepts and some very good athletes, our defense has been able to accomplish its objectives. Our defensive objectives aren't much different from most programs. Those objectives are:

- Control the opponent's running game.
- Force the opponent into pass situations.
- Prevent the long run or pass.
- Score or set up a score.
- Keep the opponent from scoring.

We emphasize the first objective—to control our opponent's running game. If we control the running attack, we can force the opponent into

long-yardage pass situations. This is a high-risk, low-percentage situation for the offense—the type of situation where the defense is in control.

We believe in the "gap control theory" of defense. We want each man in our defensive front to be responsible for controlling one gap. Each gap and the corresponding techniques that our front people play are numbered according to the numbering system made famous at Alabama by Coach Bear Bryant (see Figure 1).

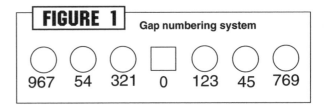

FIGURE 1 | Gap numbering system

967 54 321 0 123 45 769

We want simplicity and repetition in everything we do. If we're going to ask our front people to control a gap, then we want to teach them the simplest and most effective way to control that gap. We do this by asking our front people to play with their hands in order to defeat one side of a blocker. It's easier to control one side of the blocker rather than to play head-up and work to the play-side gap.

By teaching the use of hands to defeat a block, we can play on either the inside or outside half of the blocker. This allows us to switch personnel from right to left or vice versa. Also, by teaching the same technique, we can improve our fundamental techniques and increase our repetitions at recognizing blocking schemes.

Besides keeping our fundamental techniques to a minimum, we align in one basic front—the Eagle defense. We do this in order to eliminate mistakes and the chance of the long run or pass (objective #3). Teaching from one basic front allows us to spend more time in practice defending those plays we must stop, plus it affords us more time to work on adjustments, special plays, stunts, game situations, etc.

Setting Up the Eagle Defense

Our method of playing the Eagle or 50 shade defense is technically the same as most programs, but we differ in our alignment of the Eagle-side personnel and how we deploy our defensive front.

We always align our strong safety, Eagle end, and Eagle-side linebacker together. We then declare where we want the Eagle side of our defense by making a directional call such as "Field or Short Eagle," "Strong or Weak Eagle," or "Tight or Split Eagle." We align our Eagle front versus a tight end side and a split end side (see Figure 2).

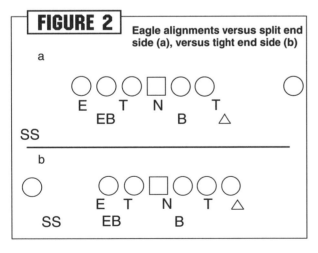

FIGURE 2 Eagle alignments versus split end side (a), versus tight end side (b)

Our Eagle end will learn to play basically two techniques—a 7 technique versus a tight end and a 5 technique on an offensive tackle on the split end side.

The Eagle linebacker aligns in the offensive tackle-guard area with one set of key reads and gap responsibilities. He never has to take on the tackle's block. He's the alley player with flow to him, or he runs to the 1 gap with flow away from him.

The strong safety is a 9 gap player with contain responsibility versus the run to him and flat responsibility versus pass.

The T-N-Ts have their respective gaps to control. The tackles play a 5, 3, and 4 technique while the nosetackle plays a shade 0 technique on the center.

Our drop end is another strong safety except he must learn to play 9 technique versus a tight end to his side. The drop end will play just like a SS when he is aligned on a split end side. He has contain responsibility versus run and flat responsibility versus pass.

The Eagle Front

Every offense has tendencies. It is our defensive staff's responsibility to find those tendencies and design our game plan accordingly. We determine which defensive look will present our opponent with the most difficulty, either the 50 shade look or the Eagle look. We then attempt to deploy the particular look that's best suited to our opponent's tendencies. Those tendencies could be to run either to the field or the boundary, to the tight end or split end side, or to the formation's strongside or weakside.

Field or Short Eagle

If we find that our opponent has a strong tendency to run to the field or to run into the boundary, we simply call "Field Eagle" or "Short Eagle" depending on which look we want to the field.

In Figure 3 we have declared Field Eagle. Therefore, we expect our opponent to attack our Eagle look.

If we want our opponents to run at our 50 look, we then call Short Eagle as diagrammed in Figure 4.

Strong or Weak Eagle

When the ball is in the middle of the field or on the hash mark, and we find that the offense has a tendency to run to the formation side, we then call either "Strong Eagle" or "Weak Eagle," depending on which look we want on the strongside (2-receiver side; see Figure 5).

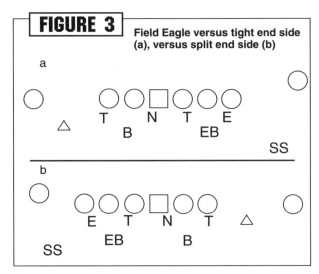

FIGURE 3 Field Eagle versus tight end side (a), versus split end side (b)

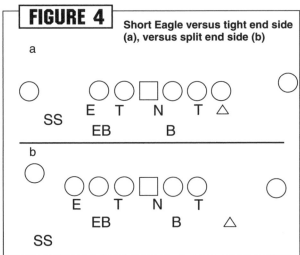

FIGURE 4 Short Eagle versus tight end side (a), versus split end side (b)

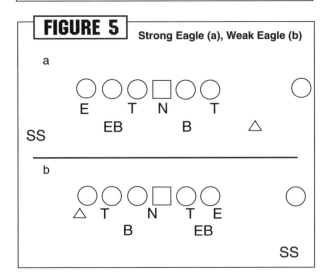

FIGURE 5 Strong Eagle (a), Weak Eagle (b)

Obviously, if the offense has a tendency to run weakside, we can make the same calls to get the 50 or the Eagle look on the weakside.

Tight or Split Eagle

If we find that a team likes to run the tight end side, we can call "Tight Eagle" or "Split Eagle," once again depending on which look we want (see Figure 6). Just as with the Strong Eagle or Weak Eagle calls, we can align the Eagle look or the 50 look to the split end side by making the same Tight Eagle or Split Eagle calls.

In today's game of defensive football, everyone is concerned with adjustments to motion and to shifts. We ask only our front people to adjust to a tight end or split end alignment, while our secondary handles all changes of strength.

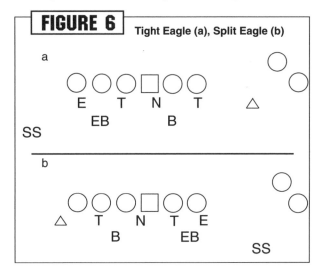

FIGURE 6 Tight Eagle (a), Split Eagle (b)

Eagle Advantages

Let me review with you why we deploy our defensive front as we do:

- We can take advantage of offensive tendencies.
- We determine where we want our front to align; the offense cannot dictate to us where to align.
- We can get the personnel matchup we want.
- We can adjust to changing game-situations. We don't add fronts or stunts to stop an opponent's attack. We simply find out where our opponent is trying to attack us, and then we make the appropriate directional calls, thus getting the 50 or Eagle look where we want it.

Overall, we've derived many benefits from playing the 50 shade defense the way we do. These benefits include flexibility to make proper adjustments in personnel, alignments, and coverages, and the simplicity of learning the overall scheme and particular techniques.

—1985 Proceedings. Coach Dooley was head coach at Virginia Tech.

Adjusting the Eagle Defense
ROCKY HAGER

Our defensive philosophy emphasizes the importance of hustle and pursuit. We grade our players' pursuit with the objective of reaching a 90% grade as a defensive unit. We want 11 players to the ball on every play.

When we talk about our defensive team's performance, we do not talk about points the opponent scored—we talk about our pursuit grade. We stress great pursuit on every play of every practice, and we expect results.

Now, we're not foolish enough to think pursuit is the only thing a defense has to do well to be a success. We also drill the fundamentals, the same as every other program in the country. We are very particular about our technical play, and our players have developed good technique.

We're constantly referring to SAKRAT with the defensive team. This acronym stands for stance, alignment, key, read, assignment, technique. Our Eagle package begins with the most basic, the Strong Eagle, shown in Figures 1 and 2 versus the pro and twins formations, respectively.

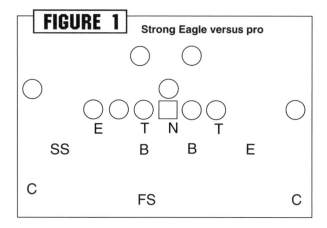

We work this base front frequently and drill on a daily basis the techniques for success. We believe that the development of the techniques will progress at a rate relative to the level of practice competition. Therefore, early in spring and fall practice periods, we often work our first defense against the first offense in group sessions.

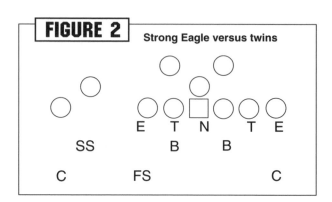

Although we do this for only short periods, it has proven to be most beneficial.

To keep this important part of our package from becoming predictable, we always employ movement in our defensive line. This is a residue of our old Okie defenses and has its roots in the "three-way-go" principle.

These movements help to solidify the offensive line schemes and usually keep them honest in their design. Our one-man movements are used most frequently, and obviously are the foundation for any multiple movements. Each position player has several movements to learn and execute. Knife, tag, and fire in are examples (see Figure 3).

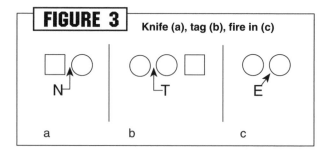

However, movement on our defensive front was not enough to keep offenses from locking us into a desirable look. Opponents understood our design and found ways to attack us. So, we've moved the noseguard from his usual alignment over the center to a shade look over the offensive guard.

This is a common adjustment made by Eagle teams, and puts us into a 40 defense, which is a completely different part of our package (see Figure 4).

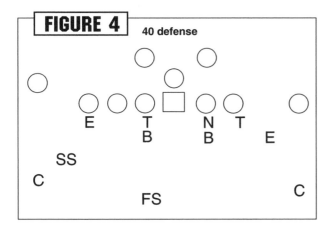

FIGURE 4 40 defense

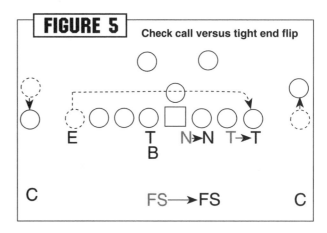

FIGURE 5 Check call versus tight end flip

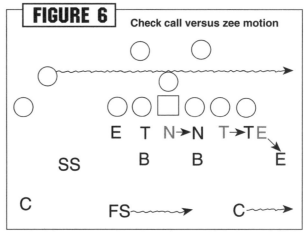

FIGURE 6 Check call versus zee motion

With this basic adjustment, we have the flexibility to use pro-style line stunts, which have been effective for us from time to time. This combination of packages has been effective, but offensive motions and shifts can still lock us into one look or another. To compete against sophisticated audible systems, we felt we needed to find a way to keep the chalk in our hands.

Our check system has kept us from being predictable by alignment and it combats tight end flip and zee motion (see Figures 5 and 6).

The addition of the check system to our package has been very beneficial. It has enabled our secondary to play nearly any coverage versus any formation. We'll change the coverage checks within this part of our game plan and understand we must be sharp with our recognition of the various formations and adjustments.

When we first started this part of our package, we made frequent mistakes. To insure error-free play, we now drill the entire defense for 25 to 30 minutes per week on formation recognition only. We also incorporate this same concept when we're working on pursuit drills.

Our coaches work exceptionally hard at teaching our athletes our package, the fundamentals, and their techniques. This has allowed our defensive players to perform with much confidence, high efficiency, and great pursuit within our team concept.

—1989 Proceedings. Coach Hager was head coach at North Dakota State University.

Stopping the Run With a 7:6 Advantage

JIMMY JOHNSON

In setting up a defensive scheme, you first need to analyze what you need to stop offensively. Against most teams, and in most conferences, the first thing you need to stop is the running game. Our defense is set up to stop the running game and force the opposing offense to throw the football. We do this with what we call the "hit-man principle." We developed this type of defense from coaching at various universities through the years. I'd like to give you a little background on how we go about it.

I was fortunate enough to work with some outstanding athletes at the University of Oklahoma during 1970 to 1973. We had players such as the Selmon brothers, Sugar Bear Hamilton, and Roderick Shoate, so we could be highly successful by being very basic and taking full advantage of the talent we had.

In 1973, I went to the University of Arkansas, where we didn't have the same type of talent and we had to come up with something to support our defense. For years, I had listened to offensive coaches talk about how they wanted to get a 3:2 ratio with their option offense; in other words, they wanted isolation on the corner, where the quarterback could read pitch or keep, depending on the reaction of the defensive end and secondary run support. Various blocking schemes were set up to veer everything to the inside, with the exception of the defensive end and the secondary run support. They felt that any time they got the 3:2 ratio, they had the advantage.

Seven-on-Six Advantage

We're looking for a similar advantage with our hit-man principle. When applied successfully, we get a 7:6 ratio versus the running game. In Figure 1 you can see that in our 50 defense we create a situation with six offensive blockers, six defenders, and one hit man. Therefore, we get our 7:6 ratio and hit-man principle.

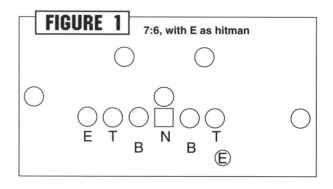

FIGURE 1   7:6, with E as hitman

In all of our schemes, whether it be the 5-2, the 4-3, or the 6-1, protecting the hit man is a priority. In order to do this we must play basically head-up alignments and must avoid stunting or running around blocks.

The hit man's only rule is that he operates up and down the line of scrimmage. He must not be committed toward the line of scrimmage until he sees the football. He must be aware that no one will block him because he's protected and he is to make the tackle. Sometimes, as shown in Figure 2, our designated hit man is the weakside linebacker.

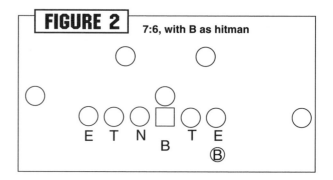

FIGURE 2   7:6, with B as hitman

We feel that the hit-man principle encompasses all the various blocking schemes (veer, zone, trap) and equalizes the offensive option ratio back to 3:3. It also gives the defense an extra man versus the basic running attack. This type of principle can be used in whatever defensive scheme you play as long as the front six read and control one-on-one blocks and you protect your hit man. Defensively you have to be patient and disciplined and let the offense make the mistake. At times, there is a need to stunt and force something to happen, but this scheme gives you a sound defense to work from. Protect your hit man, put some points on the board, and you'll come out on top.

—1980 Proceedings. Coach Johnson is head coach for the Miami Dolphins.

Stopping the Wishbone

DAVE WANNSTEDT

Too many coaches underestimate the Wishbone attack's complexity because the ball is not thrown 30 times a game. Our philosophy against the Wishbone is to slow it down and force the opponent to drive as long and as far as possible on each possession, forcing the offense to execute as much of the triple option as possible. We try to make them run east and west, not north and south. By forcing total execution, it puts the percentage for negative plays and turnovers to the advantage of the defensive side.

We play with four down defensive linemen, which gives us the flexibility to slide into different fronts without changing personnel. When defending the Wishbone out of an even front, we start by covering the guards and use our 4-3 scheme. The 4-3 even front gives us the best advantage in taking away the fullback and slowing down the Wishbone.

It's very important when playing a Wishbone team to understand the importance of the fullback play in correlation to the success of the offense. The fullback is the Wishbone's starting point, and it also must be yours as a defensive coach.

Linemen Responsibilities

Our tackles cover the guards and play 6 inches off the ball. This allows us to crowd the football as much as possible and get penetration in the backfield to disrupt the mesh point between the quarterback and fullback handoff. By getting this penetration, you'll force the offense to use blocking schemes that will help free up your linebackers.

We'll usually play a 3 technique to the tight end and a 1 technique weakside; each must un-derstand his responsibility and how the offense can attack him. The 3 technique must never get reached by the guard and must always force the fullback to cut back inside him (see Figure 1).

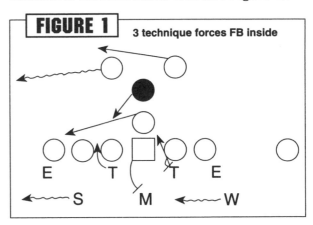

The 1 technique can expect one of two different blocking schemes. Against man blocking, he must be prepared to never get cut off inside and to help on the fullback winding back. Against a Charlie block (see Figure 2), where the center

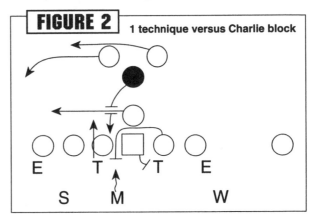

blocks back and the guard pulls for the middle linebacker, he must not be in too big of a hurry to cross the face of the center. We want to squeeze the center into the hole as much as possible. Although this scheme is tougher on the 1 technique, it's an easier read for the middle linebacker and should put him in a better position to make the play on the fullback.

Linebacker Responsibilities

We play our middle linebacker a little tighter versus the Wishbone than we do against a conventional running offense. Normally, we have his toes at 5 yards. Versus the Wishbone, we'll tighten him up to 3 yards from the ball.

The middle linebacker's only responsibility, and his total concentration, must be with getting the fullback. *Every* play. The minute he gets too concerned about the other phases of the option game, the quarterback or pitch, the defense suffers. He must key the fullback. If flow goes strong or to the 3 technique, he must step up attacking the center, keeping his outside arm free, and try to force the fullback to commit behind him (see Figure 3).

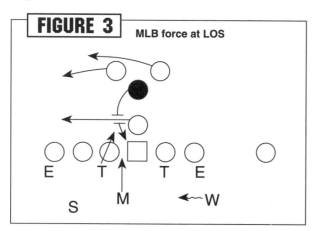

If they hand the ball off strongside, he must be in position with his outside arm free to make the tackle. If he's too soft or aligned too deep, the cutback lane becomes too big for the 1 technique to cover (see Figure 4).

If flow goes to the 3 technique and they Charlie block it, he must step up and attack the guard in the same manner as he would the center on a base block, again forcing the cutback by not getting stretched (see Figure 5).

If flow goes weak or to the 1 technique, the middle linebacker must beat the center and make

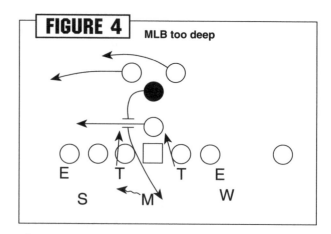

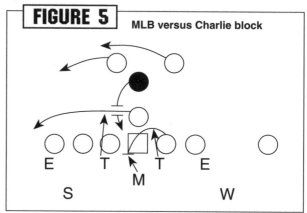

the tackle in the B gap. This is somewhat tougher, especially if he gets tied up with defeating the center's block. It's important that the 1 technique gets penetration (see Figure 6) and doesn't get knocked back into the scraping path of the middle linebacker.

The two tackles and middle linebacker in an even front must work together, not only scheme-wise, but also technique-wise, to stop the Wishbone dive effectively.

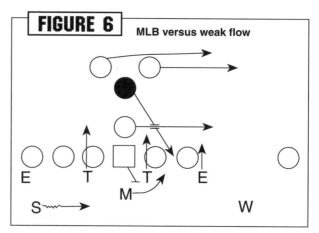

—1988 Summer Manual. Coach Wannstedt is head coach for the Chicago Bears.

Getting Linebackers
to the Point of Attack
DENNIS GREEN

"Getting to the point of attack" is a phrase we all use in discussing defensive football. To me it applies to every defensive player once the ball is snapped. In this article I'll show how we try to get the outside and inside linebackers to the point (where the ball will be), and then to attack.

Let's start with the linebacker responsibilities. An outside linebacker has to get out of his stance, read his key, and determine what technique to use according to his assignment and play confrontation. The inside linebacker has to read his key, diagnose the play, and get to the point of attack.

Linebackers Versus the Pass

Now, I want to deal first with the role that a linebacker can play against the pass. One approach is to attack from the perimeter and rush the quarterback on his drop. Figure 1 shows a basic 3-4 defense with a weak outside linebacker pass rush. The outside linebacker to the tight end side has the pass rush versus a dropback and sprint-out pass.

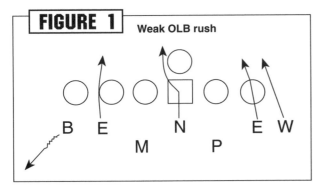

I don't feel that enough emphasis is placed on the linebacker's ability to get to the quarterback. Remember, if the defense is facing a pass play, the outside linebacker has to blitz, drop to an area of responsibility, or cover a man. I like to refer to a linebacker's pass rush as a blitz because then everyone knows that his responsibility is to make a maximum effort to get to the quarterback.

Before the outside linebacker can effectively force the quarterback, he must try to get to a spot up the field. Too many times the outside linebacker does not aim for a point that is deep enough to force the quarterback to step up into the pocket.

The advantage that the weak outside linebacker has when rushing against an offensive tackle is that he can get as much width as he wants. The width allows him the opportunity to try to beat the offensive tackle up the field with quickness off the line of scrimmage. The wide split forces the tackle to jump to the outside, which many times will offset his balance. The backer can now try to use a swim technique and go inside or use the inside arm to throw him to the outside, as you see in Figure 2.

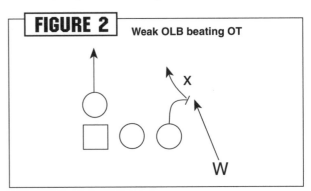

The backer must make sure that anytime he goes inside of the tackle, he has to get his width back. His pass blitz responsibility always carries a contain assignment. The quarterback cannot be allowed to break containment. Thus, he has to keep the quarterback on his inside shoulder as he applies pressure.

If when rushing, the weak outside linebacker is confronted by a back, the best technique to use is to force, strike a blow with the inside shoulder, and squeeze toward the quarterback (see Figure 3).

This can be a problem because so often these days defensive players are taught to play with their hands only, and never learn to strike a blow

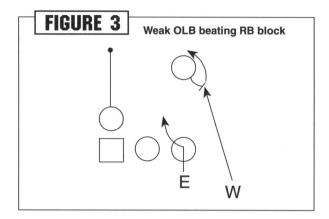

FIGURE 3 — Weak OLB beating RB block

with the forearm shiver. Don't get me wrong. Defensive players have to be very proficient at using their hands in this era of football. However, I believe that the best way for a linebacker to attack a pass blocker is to let the situation dictate his technique. For example, using the hands to strike a blow requires a lot of upper body strength, whereas a forearm blow can be more explosive and is definitely more aggressive.

If the outside linebackers don't apply the pressure in an Okie defense, the quarterbacks are going to have too much time to throw. There should be a mismatch with the weak outside linebacker rushing against a halfback, and that's the way it should be introduced to the backer.

The inside linebacker is rarely involved in a pass blitz against the dropback pass, unless the defense is playing some form of straight man coverage with the free safety covering one of the remaining backs. When the quarterback is running a designed pass play to break the contain and challenge the defense at the perimeter, the inside linebacker must now support, get to his point, and attack. The sprint-draw pass play is the most effective way to do this, because the fake to the halfback affects both linebackers (see Figure 4).

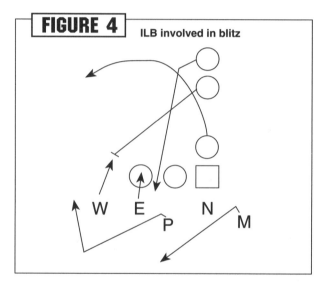

FIGURE 4 — ILB involved in blitz

If the outside linebacker is not able to contain the quarterback, then he has to get help from the inside linebacker. The inside linebacker has to make up his mind to support and then attack the quarterback. The inside linebacker now becomes the contain man, and he must force the quarterback with inside leverage on the ball. If he misses him, the quarterback at least has to cut back inside where the inside linebacker should get help from pursuit (see Figure 5).

For the inside linebacker to get to the point of attack, he must precisely read his key and diagnose the play. Film study should tell him whether he is seeing sprint draw or sprint-draw pass. His first key is the guard, and his second key is the ball. The angle of the ball can also be a factor.

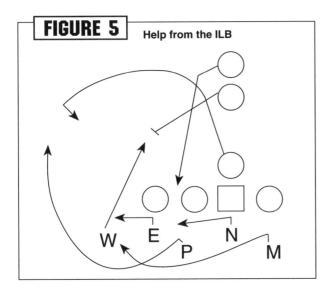

FIGURE 5 — Help from the ILB

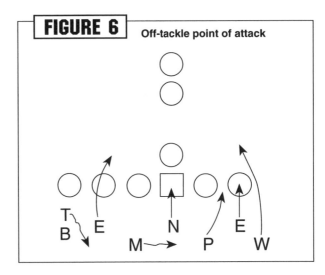

FIGURE 6 — Off-tackle point of attack

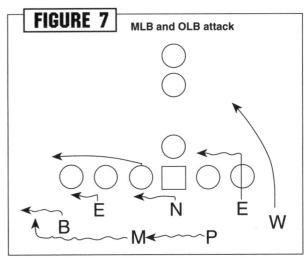

FIGURE 7 — MLB and OLB attack

Linebackers Versus the Run

So far, I have talked only about pass rush, support, and contain principles. But teams that can consistently win have an effective running attack.

For every run play there is a determined point of attack. This area is where the play is designed to go, and all of the offensive blocking schemes are designed to get the ball carrier through that area. The team that gets to that area with the most people has the best chance for success. For defense to win this battle, they have to have at least one defender moving forward to fill the area.

In Figure 6, the point of attack is the off-tackle area. For a defense to have success (a) the nose guard cannot be hook blocked or scoop blocked; (b) the outside linebacker has to go meet the fullback as far in the backfield as possible, attacking with his inside shoulder and keeping his outside arm free; and (c) the middle linebacker must shuffle and attack the guard, not wait for him.

In Figure 7, both the middle and outside linebackers have to attack in order to turn the play back inside.

I view the point of attack as that area where the defense has to apply pressure with defend-

ers. It does not matter if it is a quarterback throwing from the pocket or sprinting out and challenging the perimeter. At least one linebacker has to be assigned to contain the play and feel that it's his responsibility to attack with leverage.

On run plays, you can't be passive and wait and see how you are going to be blocked. By getting defenders to the area where the offense wants to attack, you have a much better chance of stopping them.

—1983 Proceedings. Coach Green is head coach for the Minnesota Vikings.

Getting Run Support From the Secondary
HAYDEN FRY WITH BILL BRASHIER

It is our belief that the most important thing about run support is the position that the defensive backs assume and keep on the ball. If they understand the position that they must have and then do everything they can do at that position, the chances for a long run are greatly minimized.

The following diagrams and comments illustrate the basic principles we try to adhere to regardless of the coverage we are using. Although we're focusing on the position of the defensive backs, it's important to understand that the front people must remain on their feet and pursue with good angles to allow the defensive backs to get to their desired position. All defensive secondary support depends on proper pursuit from the front seven people.

Wide Play Run Support Objectives

The two main objectives are to funnel the ball into the YES areas, and prevent the ball from getting into NO areas (see Figure 1). All secondary coverages will be designed to funnel the ball into areas where the defense wants the ball. The quicker you can force the ball into the desired areas, the better off you are.

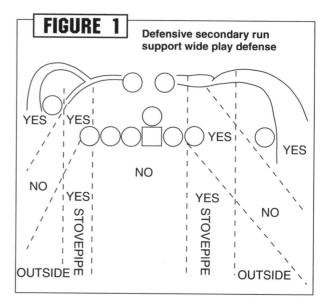

FIGURE 1 Defensive secondary run support wide play defense

Run Support Positioning

In primary run support, the player responsible for taking the pitch or forcing any wide play back to the inside is a defensive back or a defensive end. Secondary run support responsibilities of the defensive backs are to:

- Keep the ball from going inside the primary support and back to the outside.
- Keep inside position on the ball as you approach the stovepipe.
- Be the last man to make play, deep in stovepipe or on the boundary (see Figure 2).

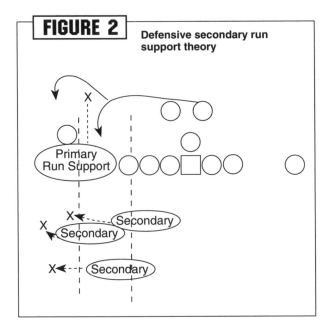

FIGURE 2   Defensive secondary run support theory

The desired results of primary and secondary run support are to (a) force the ball inside with position on both sides of the stovepipe to make the ball go perpendicular to LOS; and (b) force the ball to bounce outside deep, allowing the secondary run support to make the play on or near the LOS.

Run Support Example

Now let's look at how the objectives and positioning for run support apply to an actual play, in this case, against the veer run to the strongside (see Figure 3).

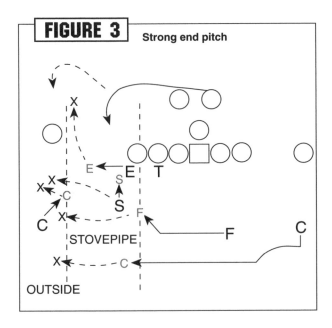

FIGURE 3   Strong end pitch

The defensive run support responsibilities and position are as follows:

Strong end—For veer call-TE release, you have pitch; sky according to block you're facing; if the TE blocks down, play first threat in your area (dive or QB).

Strong safety—For veer call-TE release, play dump pass first, then support inside defensive end for first threat. If the TE blocks down, you have pitch. Play according to block you're facing. Play sweep aggressively, forcing it inside or bouncing outside deep.

Strong corner—Secondary run support. Don't let ball inside the primary run support (SS or SE) and back to the outside. If ball bounces, support outside on or near LOS.

Free safety—Secondary run support. Always keep inside position on ball. Make approach to ball as you pass the center. You should be able to take a QB keeping and be in stovepipe on all wide plays.

Weak corner—You're the last man. You must make play deep in stovepipe or on the boundary.

Inside Play Run Support Objectives

The run support strategy versus inside runs is much the same, but the positions obviously change. Again, you want to keep the ball in the YES area and never allow it in the NO areas (see Figure 4).

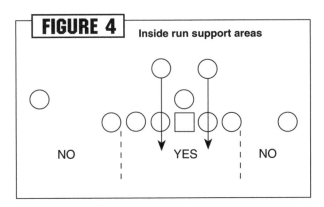

FIGURE 4   Inside run support areas

Defenders must maintain their initial outside position to the ball. The stovepipe must be squeezed down as much as possible and defenders must still maintain the proper position on the ball. Positions move as the stovepipe moves (the

Xs in Figure 5 show how positions move as the ball moves).

Good run support is essential for a successful defense. By keeping the ball in the areas where you want it, you greatly reduce the chances for a long run or a big play.

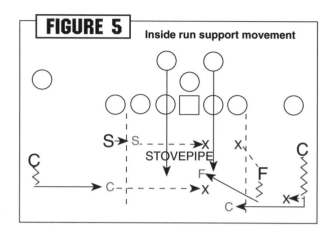

FIGURE 5   Inside run support movement

STOVEPIPE

1991 Proceedings. Coach Fry is head coach at the University of Iowa. Coach Brashier is his assistant.

The Stunting 4-3 Front
GEORGE PERLES

We run the same type of defense that I ran as defensive coordinator of the great Pittsburgh Steeler teams—the 4-3 stunting defense. It's different, and I don't know many people who use it.

Some people will tell you that you can't play the stunt 4-3 without a Joe Greene. We seldom have those type of people, but the defense still works.

4-3 Alignment

We take our strongside tackle and put him in the gap between the center and guard. He gets into a stance that allows him to hug the ball. He keeps his inside leg back to a point where we don't worry about lining up offside. Normally, we can hug the ball as much as we want. The center can't back off the ball, so he can't do much about it.

The tackle gets into an angle charge with his rear end in the way of the offensive guard. The middle linebacker is also behind our tackle. The strong end plays a 5 technique on the outside shoulder of the offensive tackle. The strong linebacker either plays head-up or outside the shoulder of the tight end, depending on the support responsibility. The weakside tackle plays on the

outside eye of the guard, which we call a 2-gap technique. The weakside end is in the 5 technique, with the weakside linebacker on the outside.

In defense, someone has to have two gaps. In the 4-3, the middle linebacker has two gaps. In the odd front, the noseguard has two gaps. What we try to do is give our down tackles a gap and a half each. What can hurt this theory is the offense continually running the fullback in the inside gap. However, the offense usually doesn't have the personnel or the patience to do it.

Stunts

When people see what we are doing, they give us big splits between the center and guard. When that happens, we can't cover the inside gaps with our tackles. We go into an automatic stunt called our "Tom game." In this stunt, we slant our weakside tackle into the center-guard gap and loop our strongside tackle into the face of the weakside offensive guard (see Figure 1).

People try to run the inside isolation to our strong side. They double down on the tackle, single out on the defensive end, and isolate the linebacker. Our coaching point for the linebacker

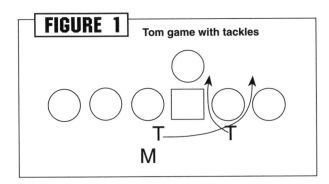

FIGURE 1 — Tom game with tackles

is to fill the hole, taking on the fullback with the outside shoulder, and making the running back run into our single-blocked lineman. If they try to reach the gap tackle and lead the guard up on the linebacker, his technique is different. He takes on the fullback with his outside shoulder on a down block. By doing this, he forces the back to run into the reach block of the center on our tackle—an extremely hard block for the center.

Also, we run the "three game" against the isolation game. We call it the three game because it is to the weakside. It is run like the Tom game, except the defensive end also runs an inside slant. This gives us great penetration because of the reach blocking scheme run by the offensive team. You have to have penetration. There is only one problem with penetration, and that is the trap. If you are going to penetrate, do it on an inside slant with people coming to the outside (see Figure 2).

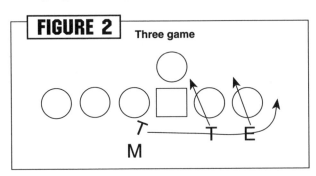

FIGURE 2 — Three game

When we were in the pros, the ball was in the middle of the field all the time. Even with the ball on the hash mark, it was always within a few yards of the middle. In the college game, we definitely have a short side as well as an open side of the field. For this type of game, we developed the "open scheme." That simply meant that we stacked and shifted to the open side of the formation.

We still had the Tom game, which now was run into the strong side of the defense. We had our three game, but now it was called "four game,"

run into the even side of the defense. What that does is to bring four men into the strong side on a stunt. This scheme eliminates trap blocking, isolation, and cutback running. This defense is excellent against the I-formation. The stunt tackle isn't stunting upfield. He's stunting into men so that he can read the down block and play the trap (see Figure 3).

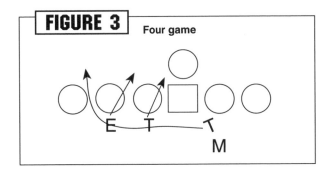

FIGURE 3 — Four game

Another game we run is called "storm." This is like the four game, except the outside linebacker comes on the inside slant (see Figure 4).

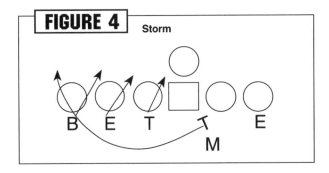

FIGURE 4 — Storm

We have a number of combination stunts that can be run. To the open side we run a "ram." It involves the weakside end and linebacker. The end and linebacker stunt to the inside, with the middle linebacker on a scrape off to the outside (see Figure 5).

We use the "me" call between the weakside end and linebacker. All these stunts are used for

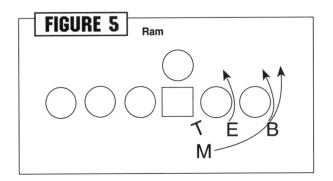

FIGURE 5 — Ram

penetration; however, you cannot penetrate without being covered from the back side, or you will get trapped. And anytime you involve one of your outside linebackers in a run stunt, then one of your short pass zones is left uncovered. We try to get away with that to the short side. If we call the "open me," that involves the strongside end and tackle. In the stunt, he steps to the offense and then loops to the outside while the linebacker comes on a down slant (see Figure 6).

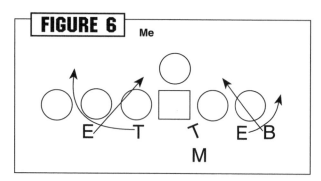

FIGURE 6 Me

If we wanted to run strongside, we called "open." One good thing about it was it allowed us to play the I-formation play pass. When we ran the Tom game, the guard blocked down and the fullback picked up the stunting tackle. Coaches don't like their fullbacks picking up tackles, especially if the tackle is someone like Ernie Holmes. It helps us when we find teams that like to run the play pass to the strongside (see Figure 7).

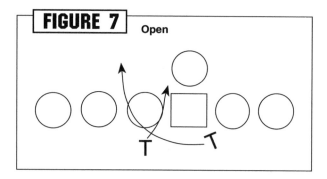

FIGURE 7 Open

The "open storm" is good against the play-action pass into the strong side. You give up the strong flat zone, but we get the pressure and let the strong safety play both zones into the boundary (see Figure 8).

The ram stunt can be run with a number of other stunts. The ram can be run with the Tom, four game, and the open me. The middle linebacker in this scheme stays free.

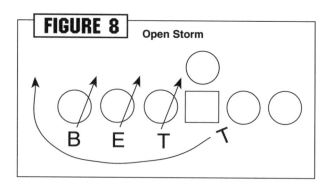

FIGURE 8 Open Storm

Remember, technique is one of the keys in playing this defense. The tackles crowd the ball as close as possible. The center can do only three things. He can block straight. When the center has to snap the ball and block the tackle straight, we usually have the advantage. It is difficult because the tackle is hugging the ball in alignment. Another thing the center could do is the slip block. In this block, the center slips past the tackle and blocks the middle linebacker. The last thing the center can do is try to reach the tackle. To do this, he has to step, open his hips, and move down the line. We drill these three blocks time and time again until our tackles learn how to react to them.

The middle linebacker is reading the triangle of the center, guard, and QB. The guard can't take an abnormal split to block the middle linebacker. We have stunts where both the tackle and linebacker come on a stunt, so it becomes dangerous to split too much. When the guard cuts his split down to protect the gap, the butt of the defensive tackle is in the guard's way and he can't get the shop on the linebacker. That's why we angle the tackle. At times, we put both tackles into the gaps and let the middle linebacker move just before the snap from one stack to the other so that it confuses the offense as to who's involved in the stunt (see Figure 9).

This confuses the offensive line, and we get big plays in the backfield. This screws up the blocking assignment. This isn't something that I

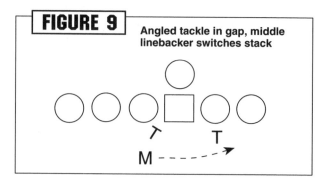

FIGURE 9 Angled tackle in gap, middle linebacker switches stack

dreamed up last night. This scheme has been tested, and very great coaches have had an opportunity to beat this defense and came up light.

4-3 Versus Offensive Sets

When we face the halfback set, we don't like to run the three game. The reason is that the halfback can get to the outside too easily and too quickly, before the stunt tackle.

If we run the Tom game and the offense runs away from the stunt, we're still in good shape. The center's rules have him reaching on that type of play. The further he reaches, the more penetration we will get from the back side (see Figure 10). It doesn't make any difference if the offense runs away from the stunt. There isn't a coach in this room who will coach his offensive center to disregard the tackle in the playside gap and block back. Coaches will not change their blocking scheme to block a stunt.

FIGURE 10 Tom game, offense runs away from stunt

If we face the halfback in the strong set, we adjust differently (see Figure 11). The strong tackle lines up in the gap and comes upfield. The middle linebacker moves into the stack behind the strong end. The weakside tackle comes to head-on the offensive guard. The weakside end

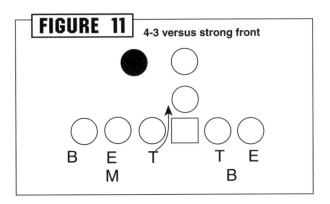

FIGURE 11 4-3 versus strong front

loosens up and the weakside linebacker moves to a stack behind the tackle.

The adjustment to the split formation involves some automatic stunts. We don't need to adjust toward the tight end because we are already strong that way. The weakside doesn't have a strong running attack, and the only play we look for to that side is the sprint draw. On the weak side, we use a "your" call. The your call involves the weakside tackle and weakside end. It is the reverse of the me call. The tackle loops into an offensive tackle, and the end crosses behind and to the inside (see Figure 12).

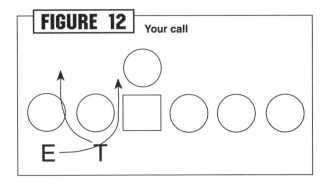

FIGURE 12 Your call

From this defense we have an open Tom, open four game, storm, ram, me, and any combination of these stunts. The "open, ram, Tom" is a combination stunt shown in Figure 13.

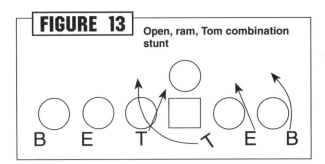

FIGURE 13 Open, ram, Tom combination stunt

We can run the Tom game on formation. The fact that the running back is so deep gives us that flexibility. When the center tries to reach, this opens the center of the line for the slant stunts and eliminates the bubble in the middle which running backs look for in the cutback. Earl Campbell was a cutback runner. We played him ten times while I was with Pittsburgh, and he averaged 42 yards rushing. Our scheme could penetrate and keep him from cutting back.

If a team plays two tight ends, we make our adjustment with our secondary people. We either play the regular 4-3 and move the weak safety into a linebacker position or go to the "open" with the strong safety in the linebacker position (see Figure 14).

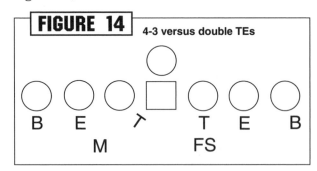

FIGURE 14

4-3 versus double TEs

With the one-back backfield and the double tight ends, we go to a regular 4-3 and run all kinds of stunts with our tackles and ends. If the one back is in the middle, we run the stunt 4-3 and play normal.

Problem Plays for the Stunting 4-3

The play that gives us some trouble is what we call 36 power. This is tough on the middle linebacker. The offense blocks back and pulls the offside guard through the off-tackle hole. The offensive tackle and tight end run a blocking scheme on our defensive end that allows the right end to come off and seal our middle linebacker. We have a coaching point for the middle linebacker. If the tight end is waiting for the linebacker in the off-tackle hole, we run the linebacker through the guard-tackle gap (see Figure 15).

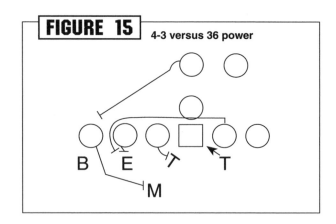

FIGURE 15

4-3 versus 36 power

A big play people are running out of the I-formation is the counter sweep with the backside guard and tackle pulling (see Figure 16). If we play it straight, the coaching points are the same for the middle linebacker. However, we aren't going to play the I-formation straight too often.

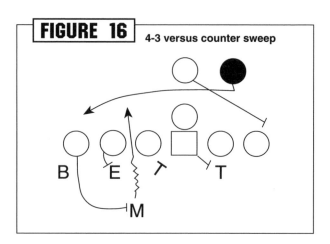

FIGURE 16

4-3 versus counter sweep

—1988 Proceedings. Coach Perles was head coach at Michigan State University.

Slanting Defense for an Advantage
CHUCK BROYLES

We like to move our defensive linemen. In running situations, we may call a slanting defense almost 50% of the time.

There are a number of reasons to slant. Some teams slant to confuse blocking schemes, some to avoid mismatches, others to get penetration. We probably slant for those reasons also, but the biggest reason we slant is to gain an advantage.

The advantage we wish to gain is slanting our defensive linemen in the direction the offense is running the football. Therefore, we put a lot of time and effort into determining the directions we are going to slant versus particular offensive sets.

Base Defense

When we are not slanting, we base out of an Eagle defense. We have convinced our defensive linemen that in our Eagle defense, they are role players. Their job is to keep the LBs free to make tackles. We play with four down linemen—two ends and two tackles. We usually make only two calls in our Eagle defense. When we are on the boundary, we make a field call (Field Eagle) and when we are in the middle of the field we make a TE call (Tite Eagle, see Figure 1).

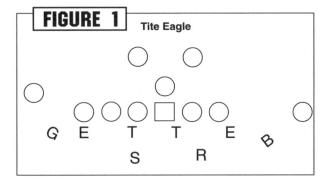

FIGURE 1 Tite Eagle

Our basic alignments for our down linemen in Tite Eagle are a 6, a 3, shade, and a 5. We play with four linebackers in our scheme. Our wideside of the field player is named Gorilla (strong safety); our shortside of the field player is Bandit (drop end); our strongside linebacker is Sam (Eagle backer); and our weakside linebacker is Rambo (Fifty backer).

Slanting Defenses

Most of the time when we call a slanting defense, we are talking only to our tackles. We play a heavy 6 technique. He is a C gap player, and he is so conscious of the C gap that we usually do not slant him, unless we would give him a fire call.

There is one exception: When we slant strong, we will slant our DE when he is a 5 technique to the strength call. Our call is either Tite/Field Slant (see Figure 2), or Tite/Field Slant Weak. We slant only the two tackles, not the 6 technique.

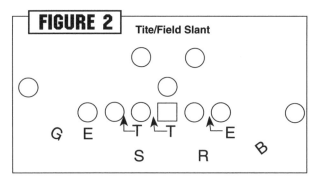

FIGURE 2 Tite/Field Slant

Versus two TEs, our Bandit would be forced to play a loose 9 technique. A variation in our Eagle defense is to play Tite/Field 2 (see Figure 3). The 2 call moves our shade to a 2 technique, so versus two TEs we would be in a 6, a 3, a 2, a 5, and a 9. From this alignment, our call would be Tite/Field 2 Slant or Tite/Field 2 Slant Weak.

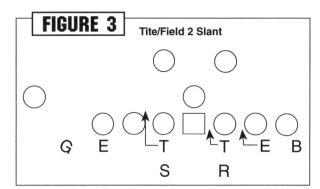

FIGURE 3 Tite/Field 2 Slant

If we do not want two TEs forcing our Bandit to play a loose 9 technique, then the call would be Tite/Field G. G moves our shade to a 2 technique and also alerts our DEs versus two TEs to play double 6s. From this alignment, our call would be Tite/Field G Slant (see Figure 4), or Tite/Field G Slant Weak. When G is the call, we slant only our tackles, regardless of the direction of the slant. If we were to slant the DEs, we would have to give them a fire call.

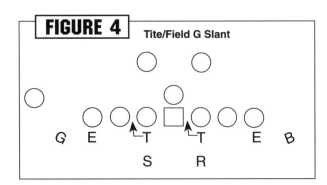

FIGURE 4 Tite/Field G Slant

Besides our Tite/Field slants, we will run a 50 Slant with several change-ups. We call this defense simply Slant. Slant defense is used only as a boundary defense.

Our basic alignment in Slant defense is a 6, a 4, a 0, and a 5 (see Figure 5). In this defense, when we slant we are referring only to the tackles. This defense is called only on the hash; therefore, the strength of the defense is always a wideside call.

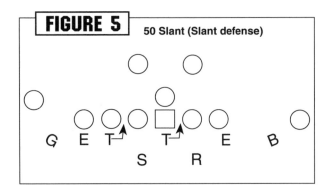

FIGURE 5 50 Slant (Slant defense)

In Slant defense, it is imperative that our 4 tackle not get cut off. He becomes a B to A gap player. He is to read the guard on the move and adjust to his block.

Our 0 tackle, or nose, does not have to slant quite as hard. We refer to this technique as a shave technique. We want him to crowd the center and quickly avoid his block with a slanting motion. He is to read the center on the move.

We do not accept the excuse, "Coach, I slanted away from the play." We expect these two players to be able to slant away from the strength call, and at the same time be able to plant and play back across the face or use run-around technique.

Slant Stack

A variation of our Slant defense is Slant Stack, shown in Figure 6. In Slant Stack, we pinch our 5 technique, and we widen our Rambo LB to a 4 eye. Slant stack helps us protect the Rambo backer. It is simply a change-up of assignments between the 5 technique and the Rambo LB. The 5 technique becomes a B gap player, and Rambo becomes a C gap player.

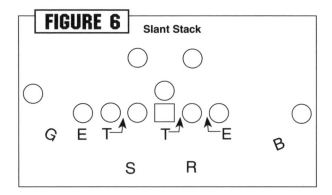

FIGURE 6 Slant Stack

Also from Slant Stack, we will run Slant Stack/Rambo Loop (see Figure 7). Slant Stack/Rambo Loop brings the Bandit on a QB stunt, 5 technique to B gap, and Rambo becomes QB to pitch.

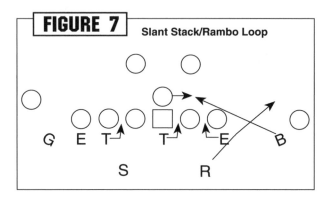

FIGURE 7 Slant Stack/Rambo Loop

Rambo only loops if flow is weak. The QB stunt by Bandit is on, regardless of direction of flow. If flow goes away from Rambo, he becomes overlap LB. We feel like Slant Stack and Slant Stack/Rambo Loop give us two good change-ups to the weakside in the 50 slant.

Our change-up to protect our strongside is to make a Slant Nose call (see Figure 8). By calling

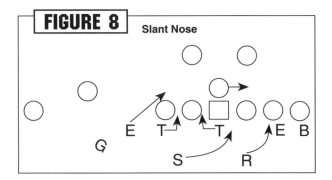

FIGURE 8 | Slant Nose

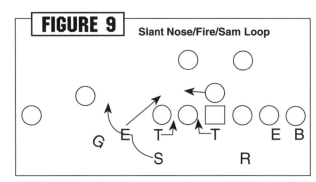

FIGURE 9 | Slant Nose/Fire/Sam Loop

Slant Nose, our 4 eye tackle is more conscious of the B gap, and our nose becomes a callside A gap player.

Sam must read flow of the football. If it flows his way, he becomes a scrape LB very similar to the old Arkansas monster defense. Sam's responsibility becomes flow his way C to D gap. If Sam reads flow away, he must check for the counter and then become an overlap player.

If we want to insure a quick force by our DE, our call would be Slant Nose/Fire/Sam Loop (see Figure 9). Sam would loop and become QB to pitch. He still must be an inside-out player.

If an offense gives a wide slot or twins to the field, we crash up our DE and bring him on an automatic fire call.

There is a lot of time and preparation that goes into our slanting defense. We work pre-practice four days a week in our stunt and slant period. In order to be a successful slanting team, you cannot just slant to be slanting, but must slant for an advantage.

—1991 Proceedings. Coach Broyles is head coach at Pittsburg State University (KS).

Coaching the Front Seven in the 50 Defense

RON SCHIPPER

I've been a head coach for 30 years, and the 50 defense has been our defense for each of those 30 years. During these 30 years, I've tried to read every word written about the 50 defense. I've gone to clinics across the country to hear people speak on the defense, and I've attended spring practices at many of the major colleges in the country that run the 50.

The defense has gone through many model changes. It's been called the 54, 52, 50, 34, as well as many other special names given to it by coaches who have added different stunts, alignments, and adjustments. New secondary coverages have added to its flexibility.

We begin with the Base 50 (see Figure 1). We want our players to understand this defense inside out. We must be able to run this defense against anything the offense shows us.

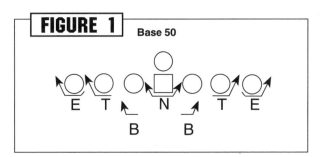

FIGURE 1 | Base 50

This is a read defense. We move on the snap, hit, read keys, protect our gaps, find the football, and go to it. If I felt we were physically superior to all of our opponents, I would run this defense most of the time. But that is not the case. We're not going to have the big physical player in Division III, so we're going to use multiple alignments, a variety of techniques by our front seven, and various coverages in the secondary.

Front 7 Techniques

For us to accomplish the multiple-penetrating-aggressive style of defense, we must teach our front seven a variety of techniques. Just as all seven of them must learn the "read technique," all seven must learn to "go." Go is very important to our defensive philosophy. It means attack, penetrate, get to the football as quickly as possible, and read on the run. We still want to have the correct stance, have perfect alignment, and know our gap responsibilities. This is demonstrated by our Basic Blitz (see Figure 2), in which our players show a base 50 look, but are in a go technique.

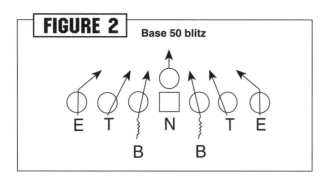

FIGURE 2 Base 50 blitz

Any one member of the front seven can be sent on a go by a simple call. We have a variety of combinations that involve two or three members of the front seven. In each of these combinations, the call is designated by strong or quick side; tight end or split end; right or left.

We also have a number of defenses that involve all seven men beginning with our two slant defenses: Rover—slant away from strong safety (see Figure 3a), and Angle—slant to the strong safety (see Figure 3b).

With the simple addition of go to any of our defensive calls, we place emphasis on attacking, reading on the move, and getting to the football. Figure 4 illustrates Rover 4-Man Go.

One of our real favorites to rush the passer is Rover Squeeze Bang Strong 6-Man Go (see Figure 5).

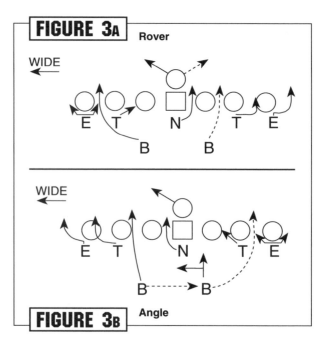

FIGURE 3A Rover

FIGURE 3B Angle

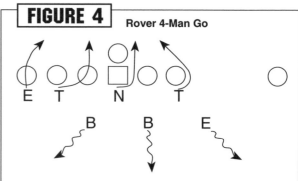

FIGURE 4 Rover 4-Man Go

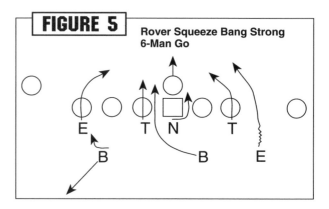

FIGURE 5 Rover Squeeze Bang Strong 6-Man Go

We've also had success by moving our slant tackle and noseguard to their new gap responsibility in the Rover and Angle defenses and stacking the linebackers behind them. For example, we run Rover Stack 5-Man Go (see Figure 6).

Obviously different offenses present different problems to the defense. For example, we've stopped the option by using a combination of defenses. Using the "choke" on the tight end side

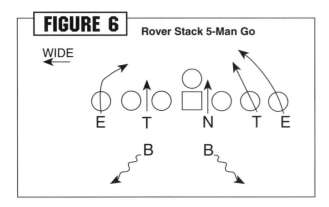

FIGURE 6   Rover Stack 5-Man Go

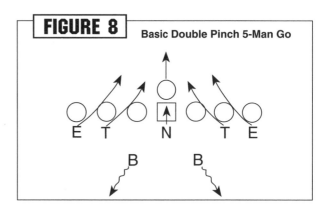

FIGURE 8   Basic Double Pinch 5-Man Go

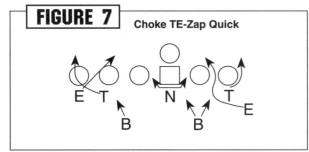

FIGURE 7   Choke TE-Zap Quick

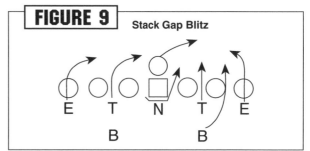

FIGURE 9   Stack Gap Blitz

and the "zap" on the wide end side allows us to put quick pressure on the quarterback (see Figure 7).

Another scheme used to attack an inside running game and give us a different pass blitz look is the Double Pinch. In the Double Pinch 5-Man Go, shown in Figure 8, the linebackers will read, while in the blitz they will go immediately.

Some of our tackles are very effective in the gap because of their quickness. So we put them in the B gap, allow our noseguard to play soft and control the center, and run a Stack Gap 4-Man Go or turn them all loose in Stack Gap Blitz (see Figure 9).

Like so many other 50 teams, we also use the overshift with a hard corner, 2-deep zone, playing four or five men in under coverage. This type of front seven alignment allows the defense to overload the offense inside and force some changes in blocking patterns. We also like to use an inside stack alignment in our overshift scheme and blitz from this alignment. The number of different combinations we can use is just about unlimited. We don't claim to be original, but most important, we believe in what we are doing and it's successful.

—1985 Proceedings. Coach Schipper was head coach at Central College (IA).

Defending Against the Pass
JERRY SANDUSKY

Defending the pass has become increasingly difficult in recent years. Liberalized blocking rules, outstanding skilled athletes, and a greater emphasis on the throwing game have created this situation for defensive coaches.

Before you put together a defensive scheme to defend the pass, you must address some personnel factors that are vital to the development of any defensive package.

Personnel

The first priority has to be pass rush. It's vital to be able to apply pressure on the quarterback without blitzing linebackers. Speed and quickness are especially important on the outside. Power and force are more vital on the inside. The next priority is to have at least one excellent cover corner. And because of all the spread formations with one or no backs, the third priority is to have linebackers who are capable of playing man-to-man pass coverage.

Our defensive scheme is a multiple one that involves predominantly a seven-man front with a four-deep secondary (see Figure 1). We look for personnel with specific qualities to play this scheme.

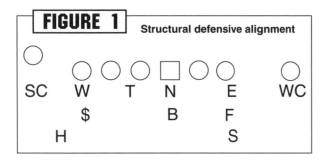

FIGURE 1 Structural defensive alignment

Down Linemen

Noseguard (N)—Explosiveness, probably a little more compact than the other down people, quick enough to handle the scoop blocking schemes

Tackle (T)—Same explosiveness as the nose, possibly a little bigger and more pass rushing skills

End (E)—Big, active player who is strong enough to play on an offensive tackle, yet agile and quick enough to play the option, contain a sprint out, and rush the passer

Linebackers

Willy (W)—Usually the strongest linebacker versus a tight end and an excellent pass rusher

Sam ($)—The most active linebacker, an outstanding open-field player and pass defender (a combination of a linebacker and a strong safety)

Fritz (F)—The second-most active linebacker, usually a little bigger and stronger than Sam (a combination outside and inside linebacker)

Backer (B)—Solid, alert player who is the quarterback of the defense, handles front adjustments in the huddle

Secondary

Strong corner (SC)—The best one-on-one pass coverer on our team

Weak corner (WC)—A good cover player who is a little better at run support than the strong corner

Hero (H)—The strong safety, both an underneath and deep defender, a very good run support player

Safety (S)—The centerfielder, a good tackler and instinctive player who has excellent judgment

Pass Rush Principles

The ability to rush the passer is predominantly innate, but there are some general coaching points that we have learned through trial and error that can help:

- Get a great jump on the football. Anticipate, know the situation, study the stances of the opponents.
- Get on a corner, if possible.
- Be offensive, attack. Get the offensive player into an awkward body position. Cause him to move either laterally or forward. Get the blocker turned or overextended.
- Outside people establish a speed rush, and inside people develop a ball rush.
- Do not get hooked up with the blocker. Keep his hands off of you with slaps, pushes, etc. Use quick fakes, then head upfield.
- Keep your elbows close to your body, and your hands inside the opponent's hands.
- Develop a sense of timing. Know when opponent is off-balance, when to push or pull, and when to accelerate by the defender.
- Use arm and under or over when appropriate, depending on your height. Develop a counter off of your best move (e.g., club off of arm under).
- Keep heading upfield, maintain constant pressure on the quarterback.
- Get your hands up when the quarterback is ready to throw the ball.
- Keep position relative to one another. Develop a feel for one another versus dropback pass. Inside rusher should sense when the outside rusher has made an inside move. T and W, N and E align next to each other in order to develop familiarity with each other.

Pass Rush Twists

Twists are used to take advantage of pass protection schemes and to keep the offensive blocker off-balance.

- *Twist on the snap.* Two defenders change lanes on the snap (see Figure 2). This is more effective versus man-to-man protection.

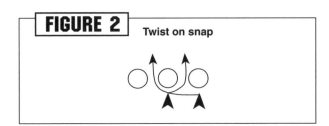

FIGURE 2   Twist on snap

- *Twist on key.* Two defenders exchange pass rush lanes on key (see Figure 3). Use only versus a dropback pass.

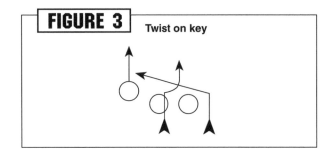

FIGURE 3   Twist on key

- *Combination twist.* One defender drives into a gap on the snap. The other defender reads to determine run or pass, then exchanges rush lanes versus a dropback pass (see Figure 4).

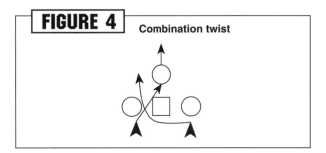

FIGURE 4   Combination twist

Coverages

Because of the sophistication and the intricate timing of today's passing games, the two most significant factors in a coverage scheme are disruption of receivers and disguise. With that in mind, we begin our teaching with a 2-deep zone (see Figure 5).

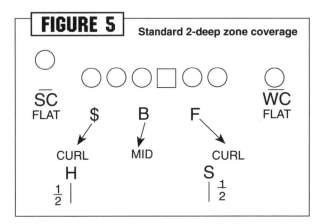

FIGURE 5   Standard 2-deep zone coverage

Both corners are responsible for the flat zone. They assume a press alignment slightly outside the wide receivers, as close to the line of scrimmage as possible. Their feet are parallel and shoulders square to the line of scrimmage. As a first priority, they try to jam the receiver (disrupt his release). This is accomplished by sliding laterally and striking the receiver with their hands. They must not get overextended or let the receiver have an easy outside release (see Figure 6).

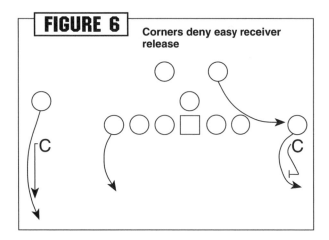

FIGURE 6 Corners deny easy receiver release

We want to disrupt or cause a very flat release in any direction. If the receiver inside releases, the corner slides, then opens to the inside and retreats laterally to a depth of about 12 yards, depending on the situation. If necessary, the corner should be ready to sink to the outside and be ready for a corner route. When the defender has gotten enough depth, he should be ready to drive off his back foot and attack any receiver that shows in front of him.

If the ball is thrown over the defender's head, he should turn his shoulders and sprint at an angle to make the interception. If the receiver takes a flat outside release, the defender should slide, then pivot back to the inside. Again he retreats laterally and sinks slightly outside to protect the hole between him and the safety.

The Sam and Fritz are responsible for the curl pass zones. If the ball is in the middle of the field, the curls are 1 yard inside the hash, 12 yards deep. When the ball is on the hash mark, the open field curl is 3 yards inside the hash, and the boundary curl is 3 yards outside the hash.

Before they go to the curl zone, they must not let the number two receivers go straight down the field easily. They should force these receivers wide to the curl zones as shown in Figure 7.

The only people who curl are the wide receivers. Enroute to the curl, the defenders should run laterally and glance for the widest receiver. They should settle at the angle they have retreated to, stopping approximately 3 yards in front of and to the inside of the receiver threatening the curl.

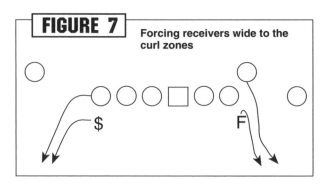

FIGURE 7 Forcing receivers wide to the curl zones

The backer is responsible for the middle zone. The location of the middle zone is 15 yards deep in the middle of the field, 5 yards inside the hash if the ball is on the hash. The first threat to the middle zone is the number two receiver. Attention should be focused on number two first, then number three. The hero and safety align on the hashes and retreat straight down the hash, reading the inside receivers. When they're sure that there isn't a deep middle threat, they can widen and play over top the wideout.

Two-Deep Man Coverage

As a complement to the 2-deep zone, we incorporate the 2-deep man coverage (see Figure 8).

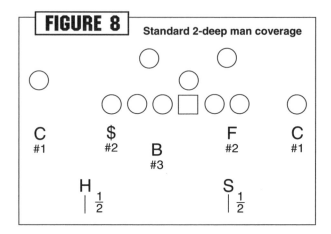

FIGURE 8 Standard 2-deep man coverage

Trying to disguise the coverage as much as possible, the corners move to inside alignments on the wide receivers. Now the corners set and take away the inside release of the receiver. They must not overreact to any outside fakes. When the receiver has gotten beyond the defender's outside shoulder, he turns and runs with him, mirroring him from underneath. He should concentrate on the receiver, especially his hands. When his hands go up, the defender should bring his hand up through the receiver's hands and turn to look for the ball. The safeties should shout "ball."

The Sam and Fritz play the number two receivers in the same manner. The backer is responsible for handling the number three receiver. If playing a receiver who is aligned in the backfield, the defender attacks the back through his inside half, then mirrors him, staying underneath and to his inside (see Figure 9).

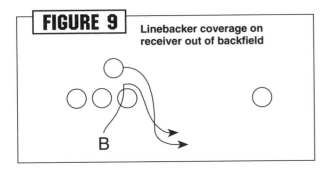

FIGURE 9 Linebacker coverage on receiver out of backfield

Three-Deep Roll Weak Coverage

Disguising from a 2-deep look, our next progression is to have the strong corner finesse out of his press alignment, and we roll weak to 3-deep (see Figure 10).

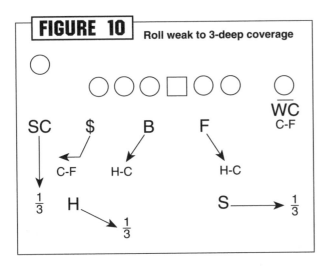

FIGURE 10 Roll weak to 3-deep coverage

SC—Back out and play outside one-third zone.
H—Roll to deep middle one-third zone.
S—Roll to weak number one recklessly, unless number two shows flat, then play up to number two.
F—Start to curl zone reading number two. If number two goes flat, continue to the curl. If number two comes straight down, latch on to him in the hook area. If number two blocks or goes strong, go to the middle.

B—Start to the curl, reading number two. If number two goes flat, continue to get width to the curl. If he comes straight down, latch on to him in the hook area. If number two blocks, hang in the middle.
$—Start for the wide curl, top of the numbers in the middle of the field, hash mark if the ball is on the hash. Read number two. Hang in the wide curl and play up to anything that shows flat.

In order to get to an 8-man front, the weak corner can move into an alignment 3 yards outside the nearest defender at a depth of 3 yards. Safety moves out to a position slightly outside the widest receiver on the weakside. The hero moves closer to his middle one-third zone. Obviously, the disguise is very limited.

Deep Man Coverage

Having eight people around the ball provides the opportunity for quick perimeter pressure. By rushing both Sam and the weak corner, the coverage that is played is 3-deep man-to-man (see Figure 11).

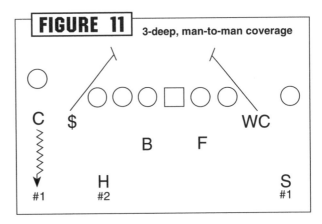

FIGURE 11 3-deep, man-to-man coverage

In this coverage, the strong corner and the safety play more cautiously when covering the receiver. They start to backpedal, then run laterally, striving to maintain inside position and keeping a cushion of 2 to 3 yards. The inside linebackers play the same as in 2-deep man.

Three-Deep Rotate Strong Coverage

In addition to the roll weak to 3-deep, we rotate to a strong 3-deep (see Figure 12).

The hero and strong corner can either roll or invert. If a roll call is made, the corner presses

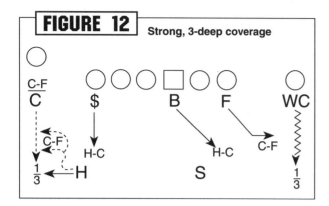

FIGURE 12 Strong, 3-deep coverage

and plays curl to flat, while the hero plays the outside one third. If an invert call is made, the hero plays curl to flat and the strong corner has the outside one third. The Sam and backer handle hook to curl. Fritz plays curl to flat. The safety has the middle one third while the weak corner retreats and plays the outside one third.

Regardless of the defensive scheme, it is very important to have a sound system. Don't try to do any more than is necessary. Success comes with good players, discipline, concentration, and aggressive play.

1992 Summer Manual. Coach Sandusky is defensive coordinator at Penn State University.

Making the Secondary Primary
BILLY JOE

Our base defense is a variety of the 40 defense, which gives us balance with the flexibility to show different looks and make adjustments with minimal coaching points. The pro 4-3 makes our defensive line play, linebacker play, and secondary play very easy to incorporate into the total concept of our defensive philosophy. Figure 1 shows our basic alignment.

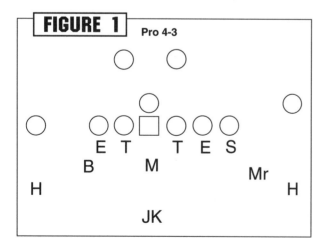

FIGURE 1 Pro 4-3

We present many different fronts within our system to cause distraction, misconception, and unnecessary thinking by our opponents. It's extremely difficult to handle pressure if the offense

is not certain of their assignments and responsibilities. By applying intense pressure, our defense will prevent the easy touchdown, obtain possession of the ball, and score.

A successful member of our defensive team must have the knowledge to perform his techniques and duties with maximum accuracy and persistence. Proficiency in the execution of technique and fundamentals is especially important in our secondary.

Defensive Back Responsibilities

Our defensive backs must be excellent athletes. Our defensive pressure concept often places secondary personnel on an island. They must be great cover men and hitters. They must be proficient and efficient without requiring a lot of help.

Our stunting, dealing, dogging, and blitzing require a secondary that must enjoy the role of the "lone ranger." They must possess that uncanny ability of having great range and must enjoy our pressure concept.

In most cases, our dogs (see Figures 2–5) require some form of man coverage. However, there are times when we will "zone-up" behind an up front dog.

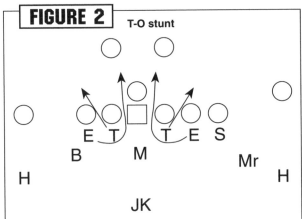

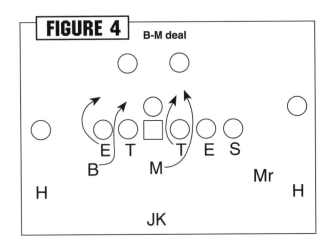

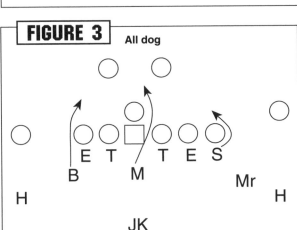

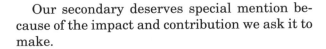

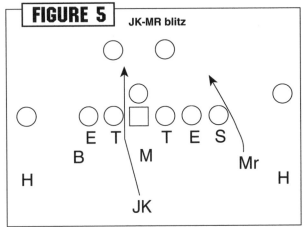

Our secondary deserves special mention because of the impact and contribution we ask it to make.

Man Coverage and Techniques

In our basic man coverage, the defensive back aligns in a 1 alignment facing the inside eye of receiver. We ask him to set up 4 yards deep on the inside shoulder of the receiver, always conscious of the sidelines.

Whenever possible, the defensive back should use the sideline as a 12th defender, and in doing so, apply the 7-yard rule: When a receiver splits to within 7 yards of the sideline or closer, let him gain the outside position and force the fade route, making sure to turn to the receiver's downfield shoulders.

It's been said that 75% of man coverage is concentration. A defensive back must concentrate on the receiver by focusing the eye on a chosen spot just at the base of the jersey number. Defenders must learn to discipline themselves to the point that they can ignore everything but the receiver.

At the snap of the ball, square up by keeping the shoulders square to the LOS and begin the backpedal, keeping the weight on the balls of the feet; do not rock back on the heels. The body should be bent and balanced, with the arms hanging loosely and the feet approximately shoulder-width during the initial backpedal stage.

We coach our players to maintain position by keeping a slight cushion, which is determined by the receiver's speed. The defensive back must keep his feet moving, regardless of how fast or slow the receiver is moving. Keep in mind that most receivers will make their cuts early from the LOS and anticipate the pattern tree.

When the receiver shows a sign of slowing down or when he straightens up, he will usually enter what we call a "faking stage." When this happens, the defender should stay low and be ready to sprint once the final cut is made. As a general rule, he can ignore the first fake.

As the receiver makes his final break, the defensive back should react by stepping quickly with his break. He should drive off hard with the receiver, maintain inside leverage on him so that he has to make contact with the defender in order to cut back. After the receiver has made his drive, the defender should get in stride with him step for step, look for the ball through the receiver, and prepare to turn toward the receiver, anticipating the ball or the strip. Then, he should react to the ball. The first thought should be to intercept the ball. If this is impossible, the defender should do the following, in this order:

1. Knock the ball away from the receiver.
2. Strip the receiver.
3. Tackle the receiver.
4. As a last resort, if a touchdown is unavoidable, take a penalty.

Zone Coverages and Techniques

Zone coverage is also a very important component of our defensive package. The 3-deep, or stay zone, provides a true 3-deep with no rotation, regardless of play-action.

In zone coverage, the secondary personnel must align at a specified depth in their assigned areas, keying specific receivers and then the ball. They must learn to recognize the formation and the passing potential of each in order to pick up their keys quickly.

We use two basic keys in our zone coverage: an initial key to determine the route—when and where the ball will be thrown—and the quarterback's release of the ball. Therefore, the initial key is usually the receiver's route, while the secondary key is the quarterback's release of the ball.

The cornerbacks align and locate their key quickly. They should set up in a position 7 yards deep and on the outside shoulder of the outside receiver, with the outside foot back or up, in whichever stance they feel comfortable. They should drop the hips by bending slightly at the knees and waist. Also, they should skate when the receiver releases across the LOS.

If the receiver aligns to the wide side of the field 7 yards from the sideline, the defensive back must gain a heads-up position. The further outside towards the sideline the receiver aligns, the further inside the defender adjusts, but never more than a 1 alignment.

Use the sidelines as a defender. Your free safety should align in the middle of the formation and key through the interior part of the line (i.e., the uncovered man to the quarterback and the ball). At the snap of the ball, the free safety tries to get an overall picture of the action by reading the center, and then focuses in on the quarterback.

We teach each corner and free safety to skate, looking for the pass after the snap of the ball. If the keys show pass, the free safety moves quickly to the middle of the zone, while the corners adjust to the receivers' routes. You must make sure your players are at a point in their assigned zone that will enable them to cover all route variations in that zone equally, and as quickly as possible. Defensive backs should always locate the deepest route in their zones. (At times, we do not play a true zone; we allow the defenders to favor the receivers who enter their zones.)

We ask our DBs to maintain a slight cushion and skate as fast as the receiver moves downfield. This helps eliminate the gaps between the underneath and deep routes. We prefer to expand as needed, and be prepared to turn, cut and run, or break at the BP (breaking point) of the route. Tell your DBs to work to the receivers' "downfield" shoulders.

As a general rule, if a receiver is entering your zone, coming straight at you, do not let him close the gap to more than 3 yards. If the receiver is running a route parallel to the LOS, cut the cushion about 4 yards and keep the outside position on him. The distance between the passer and the receiver will also be an influencing factor. The greater the distance, the deeper you must play, while adjusting to the route and strength of the quarterback's arm.

As the defensive back moves through his zone, have him focus in on the quarterback and the ball. He should try to read his eyes, arms, and head for a tip that may give away his intentions prematurely.

Tell your players that when the ball is released, to sprint to a point where they can jump and intercept the ball at its highest point, and think in terms of interception first. However, there are exceptions to this rule. If they cannot make the interception, they should turn toward the receiver and knock the ball away from him. If the receiver catches the ball and the defensive back is close to him, strip him of the ball. If the receiver has the ball, the defensive back should break down and make the sure tackle.

Team Principles of Defense

- Development of positive morale.
- Proper angle of pursuit.
- Gang tackling.
- Sound pass defense.
- Defensive football is *reaction* football: You will get blocked, but *don't* stay *blocked*!

—1991 Summer Manual and 1993 Proceedings. Coach Joe is head coach at Florida A&M University.

Defending Against the Run-and-Shoot

DEL WIGHT

The run-and-shoot offense is difficult to defend. Each team that uses this offense has different characteristics and philosophies. One constant is that the quarterback is the key. If he's a good passer and has the ability to run and attack the containment, this puts added pressure on the defense. If the option and counter option have been included in the run-and-shoot package, that gives defenses still another dimension to defend.

In order to win against the run-and-shoot, a defense must stop the ace back draw play. It also must successfully defend against the ace back screen, another major feature of the run-and-shoot. The ability of the ace back determines how we deploy our front seven alignment.

Because the run-and-shoot utilizes four receivers—with motion of a receiver on almost every play—the secondary is required to move and adjust. This can cause defenses many problems.

Our approach to stopping this offense is that we will "shoot" the run-and-shoot. In other words, we'll pressure the passing game and defend the option, draw, and screen with our front seven. We'll play good man-to-man coverage and force the quick pass, but at the same time defend against the option, draw, and screen.

Setting the Defense

The alignment we deploy is shown in Figure 1—man coverage with pressure concept.

The key to pressuring the half-roll pass is for the frontside linebacker to recognize pass and to allow him a free rush. We don't want him to contain the quarterback; he has freedom to force the passer in any lane possible. The responsibility of containing the quarterback is left to the defensive end aligned over the offensive tackle. The linebacker and defensive end must put quick pressure on the quarterback.

Additional pressure on the quarterback can come from the defensive tackle aligned over the

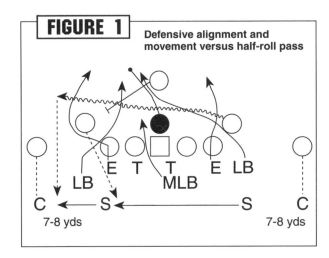

FIGURE 1 — Defensive alignment and movement versus half-roll pass

7-8 yds   7-8 yds

offensive guard. In addition, the outside linebacker away from the half-roll must chase hard in a flat angle—he also has no contain responsibility. The defensive end away from the half-roll has contain on the quarterback. The tilt tackle has spy responsibility for the draw and delayed pass rush.

As indicated in Figure 1, the defensive backs align 7 to 8 yards deep and straight across in the invert position. This allows us to move and adjust to receiver motion. It also gives us the matchup our secondary coach desires versus the man-to-man concept. We try not to have any mismatch on fast wide receivers; therefore, we can adjust easily to the motion from this alignment and match our cover men against the opponent's best receivers.

The run-and-shoot passing attack can easily read man-to-man cover, and they also can run routes designed to attack the man cover. However, with tight man cover and pressure on the quarterback you have at least an equal chance to stop it.

The middle linebacker has the ace back man-to-man. He's also responsible for the draw play and ace back screen. This allows the defensive

tackles to be more aggressive on the pass rush. We need the bonus pressure from the defensive tackle positions.

Versus the Trap and Trap Option

In Figure 2 you see man responsibilities versus the trap and trap-option reads. We have one man on the pitch back and two men responsible for the quarterback, so he can't run the football. If the outside linebacker keys run to him, his responsibility is to get into the pitch lane and maintain pitch responsibility. The defensive ends cannot allow the offensive tackle to block the middle linebacker. The defensive end must play the trap and try to help on the quarterback keep. The middle linebacker must then "skate" and make the quarterback pitch the ball.

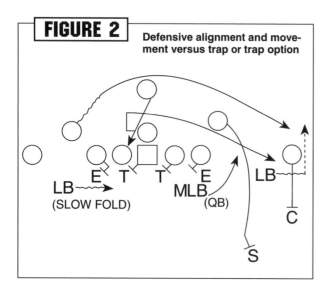

FIGURE 2   Defensive alignment and movement versus trap or trap option

Defensive tackles play a major role in concealing the ace back runs off tackle. In addition, the outside linebacker away from the run action must read run or pass, and slow fold to help on any inside run. This technique is a disciplined and slow fold assignment; the linebacker must read the differences between run and pass.

Versus Ace Back Draw

The defensive tackle away from the ace flow and the middle linebacker have major roles in stopping the ace back draw (see Figure 3). They have the spy responsibility. This isn't difficult for the middle linebacker, since he has the ace back. The defensive tackle must spy if the back flow goes away from him, and will give LBs assistance on the draw.

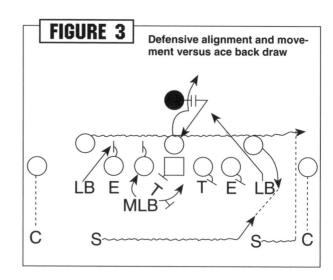

FIGURE 3   Defensive alignment and movement versus ace back draw

In Figure 4 you'll see a change-up in the backside pressure by the outside linebacker. When he reads pass, he'll drop and help the corner. Therefore, if slot motion goes away and ball rolls away, he can drop and help the corner on the crossing or short routes, or look for crossing receivers. This helps protect against the half-roll throw back pass and play-action pass.

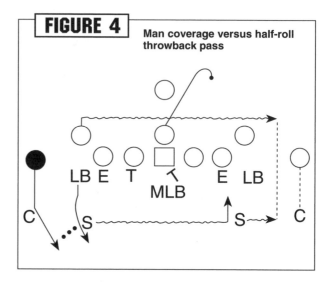

FIGURE 4   Man coverage versus half-roll throwback pass

Versus Ace Back Screen

To defend against the ace back screen, a common and difficult play, we double cover the ace back with outside linebackers and middle linebacker (see Figure 5). The outside linebacker on the side of the half-roll starts his pressure move upfield and then reads the FB setting for screen. On this upfield move, he's in position to be behind the screen blocking. In addition, the middle linebacker who is still spying the ace back allows for double cover. This is much more successful than relying on the middle linebacker to play the ace screen, because he can be easily blocked when he has sole responsibility.

The run-and-shoot offense is designed to throw on the move. To defend it, we give our front people a very simple and aggressive plan to pressure the quarterback into a hurried pass. However, you must have a quick and active front four to make the man-pressure concept work. By employing outside LB pressure, you can create one-on-one blocking situations. And always be prepared to use zone coverage if necessary.

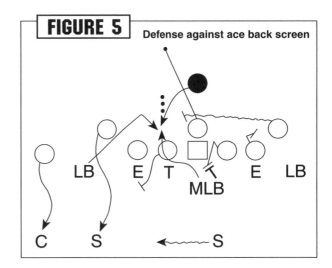

FIGURE 5 — Defense against ace back screen

—*1988 Summer Manual. Coach Wight is assistant coach at the University of Kansas.*

Applying Pressure Without the Risk
FRANK BEAMER with MICHAEL CLARK

Pressure!! On the defensive side of the ball, you can't be afraid to make this call. In our basic eight-man front, we will base a game plan on pressure and then react to the offense's response to it.

With pressure comes risk, particularly if pressure is always matched with man-to-man coverage. Much of our attack will entail this risk, but we try to keep a mix of pressure in our defensive package to keep the offense off-balance.

To pressure the quarterback with four people requires a great commitment and a selling job on the part of the coach. Four-man pressure involves a reliance in your people, not in your plan. Putting trust in your people will always pay dividends, and here is how we help them.

We maximize our matchups and get out good people going one-on-one. Winning the individual matchup is the key. Our players who we get isolated know their importance to the total defense, and are extremely motivated and individually coached to win their fight.

We also help our linemen pressure by aligning properly and allowing them to focus on the quarterback. We have them crowd the LOS and adjust their stance as needed to get off the ball

quickly. When we jet stunt upfield with our line, we assign screen and draw checks to one of our LBs on the second level, not a lineman. Although good players will always react to or feel out these long-yardage change-ups, they'll be more aggressive if they know it is not their primary responsibility.

In the "80 Look" shown in Figure 1, the W-end is using an under move which he sets up by

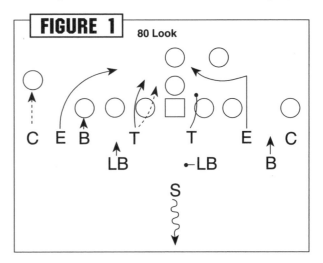

FIGURE 1 — 80 Look

selling a hard jet rush. Whether he spins or clubs under is his call, but taking contain away from a wide DE can compress a pocket and keep an OT off-balance. We shade the weak DT and, hopefully, dictate the double team look by our alignment.

On the snap, the shaded DT must drive to the inside shoulder of the OG. Staying square, he must draw two offensive linemen to him to prevent them from picking out on the DE's stunt. Once the double team is drawn and he feels the DE clear, he'll loop out on a late contain.

On the strongside, we give the DT shaded in a 3 technique the option to beat his guard over or under. A change call by our outside LB gives our strong DE a wide jet rush. This forces the OT to fan out and block him in space, or a RB must pick him up in the backfield.

Any time we can deny or make the offensive line work to keep the "big on big" matchup or tie RBs or TEs into the protection quickly, we then gain a coverage advantage. Also, from a technical point, the DE is No. 4 strong rushing or strong safety blitz. This read in itself can cause problems for an offense. Using the 1-Free coverage, we use the weak ILB to slide and check draw and screen before dropping off.

In Figure 2, we use the same 80 pre-snap look but add a defensive line twist to pressure. Much as an offense will run the same play from differ-

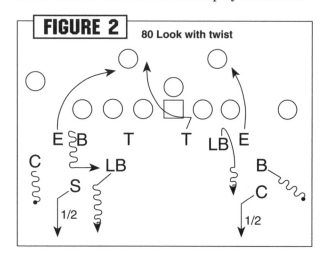

FIGURE 2 80 Look with twist

ent formations and motions to cause confusion, on defense we will try to base rush, twist, and max blitz from the same look.

In this simple X-stunt adjustment, the W-end has a true jet contain rush which earlier had set up his under move. The weak ILB walks to the LOS and will draw the O-guard's block before

dropping out. By drawing the guard's block, we insure that the inside twist has our DTs going 2-on-2 instead of 3-on-2.

The stunt has the strong tackle on the snap driving under the offensive guard. His rush lane is through the backside 2 area. It is important to sell the first man that he also is going to go free. The intensity of his rush will increase when he realizes that he is not a sacrificial lamb.

The twist tackle steps hard and upfield to the weakside. We don't hurry X-stunts; we like to X on the offensive side of the ball. The twist tackle comes tight off of his partner's tail and gets upfield once he clears behind the pick.

The strong OLB will ride the TE before spying off for screen, draw, or delay. Coverage can be matched with a standard 2-deep look.

In Figure 3 we show a four-man rush where we try to use speed personnel to pressure a QB. Ironically, although we are an even front defense,

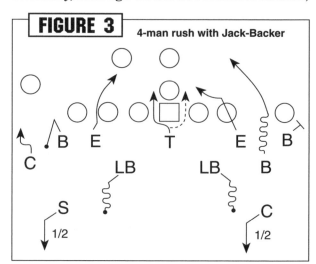

FIGURE 3 4-man rush with Jack-Backer

we get some of our best pressure from odd front looks. In our 55 front, we remove a DT and replace him with a "Jack-Backer," who is a strong-safety type player, to add speed off of the corner and cause havoc. The Jack-Backer can come from the tight or split side, and for a nice two-man change-up, he tells the D-end whether he is coming on a contain or free rush.

In our game plan, we will predetermine the Jack-Backer's rush side and responsibility to maximize our matchup, based on their protection scheme. A balanced 55 rush can be matched with any low risk coverage.

We hope these simple ideas on defensive pressure are of some help to you. Remember, good players who play hard win football games.

—1990 Summer Manual. Coach Beamer is head coach at Virginia Tech. Coach Clark is defensive coordinator.

Simple Coverages Versus Complex Passing Games

DICK SHERIDAN with BUDDY GREEN

One of the most important attributes in a defensive unit is to be aggressive. To be aggressive, our defensive players must be confident and sure of their alignment, technique, and responsibilities. To achieve that confidence and aggressiveness and to be sound as a unit, it's critical that we simplify and reduce to a minimum what we teach each position. And it's imperative that we eliminate confusion and indecision, yet include in our package the tools that we need to be effective.

We've tried to simplify our teaching process, particularly with our defensive package. For many years, our package has included

- a weakside shade 50 defense with 3-deep coverage;
- a strongside shade 50 defense with either 2-deep coverage or a weakside roll; and
- a nickel package with an easily adjusted even front with 2-deep zone, 2-deep man/robber coverages.

Six years ago, we added a stack alignment for our linebackers without changing the alignment and responsibilities of our defensive line. Our stack defense, which we call Slide, has been effective versus the running game. Versus the passing game it was OK as far as angles, alignment, and leverage, but certain sets—especially one-back sets—took us out of our base coverages.

In stack alignment or Slide defense, our down linemen slide (shade) away from the call (strength), and our three stack linebackers slide (shade) to the call. We played two base coverages with this front. Both coverages had a double call. The first call was our base call, and the second number gave our perimeter people their automatic check versus shifts, one-back sets, and motion. Figure 1 shows our alignment in cover 21, which is a 2-deep coverage with the flexibility to check to 3-deep.

Figure 2 shows our alignment in cover 91, which is a man/robber on one side and zone on the back side. Again, the flexibility to check to 3-

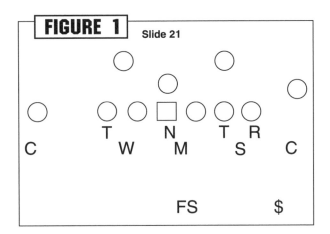

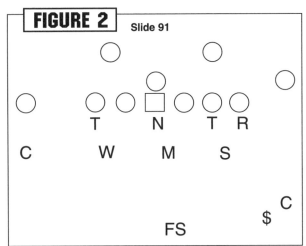

deep is built into the call. All adjustments are the same as 21.

Certain pressure calls with man coverage were built into this package. Formation recognition was the key.

In order to stay with a 2-deep perimeter (cover 2) or a man/robber perimeter (cover 9), we would use our Split (nickel) front. Our Split package was called 5, which signaled five under with 2-deep (e.g., Figure 3).

We also had a pressure package with man coverage from this front. Gaps and alignments varied from our slide front. When we evaluated this

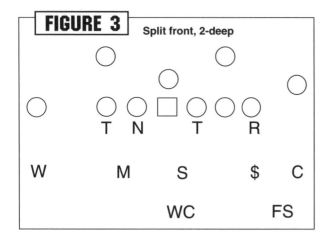

FIGURE 3 — Split front, 2-deep

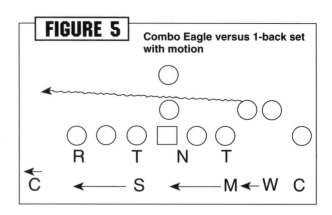

FIGURE 5 — Combo Eagle versus 1-back set with motion

system and had a change to personnel lacking experience, we decided to restructure our calls to simplify our adjustments. We wanted to keep the effectiveness of certain fronts, but improve our effectiveness versus certain one-back sets and motion. We wanted to keep each play's alignment, adjustment, and technique as much the same as possible. And we wanted to combine both fronts to maximize our effectiveness in certain situations in the running and passing game.

What we developed is our Combo-Eagle base front, shown in Figure 4. This front is a combination of Slide principles with a Split adjustment.

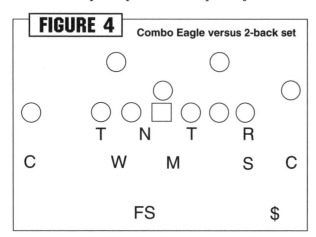

FIGURE 4 — Combo Eagle versus 2-back set

Its key feature was that it allowed us to remain in our stack alignment versus two backs, but gave us the flexibility to adjust to one-back sets, shifts, and motion (see Figure 5) while staying in our 2-deep coverage.

One phase of reorganizing our package was to have simple rules in the perimeter so that we could package more than two fronts and more than two coverages to game plan our calls to certain sets that we may see. I must admit that we stole this terminology from our offense, and our players really like it.

We called it our "check with me" package. Our huddle call was "check with me." We gave the initial coverage we wanted with the fronts, and all adjustments were automatic. The huddle call was quick, and many times a huddle was not needed. This package is game planned to match our fronts and coverages with formations of our opponents. We could communicate our Slide, Combo-Eagle, and Split calls and coverages through just one call: "check with me" (see Figure 6).

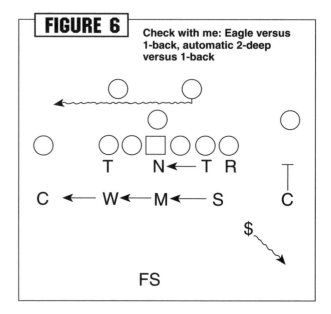

FIGURE 6 — Check with me: Eagle versus 1-back, automatic 2-deep versus 1-back

The changes we made in our defensive package have allowed our younger players to get comfortable with technique and responsibility. We're also better able to defend complex passing offenses, while still keeping the rules simple for our perimeter people.

—1992 Proceedings. Dick Sheridan was head coach at North Carolina State University. Coach Green is head coach at the University of Tennessee at Chattanooga.

PART III

Special Teams

Kicking for the Winning Edge
SPIKE DYKES

The old adage that three to five games per season are determined in the kicking game holds true—just check the records. We understand the importance and the value of a good kicking game, so we involve our very best players in the kicking game.

On punt return, extra point, and field goal block teams we use defensive players. On the kickoff and punt-coverage teams, we usually employ defensive backs, linebackers, and defensive ends.

Kickoff Coverage

Our kickoff principles differ from some theories in that we kick off from the exact middle of the field. We want a high, straight kick to the goal line. We use the waterfall approach in alignment so we can all hit the line running full speed. Our alignment is shown in Figure 1.

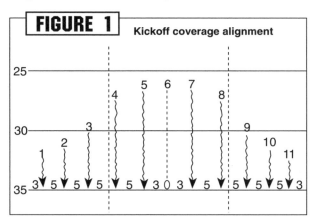

FIGURE 1 — Kickoff coverage alignment

We have three potential safeties on each kickoff: 3, 6 (the kicker), and 9. We begin covering the field with each player maintaining his relative distance between his teammates. The farther and deeper the ball goes, the longer we stay in our lanes. In the event that we get forced out of our lane, we work hard to get back in our lane. Players should be aware of who is blocking them and then beat or escape the block.

Once the ball is fielded and starts in a direction (left, middle, right), we start converging on the football (see Figure 2). This, and busting our tails downfield, are the two keys to the coverage.

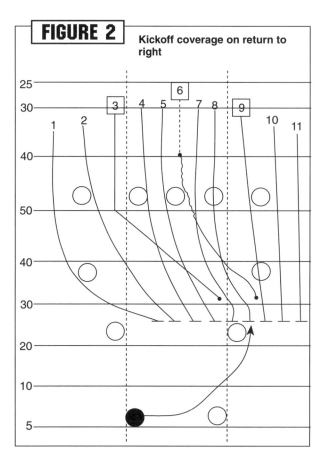

FIGURE 2 — Kickoff coverage on return to right

The safety (3) opposite the return pulls out and keeps outside leverage on the football. The outside two coverage men fill the hole created by the safety pulling out, maintaining the normal coverage lanes one gap inside. The safety to the side of the return no longer is a safety—he is a lane runner that is totally involved in coverage. The kicker faces up with the ball at a depth of approximately 8 to 10 yards behind the coverage team.

If the ball comes up the middle (see Figure 3), the kicker is the middle safety, and both safeties pull out of coverage after the ball has committed to the middle and maintain outside leverage on the football.

In our coverage, 5 and 7 maintain their leverage on the ball, even if the ball is run up the hash mark. The closer the ball gets to our coverage, the more we converge to the ball. We all squeeze

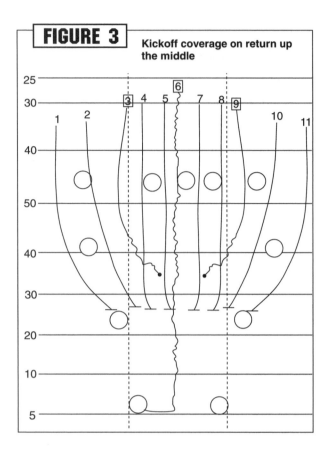

FIGURE 3 Kickoff coverage on return up the middle

not allow a lineman to catch a clean kick and return it for a big gain. The remainder of the coverage attacks! We want to force a mistake by the receiving team. Down through the years, this onside kick has been highly successful for us.

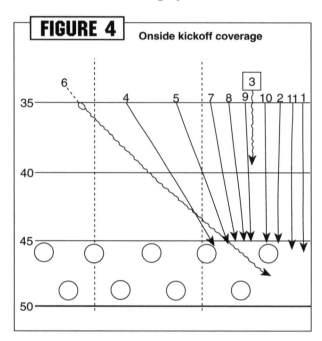

FIGURE 4 Onside kickoff coverage

down, maintaining proper leverage on the ball. Again, the ball should be kicked high and straight. We attempt to kick each kickoff so it will be returned.

This coverage team has a tremendous amount of pride. All of our defensive starters want to be on the kickoff team. It's a highly competitive situation, and that's healthy for the whole team.

Onside Kick

Another option for the kickoff team is the onside kick. This is something that you use only when your "back is to the wall"; the success or failure of an onside kick can be the determining factor in a football game.

In order to have a shot at gaining possession off an onside kick, we first must have a perfectly executed kick. Without the proper kick, you have no chance. The kick should never be kicked less than 10 to 12 yards. This is the first point of emphasis to the kicker. We strive to get the big hop out of the ball. Our alignment on the onside kick is shown in Figure 4.

Another key is to not let the kick go out-of-bounds. This is the responsibility of 1. He plays just like a shortstop covering the boundary. Another very important role is 3, a safety, who can-

Punt Protection and Coverage

The last phase of coverage is our punt protection and coverage. The quickest way to lose a football game is to get a punt blocked or a punt returned for a touchdown. This phase of the kicking game must be executed properly every time. No lapses.

We use the spread punt with zone protection. Again, we work hard to get the ball kicked straight down the field. Our alignment and splits are illustrated in Figure 5.

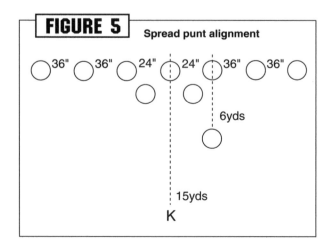

FIGURE 5 Spread punt alignment

The protection starts with the center. His job is to make a perfect snap that arrives in the punter's hands in 0.7 to 0.8 seconds. After his snap, he pops up with a good base—then he starts thinking about coverage. The guards' split is 2 feet from the center. Each guard hinges 45 degrees, with a blocking assignment from his inside foot to the inside foot of the tackle. If two people penetrate the gap, the guard should block through the first man to the second one. The hardest job for the guard is keeping his butt in the hole between himself and the center.

The tackle's job is the same as the guard's except his butt in the hole is not as strongly emphasized as the guard's. He must keep his inside foot planted as long as possible, with the same principle as the guard with two threats in the gap. The end hinges the same as the tackle, keeping his inside foot planted as long as possible. The end must re-route the rush of the outside man.

The upbacks have the responsibility of the gap between the center and guard. Two major points of emphasis: Make sure the upbackers are lined up one yard deep and stop any threat (charge) in the gap. If two people come in that gap, the upback must make himself big and get his head between the two men.

The personal protector, who we call the "searchlight," lines up 6 yards deep behind the guard (left or right depending on left-footed or right-footed kicker). The searchlight must be aware of overloads and must use good judgment, never taking a backward step. He takes on any immediate threats to the kicker, but doesn't go anywhere unless there is a reason to. After the ball is kicked, the searchlight is a safety to our right.

The kicker's job is to field the snap, know whether or not there is a rush, concentrate, and kick the football. If we have a choice, we will use a two-step punter. We align the punter 15 yards deep and work hard on stepping and fielding the ball simultaneously. We strive to get the punt off in 2.3 seconds or less. A hang time of 3.9 or better is what we want. After the ball is kicked, the kicker is a safety to our left.

We change our contain coverage week to week. Usually, and as a basic rule, the ends are our containment. Our basic punt coverage is shown in Figure 6.

Special teams are an integral part of a football team. Accompanying this article is a kicking game checklist that we cover with our team at least once a week. This is a carryover from coach Darrell Royal at Texas. He covered this with our team each Saturday morning of the season.

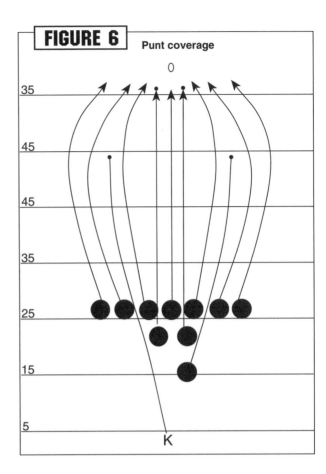

FIGURE 6   Punt coverage

Key Points on the Kicking Game

Kickoff Coverage:
A. Be onsides.
B. Sprint.
C. Stay in lanes. (If blocker forces you out of a lane, get back in lane.)
D. Locate ball. (Remember ball is live after it travels 10 yards.)
E. Converge on ball and break down.
F. We cover as a team.

Onside Kick Coverage:
A. Be onsides.
B. Attack! (We want possession.)

Kickoff Return:
A. Know blocking assignments and block above the waist.
B. Be onsides.
C. Field ball in air.
D. Know depth of ball.
E. Remember ball is live after it travels 10 yards.
F. You can fair catch.

Punt Protection and Coverage:
A. On center's snap—after command of down.
B. We must protect. (Your man will not block the kick with your head in the middle.)
C. Fan out.
D. Sprint.
E. Locate the ball.
F. Converge on the ball.
G. Ends must contain. (Alert your tackle when held up, work back to sideline.)
H. Stay on lane.
I. First man down take an uncontrolled shot if you have shot, but *not* ends.
J. Fullback covers right; kicker covers left.
K. We cover as a team.

Punt Return:
A. When we have a return, be sure ball is kicked before rolling back for the return.
B. Don't
(1) be offside,
(2) rough kicker,
(3) clip, or
(4) block below waist.
C. Field ball intelligently.
D. Call a "block" if opponents are going into a strong wind.
E. If "block" is called
(1) be ready when center touches ball,
(2) charge on snap,
(3) don't be offside, and
(4) go for "blocking" zone

F. Blocked punts that do not cross line of scrimmage can be advanced by either team. Recover ball on third down blocked punts. Advance ball on fourth down blocked punts.
G. Blocked punts that cross line of scrimmage play as any normal punt.
H. Two factors that make unsure kicking situation are
(1) field position, and
(2) score of game.
I. "Unsure" is bench call. We want them to kick. Play defense called:
(1) Normal—40,
(2) Short—short defense, or
(3) Long—long defense.

Extra Point (Protection):
A. Place kicking tee 7 yards from ball.
B. Ball in play on center's snap.
C. Linemen keep outside foot planted and block zone.
D. Upbacks keep outside foot in place and block zone.
E. On bad snaps or mishandled ball holler "fire." Upbacks and ends release outside, and holder or kicker scramble and find receivers.

Field Goal Protection:
A. (Same as extra point.)
B. Release when you hear ball kicked:
(1) Fan out.
(2) Sprint.
(3) Locate ball.
(4) Treat as punt.
(5) Converge on ball and break point.
(6) Ends must contain.
(7) Holder left; kicker right.
C. Blocked field goal attempt may be advanced by either team.

Versus Extra Point:
A. Know situation.
(1) versus extra point formation (call blocked direction), and
(2) versus run formation (automatic defense).
B. Be onsides.
C. Be ready when center touches ball.
D. Move on center's snap.
E. Go for "blocking" zone.
F. Don't rough kicker or holder.

Versus Field Goal:
A. Anticipate field goal.
B. Reminders are same as extra point.
C. Treat field goal same as punt on blocked kicks.

—1986 Summer Manual. Coach Dykes is head coach at Texas Tech University.

Developing a Complete Kickoff Return Package

BILLY SEXTON

We consider the kickoff return an offensive play—a play that is intended to score a touchdown. Our attack is based on the simplest schemes possible. We break the field down into three areas (right, middle, left) and incorporate a misdirection play (reverse or throwback).

On our kick return team, we want people that can run and hit. The players we use on the front line are a wide out, a corner, a fullback, and two outside linebackers. The end positions are manned by tight ends. The fullback positions are a fullback and a corner. The two safeties on our return are tailbacks.

Kick Return Alignment

Under normal conditions, our kick return team will align as shown in Figure 1.

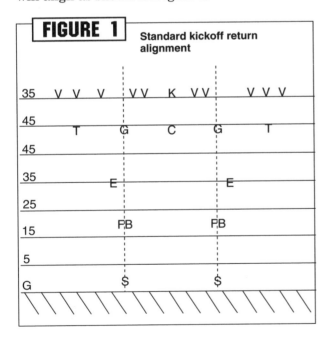

This alignment can change, depending on the strength of the kicker's leg. If he's an excellent kicker or has the wind at his back, we may drop the safeties as deep as the goal line. If his leg is

weak or he's kicking into the wind, we may bring the deep safeties up as far as the 15-yard line, on the hashes. As a rule, you want your returner to catch the kick heading toward the opponent's goal line, not catching it going backwards or going sideways.

Extremely wet conditions will adversely affect the flight of the ball, making it heavy and less likely to travel as far or as high. Adjust your safeties and back wedge people accordingly.

The front line people should be aligned 13 yards from the ball. If an onside kick attempt is indicated by the kicking team's alignment or the position of the ball on the tee, then the front five should align 10 yards and 3 inches from the line. We will adjust our ends' alignment if we anticipate a surprise onside kick, moving them from the 35-yard line to midfield to back up the five front line players.

If the ball is kicked off from the middle of the field, our center wants to offset 2 to 3 yards, 13 yards from the ball, and the tackles to align 8 yards outside the hash. The ends will line up on the 35-yard line, 5 yards outside the hash. The fullbacks align on the 20-yard line on the hash, and the safeties align on the hash at the goal line.

Alignment on Kick From Hash

If the ball is kicked off from the left hash (see Figure 2) or right hash, we adjust our alignment. The tackle and guard on the hash being kicked from will both move outside the hash on alignment. The guard will align 2 to 3 yards outside the hash, and the tackle 6 to 7 yards from the sideline. The center will slide 2 to 3 yards towards the hash being kicked from, as do the far guard and tackle.

The ends' alignment, along with FBs', won't change; they must maintain position to field the bloop kick that is kicked from the hash. You may have to adjust the safeties if you face a team that kicks from the hash and has a kicker that is especially accurate in placing the kickoff 2 to 3 yards from the sideline. Since we are in twin deep safeties, we moved the safety to the side of the kick, 1 to 2 yards alignment from the sideline. We do this so the safety can field the kick from the sideline to the middle of field. We've found that this is better than aligning on the hash and rushing to the sideline, worrying about going out-of-bounds.

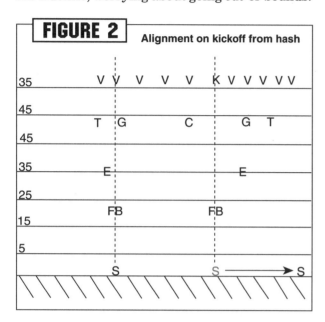

Types of Returns

We have three base returns: sideline, field, and vertical. On all three of these returns, the front wedge has the same assignment. The center sets the wedge on the 30-yard line in front of the ball, never outside the hash. The front wedge has 2-yard spacing between each player in the front wedge. After setting the wedge on the 30, their rule is to take the first man head-up to outside. The center takes the first man head-up or first man to his right. This front wedge attacks straight vertically upfield wherever they set.

The back wedge is set by the two fullbacks. Their job is to always set the back wedge 10 yards in front of the returner. Forming the back wedge, you have the two fullbacks as the focal point. Next to them, you have the safety not receiving the kick, the end to his side, along with the end on the far side. Their spacing is also 2 yards.

Sideline and Field Return

The back wedge assignment differs depending on the call, unlike the front wedge assignment. If

it's a sideline return, then the back wedge heads towards the numbers to the side of the kick, blocking head-up to outside, middle man to left (see Figure 3).

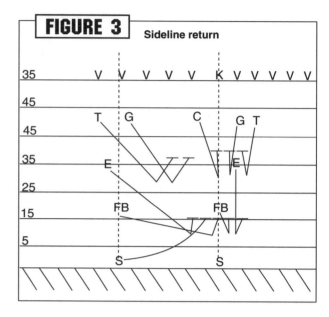

If the ball is kicked to the middle of the field on this call, then the return is predetermined by the scouting report, based on the lane disbursement and personnel. If the call is field return, then the back wedge will again set 10 yards in front of the receiver and attack the far hash mark as their aiming point (see Figure 4). Again, if the ball is kicked off down the middle, we'll return down a predetermined side.

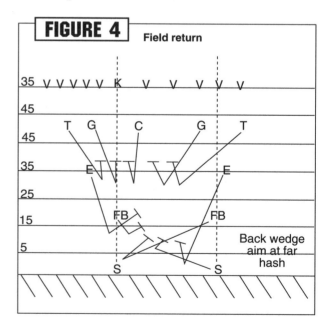

Vertical Return

On the vertical return, we are simply trying to return the ball north-south, wherever it is kicked. Here the back wedge sets 10 yards in front of kick returner and heads straight to the opponent's goal line, blocking head-up to outside.

Misdirection Return

Our main misdirection return is our throwback, shown in Figure 5. As you can see, our front people attack the coverage people and wheel to 5 yards outside the hash, setting the wall for the throw back man. There should be a man every 5 yards in the wall, beginning about the 15-yard line. The ends and fullbacks set the back wedge and attack the right numbers like a right return.

The safety that is to receive the throwback on the kick should go to a point 5 yards outside the hash and maintain 10-yard depth behind the thrower. The safety that is your thrower wants to return the kick no matter how deep it is kicked into the end zone. When he receives the kick, he wants to run right to the numbers, trying to get

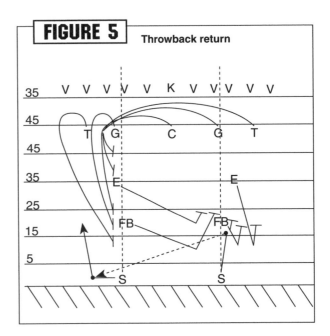

FIGURE 5   Throwback return

to the 15-yard line or until pressure forces him to throw back to the other safety. The pass is backwards; therefore, it's a lateral, so the ball can hit the ground and be advanced.

—1988 Summer Manual. Coach Sexton is assistant coach at Florida State University.

Protecting and Covering From a Spread Punt Formation

TOM COUGHLIN with ALAN PAQUETTE

We place more emphasis on punt protection and coverage than we do on any other special team unit. We devote at least 50 minutes a week in season to our punt team preparation. These 50 minutes include meetings and practice time. The fullbacks will meet with the special teams coach individually at least twice, early in the week. Whenever the punt team is on the practice field, we utilize eight coaches (including the head coach). We film punt practice from behind the punt team, as well as from the side. This enables us to closely evaluate protection (behind) and coverage distribution (side).

The capability to consistently punt the football well is a tremendous advantage in the battle for field position. The punt team has two big responsibilities. The primary responsibility is to protect the punter. The second responsibility is to cover downfield and deny the return man any positive yardage. It's for this purpose that we decided to change from a base punt formation with a zone protection scheme to a spread punt formation with man protection.

Punt Team Formations

The spread formation (see Figure 1) has allowed us to maintain our protection and at the same time improve our coverage. Spreading the formation forces the opponent to cover each end with at least one man, and our ends are often double covered. When the opponent is aligned like this, we can clearly and quickly identify the rush. This formation also gives us many punt fake opportunities.

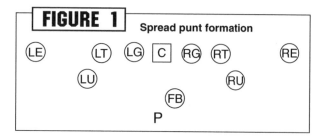

FIGURE 1 — Spread punt formation

In our man punt protection scheme, everyone from upback to upback is accountable for blocking a man. There are no free rushers. Conversely, with a zone punt protection, a rusher may enter a gray area between two zones and create indecision among the protection people, resulting in a blocked punt.

The simplicity of our protection scheme eliminates indecision and allows us to aggressively take on rushers and release into coverage. This aggressive man protection technique is much better suited to our current personnel here at Boston College.

Our zone protection scheme was run from a base punt formation (Figure 2). The protection called for big personnel who could drop step with the outside foot and lunge to the outside, keeping the inside foot anchored while extending their arms to protect the outside gap.

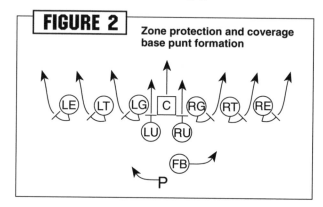

FIGURE 2 — Zone protection and coverage base punt formation

The two upbacks, aligned in the center-guard gaps, would step up into their respective gap and aggressively protect the area. After securing their gap responsibility, each punt team member would release into coverage.

Punt Team Personnel

Although we had big personnel who were capable of protecting the punter in this fashion, they couldn't adequately cover the punt. Our strong aggressive people who could cover were too compact to provide zone protection. By switching to the spread punt formation and a man protection scheme, we were getting the most out of our personnel, people who could bring their assigned rusher to a stop and cover the punt with good speed. Our ends are able to release on the snap of the ball with no protection responsibility. Our punt coverage improved tremendously!

We search long and hard to find the best player for each position on our punt team. All of our coverage drills are taped to find the player who can consistently spring downfield under control and maintain proper distribution on the field in relation to other members of the coverage team.

To quote Frank Ganz, special teams coach for the Detroit Lions: "Open field football is different. Flying down the field to make a tackle is a different skill than breaking up to make a tackle on defense." Your best tackler on defense may not be your best coverage player.

Ends

Our ends must be our best cover people. They must possess great speed and be very aggressive. They must be able to release off the ball with a defender or two attempting to keep each on the line of scrimmage. Once they are off the ball, they must beat the opponent to the return man.

Upbacks and Tackles

Our upbacks and tackles must be capable of bringing the rusher to a complete stop and releasing to contain the return man or maintain lane leverage. This calls for a more disciplined player. (The upbacks and tackles may switch coverage responsibilities.)

Guards

The guard positions call for players who are bigger than the upbacks and tackles to help the center in protection whenever possible. They need not be as disciplined as the upbacks and tackles, but they must be hitters to solidify the middle of the coverage.

Center

Our center is often involved in protection. He must be capable of not only snapping the ball accurately; he must also be able to step quickly to block left or right, depending on the protection called.

Fullback

The fullback position must be assigned to an intelligent and aggressive leader. He runs the show! He must be capable of recognizing the opponent's rush set and making the protection calls accordingly. A fullback must be an intense hitter, be able to take on rushers, and be athletic enough to execute our various punt fakes.

Punt Procedure

The punt team assembles on the sideline prior to each third down. The special teams coach will give special instructions or plays before sending them on the field.

The punt team will sprint onto the field and align quickly in punt formation. Unless otherwise instructed, there will be no huddle.

As the team runs onto the field, they communicate special instructions to members of the punt team who are presently on the field as members of the offensive unit.

Lining Up for the Punt

FB will look around to see that the team is ready and will count 11. He will call the front and alert the team if there is an overload. He will then make the protection call.

After the fullback's call, the line will make any necessary line calls and communicate their blocking assignments. After the line calls are made, the FB rechecks the team's alignment and calls for the ball to be snapped (see Figure 3).

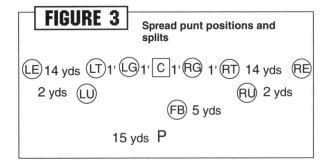

FIGURE 3 — Spread punt positions and splits

The line should assume a two-point hitting stance with hands on thigh pads, with elbows bent. Feet should be slightly staggered (toe/heel relationship) with the outside foot back. Shoulders should be parallel to the line of scrimmage. They will line up with their helmets breaking the plane of the center's belt. They must be able to see the ball.

Guards—Take a one-foot split from the center. They are responsible for the alignment of the line. Guards must be sure that their helmets are even with the center's belt. The tackles and ends will take their alignment on the guard.

Tackles—Take a one-foot split from the guard. They align on the guard so their shoulders are exactly even with the guard's shoulders and parallel to the line of scrimmage.

Ends—Take a split alignment (14 yards from the ball). Shoulders must be parallel to the line of scrimmage.

Upbacks—Line up 2 yards off the ball with their inside foot directly behind the outside foot of the tackle. Assume a two-point stance, with hands on thigh pads, cocked slightly to the outside.

Fullback—Line up 5 yards from the ball, directly behind the right guard. Assume a two-point stance, being able to block their assignment.

Punter—Line up 15 yards from the ball, directly behind center.

Punt Protection

Rock protection is called when our opponents have six potential rushers (see Figure 4). Blocking assignments will always be determined by counting the potential rushers from outside in.

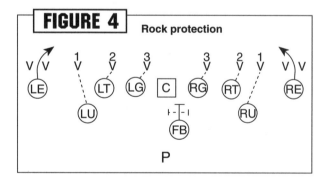

Ends—Release quickly. Go to the ball!

Upbacks—Ignore anyone on the split end. Counting from the outside, block 1.

Tackles—Block 2.

Guards—Block 3.

Center—Make a perfect snap. Sit back and block area solid.

Fullback—Scan the formation and block the most dangerous rusher.

Eagle protection is called when there are more than six potential rushers. This protection involves assigning a man to the center, and in all cases of a ten-man front, the FB is assigned a man to pick up (see Figure 5).

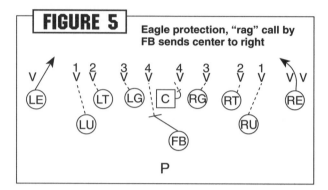

Ends—Same split and alignment. Go to the ball!

Upbacks—Ignore anyone on the split end. Block 1.

Tackles—Block 2.

Guards—Block 3.

Center—Make a perfect snap. Block 4 to the side as directed by the fullback.

Fullback—Give the center directional call and block man not picked up by the center.

Punter—Anticipate rush situation, use two-step punt. Get the punt off! Maximize hang time, but don't outkick coverage.

Punt Coverage Examples

If the ball is caught in the middle of the field, the center, ends, and fullback will go directly to the ball. The guards will be 6 yards outside of the ball, the tackles will be 12 yards outside of the ball, and the upbacks will be approximately 18 yards outside of the ball. The coverage will then squeeze to the ball, converging from *outside-in*, with the inside shoulder on the ball (see Figure 6).

Similar coverage responsibilities apply when ball is caught outside the hash area. Figure 7 shows cover responsibilities outside the right hash.

Right upback—Contain the return. Should be approximately six yards outside ball.

Right tackle and right guard—Go directly to the ball when it is kicked to their side of the field (outside the hash).

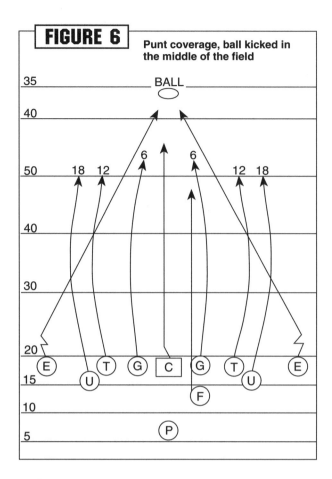

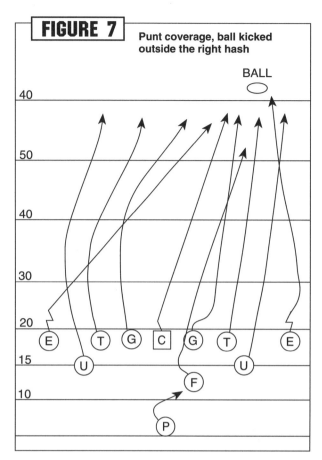

Center—Adjust coverage to be 6 yards outside the ball.

Left guard—Adjust coverage to be 12 yards outside the ball.

Left tackle—Adjust coverage to be 18 yards outside the ball.

Left upback—Adjust coverage to be approximately 24 yards outside the ball. Responsible for contain.

Ends—Go to the ball. Maintain leverage on the ball with near shoulder.

Fullback—Go directly to the ball.

Punter—Keep the ball in front at all times. Play safety role.

LU, LT, LG, C, RU—Maintain leverage on the ball. Squeeze to the ball, converging from outside-in, with inside shoulder on ball.

—1992 Summer Manual. Coach Coughlin is head coach for the Jacksonville Jaguars (NFL). Coach Paquette is special teams coach at Boston College.

Making a Commitment to Special Teams

JOHN COOPER WITH **LARRY COYER**

Every coach believes in the importance of the kicking game. Some coaches, especially those coaching winning programs, are *committed* to the kicking game. They are willing to put their best players on these teams and spend the necessary practice time on the kicking game. They don't consider the work of special teams an "after practice" activity.

Punt Team

Our defensive staff handles the punting game using the very best athletes on our team. The only player we won't use is our No. 1 quarterback. Figure 1 shows our standard punt alignment.

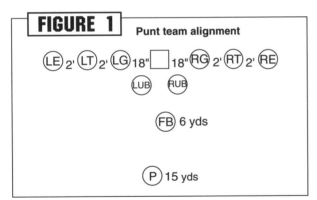

FIGURE 1 Punt team alignment

LE 2' LT 2' LG 18" ☐ 18" RG 2' RT 2' RE
LUB   RUB
FB 6 yds
P 15 yds

Center

The most important thing about the punt is the center's snap. *It must be perfect.* The center's prime job is to get the ball to the punter accurately in 0.7 seconds. He snaps at least one second after the fullback says "ready." He should vary the delay of his snap, staying aware of the 25-second clock. If an opponent is jumping around, he should snap quickly.

Assignment: Quick setup. Retain wide base and shuffle back one yard (two steps). Foot-to-foot with upbacks after this shuffle back. Be alert to "overload" call from upbacks.

Coverage: Work to get in the middle of the field. Sprint in lane. When the ball is caught, close to the ball. If first man to the receiver, attack with a high tackle. Force him to commit sideways.

Guards

Two-point stance with the outside foot slightly back. Feet slightly narrower than shoulders. Hands on knees. Lined up on the heels of the center.

Assignment: Block outside—the outside edge of protection responsibility. Responsible for the man or men in the *outside* gap from his inside shoulder (from nose to nose). If there are two men

in the gap, *block the widest man* going through the nearest gap. Thrust to outside of protection. Drag the inside foot as late as possible. If no man in area, still set, thrust, get width (shuffle), and go to lane.

Coverage: Fan out with release to cover lane, 3 yards inside hash. Cover lane point is at least 10 yards. Sprint in lane until 7 yards from ball-carrier. Then break down and shuffle in, keeping outside leg free.

Tackles

Two-point stance with the outside foot slightly back. Feet slightly narrower than shoulders. Hands on knees.

Assignment: Block outside—outside edge of protection responsibility. Responsible for the man or men in the *outside* gap of his inside shoulder to the next man's inside shoulder (from nose to nose). If two men are in the gap, or a man in the gap and a man over the end, set step and *block the widest man* going through the nearest gap. Thrust to outside of protection. Drag the inside foot as late as possible. If no man in area, still set, thrust, get width (shuffle), and go to lane.

Coverage: Fan out with release to cover lane, 4 yards outside hash. Cover lane point is at 10 yards. Sprint in lane until 7 yards from ball-carrier. Break down and shuffle in, keeping outside arm free.

Ends

Two-point stance with the outside foot slightly back. Feet slightly narrower than shoulders. Hands on knees.

Assignment: Block outside—outside edge of our protection responsibility. Responsible for man or men outside (from nose out). If man is lined up as much as 5 yards outside, set step to a cutoff spot and block the widest man going through the nearest gap. Thrust to outside of protection, get a shoulder or hip on the man. Drag inside foot as late as possible. Protect first, cover second.

Coverage: After assuring protection, release immediately. Fan out on release to cover lane, 6 yards from sideline. At 10 yards be in lane until 7 yards from ball-carrier. Break down and shuffle in, keeping outside leg free. Be contain man. Nothing gets outside. Evade all blockers.

Upbacks

Two-point stance, feet balanced, hands on knees. Align 1 1/2 yards deep, between center and guard.

Assignment: Responsibility is to block from the nose of the center to the nose of the guard. Make overload call to center, if necessary. If two men in gap, stop the first, take the second. Fullback will take the first. Fill the one-foot split by C-G gap. Extend arms like OL in pass protection. Pop them good, release, and cover. Don't be overly aggressive; can't afford to be pulled or thrown.

Coverage: Fan out on release to cover lane. Aiming point is the goal post on your side. At 10 yards be at cover point lane. Sprint in lane until 7 yards from ball-carrier. Break down and shuffle in, keeping outside leg free. If first man to the ball, attack the receiver with a high tackle.

Fullback

Man in charge. Know down, distance, field position, time, score, and *communicate!* When everyone is set call "ready." After call, center will snap ball at his leisure. If defense is jumping around, we will snap quick, early in the game.

Also responsible for audible. If open for a run, fullback indicates the direction: "Ringo" for right and "Lucky" for left.

Assignment: Count teammates—four to the right and four to the left. Ask punter if he is ready. Then call "ready." Block the first man to show—the most dangerous rusher. *Never step back to block.* Watch for twist stunts over the upbacks, your side first (especially in stack situation).

Coverage: Release downfield. If it's a sideline return, cover between the wall and the sideline. If it's a middle return, cover straight to ball.

Punter

Line up at least 15 yards deep. Always be aware of down, distance, and field position. Fourth down is must punt. Third down offers another chance if bad snap. *Always* expect the bad snap.

Assignment: Let the fullback know when ready. *Always call the direction of punt three times.* Get the punt off in *2 seconds or less* (1.3 seconds after receiving snap). Get distance and height.

Coverage: Safety man. Front up the ball at 15 yards.

Punting From Deep in Own Territory

When punting inside of our own 3-yard line, the punter will never get closer than 2 feet from the back of the end zone.

The fullback will move up 2 feet closer and then move up on the punt so that the punter doesn't kick him, but never closer than 4 yards from the punting spot. Linemen will close down splits to 1 foot and release after making good hit.

Punt Block and Return Teams

The personnel for our punt block (score) team will be the best athletes on our team. Our first priority is speed, but beyond that, we search for players with a knack for blocking kicks. We try to discover this knack with a simple kick block drill that we do throughout spring and fall practice (see Figure 2). The practice of this unit takes precedence over all other drills.

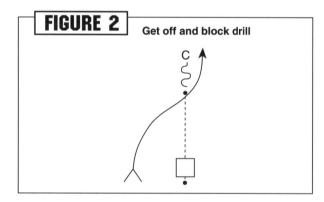

FIGURE 2   Get off and block drill

Our punt block and punt return teams look exactly the same. Our philosophy is to use the block to set up our return. We do everything we can do to block a kick from anywhere on the field. Once we get our opponent to overemphasize protection, we have a great chance to set up our return.

We operate from one type of front in our punt defense. In order to simplify our communication we refer to our positions as numbers 1–10.

Punt Return Team Alignment and Assignments

We call our punt return team "Jesse James," to emphasize the need to "hold up" the coverage. Figure 3 shows how we align in our 10-man front.

During the course of the season, we will have variations of the Jesse James return to take advantage of our opponent's personnel on punt coverage structure (see Figure 4).

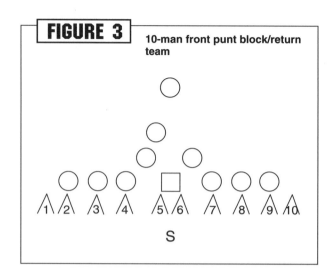

FIGURE 3   10-man front punt block/return team

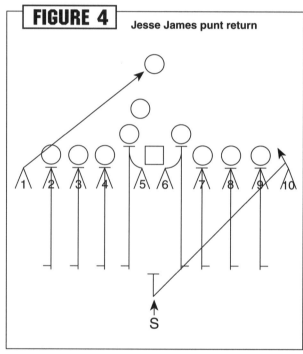

FIGURE 4   Jesse James punt return

1—Force or block kick. If ball is punted, peel around to block punter or FB.

2 and 9—Attack #4 using pop technique and return position. Release him outside.

3 and 8—Attack #3 using pop technique and return position. Release him outside.

4 and 7—Attack #2 using pop technique and return position. Release him outside.

5 and 6—Attack #1 using pop technique and return position. Release him outside.

10—Make sure ball is kicked, then turn and sprint back to the ball and block first threat. You are a "personal protector" for return man.

Returner—Go north/south right away. Get at least 10 yards.

Punt Return Blocking Principles

- Attack coverer pad under pad on proper aiming point. This enables blocker to control and release him to the side away from wall.
- The return position is on inside shoulder of cover man.
- Don't block unless able to get your head in front.
- Stay on feet. Get up quickly whenever knocked down.
- If in a wall, scan. Don't allow any penetration from self to next man in front of wall.
- As ball goes by, turn and run with the ball-carrier.
- If able to knock a man down, stay after him. Don't go to someone else.
- If about to lose a block, sprint to return man.

Punt Returner Principles

- Key punter, start moving in direction he steps. Don't wait for ball to be in air.
- Get underneath ball, use proper technique, and be in rocker position when fielding the ball.
- Don't handle punts inside 10-yard line. On kill or pooch punts, get on 10-yard line and don't back up to field the ball.
- Don't fake fair catch on kill or kill pooch punts. Instead, fake catch by sprinting up middle or either sideline in proximity to the ball.
- Field all punts in the air unless late in game and own team has lead and field position. Then let punt hit ground to consume time. Call will be made from sideline.
- Make decision to fair catch early and give the signal clearly.
- Get at least 10 yards on every punt that doesn't go out of bounds or inside the 10.
- Must break tackle or beat first coverer.

Punt Block Team Alignment and Assignments

The alignment and position responsibilities of our 10-man rush team are as follows (see Figure 5).

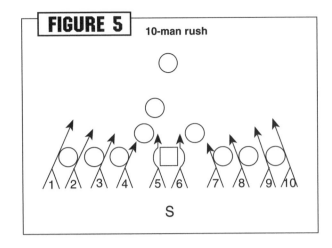

FIGURE 5 10-man rush

1, 2, 9, and 10—Drive outside of #4 for block point; block punt.

3 and 8—Drive inside of #3 for block point; block punt.

4 and 7—Drive inside of #2 for block point; block punt.

5—Finesse center left for block point; block punt.

6—Finesse center right for block point; block punt.

Safety—41 yards deep; get to the wall.

Punt Rush Principles

- Align as close to the neutral zone as possible.
- Key the ball and get a good jump on snap.
- Stay low on your charge—make yourself small. Slice.
- Block point will be one yard in front of the kicker's foot.
- Don't leave your feet to block a kick. Take the ball off the kicker's foot.
- Don't turn head. Keep eyes open. Make screaming noise.
- If ball is blocked and crosses LOS, call "Peter" and get away from the ball.
- If ball is blocked and does not cross LOS, pick it up and score.
- If picked up on charge, stay square on man, then go to the wall.
- If punt isn't blocked, it's an automatic return right.

—1993 Proceedings. Coach Cooper is head coach and Coach Coyer is defensive secondary coach at Ohio State University.

Kicking Game Gimmicks That Work

JIM WALDEN

When I talk about tricks in the kicking game, some coaches react with skepticism. That is, until they see them work and realize these gimmicks are based on fundamentals and the element of surprise. Certain gimmicks can help a punt team, a kickoff team, and a PAT team be more successful.

Punting

We put our best players on the punt team. We have one punt where we only use our first offensive team. A mistake most coaches make is with the personnel on their punt coverage teams. They tend to play six or seven defensive backs on the punt teams, putting those players in situations they don't see in the other part of the game.

What does coverage mean if you don't get the punt off? Play the people that will allow you to get the punt off. We aren't going to play all those defensive backs because they often don't want to block the opponent's linemen and linebackers.

Any good punt team will

- avoid getting kicks blocked,
- cover effectively, and
- maintain possession of the ball.

The third point is where we differ from most teams. There are two situations when the ball can change possession during a live play. One is on a punt and the other is on an interception. So, we want to put people on our punt team that will be covering a pass interception. Some coaches don't work on change of possession on the interception, because they are afraid they'll get someone hurt on the play.

Punt Team Alignment and Strategy

In our punt alignment, we line up the ends wide to the outside. We typically play our No. 2 QB in the upback position. This year we'll play our starting QB because he has played that position for the past two years, and he knows what to do at that spot.

We use three formations. We use a normal, unbalanced, and motion formation. If we put a man in motion, we have him run his regular coverage. If the wing goes in motion, the QB will take his responsibility on the contain.

The fakes we use are as follows. The upback can throw the ball to the punter, either end, or either slotback. The punter can throw the ball to the upback, either end, or either slotback. When is the last time you told one of your defensive players that they had the punter if the ball is snapped to the upback? I know, you never thought of that. You'd better be thinking about it if you play us, because I'm going to throw the ball to him.

Very seldom do we ever throw the ball to the split ends. However, someone will forget to cover the split end in a game, and the play will be open. We tell the punter to always look at the ends. If the defense tells the rushers not to go until they see the ball go by the upback, you can have the punter make the pass.

One other thing we do is move our players to change the formation. We move the running back up on the line, move the split end back one yard on the opposite side, and make our tight end eligible. It becomes a trips formation (see Figure 1). This is a frightening sight to most return teams.

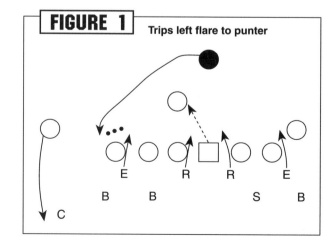

FIGURE 1   **Trips left flare to punter**

We never want to get the punt blocked. Our rules for our punt blocking are simple. We block inside-over-outside. If we face two men in our gap, we call for help. On our coverage the SEs go to the ball. The Rs have contain. The rest of the team have lanes to cover the punt return.

We can make the defense respect our kicking game. I can assure you they'll cover the two wide men; they'll cover the two wingmen; they have to assign someone to cover the upback on the pass or run. That takes care of five defenders. That leaves them with six men. They will put one man back to field the punt.

Now, they have only five men to rush the punt. We can find five people to block those five rushers. We can run the ball on the fake punt (see Figure 2). We can run the option from this set. Who has the pitch man on the fake punt? If you play us, you better assign someone to take the pitch, because we have it in our attack, and it's worked.

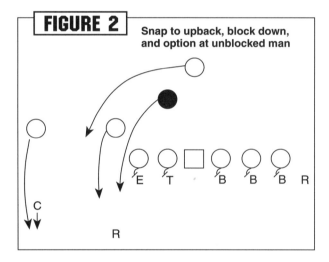

FIGURE 2 Snap to upback, block down, and option at unblocked man

If we face a 10-man rush, we can call the fake punt and run one of our trick plays. You may ask, "What do you do against teams that get in a 10-man front and then back out just before the ball is snapped?" We run a pure fake punt on them. When they turn their back as they back out, we run the screen pass with the punter throwing the ball. If you complete one of those screen passes, they'll think twice before they run it again. We can let the punter throw the ball to the upback to stop that crap (see Figure 3, for example).

They'll no longer fake the 10-man rush if we burn them a time or two. You need to have a fake punt, regardless of their set. When you are going to run a true fake punt without reading the defense, make sure you are out around midfield

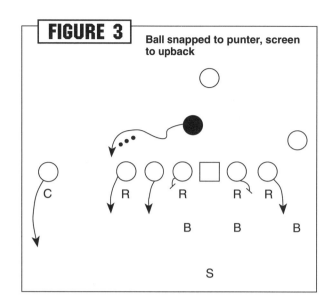

FIGURE 3 Ball snapped to punter, screen to upback

because it may not work. Don't put yourself in a bind. Don't lose your job over faking punts.

Let me tell you the truth: This approach to the kicking game is *tough* on a coach. As soon as the QB looks at the defense and calls the fake punt, you may want to cover your eyes. It's hard to watch. But it's been fun and successful for us. And our players believe in what we're doing.

Make the Call

I cannot tell you what we use as our keys. Forgive me for that. You can come up with your own plan. Let me tell you how we get a fake punt called. We use a city or state as a key word. Montana was our hot call last year.

If we're going to run our fake punt to the right, we tell them to pick any state east of the Mississippi River. (That's our geography lesson for the day!) We tell them to visualize a map of the United States. Any state west of the Mississippi River means we are going to our left.

We pick a state that is our live state. If we call a live state, we call a city. This tells the upback which way to go. It is the same setup. East cities are to the right and West cities are to the left.

This is how it would work. The punter would call "Montana-Miami-Montana." Montana means we are going to run the fake punt; Miami means we are going to our right side. If we call "Montana-Las Vegas-Montana," we would run the fake punt to the left. If we call "Iowa-Miami-Iowa" instead, we're going to punt the ball.

We can call live states or dead states. We can use colors instead of states or cities. We can change the live state, city, or color at the half or for each game. You can make up the combination that you want. We settle on a couple of live calls for each game. Next week, we can change the call to something else. We give them a hot state, a dead state, and a hot city. You need to have a system that will tell your upback which side he is going to take it to.

I'm not going to give you everything on the setup. You can work out the things that are best for your situation. I can assure you that your players will get excited. They'll get into it because it is fun. They want to get on that punt team.

Kickoff Team

Three years ago we asked our team this question: "How many of you want to go down on the kickoff?" No one raised their hand. We had to do something to change that attitude.

We have six types of kickoff alignments. One is a normal kick. We kick this from the right hash mark, which is where our kicker likes to kick from.

If we want to run the onside kick, we call it our cluster. We have 11 men that can push the ball in your face. We just bump the ball and go after it. The four inside men block out the front line to allow our two outside men to go after the ball (see Figure 4). We want the kicker to get the hell out of the way.

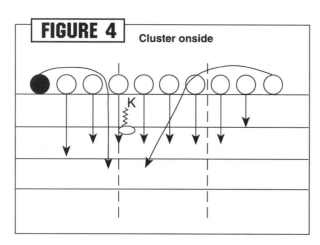

FIGURE 4   Cluster onside

We also have a running cluster spread, shown in Figure 5. We kick it to the goal line. We come out and sprint down the field in our lanes and go to the ball. If anything gets in our way, we run through them; we don't run around the blocker. The *pluggers* go directly to the ball.

On switch normal, we switch four men on each side of the ball. We change the 1-2-3-4 men on the right with the 11-10-9-8 men on the left. We

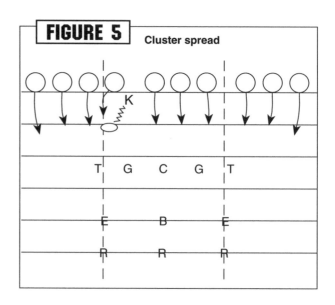

FIGURE 5   Cluster spread

kick the ball in the right corner. This screws up the blockers.

On the popover, we want to get the ball on the onside kick. We pop the ball over to the sideline and go for the ball. We pop the ball over the top and aim for the left sideline. We want our outside plugger, who is our 11 or S, to go for the ball (see Figure 6).

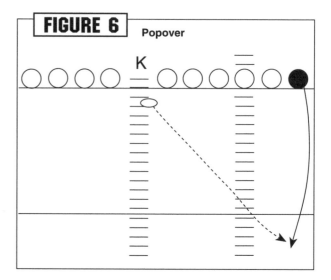

FIGURE 6   Popover

We like to build a little anxiety on the kickoffs. The rules state we have 25 seconds to put the kick in play after the whistle. What happens on most kickoffs? As soon as that whistle blows, most kickers start forward and kick the ball. We like to build the suspense. If our kicker will hold after the whistle 15 to 20 seconds, the receiving team starts thinking what in the hell is the problem. They lose their concentration. Our players know we are going to hesitate on the kick.

The last thing we do is the split and cluster. When the whistle blows, we take the front five and leave them in a cluster. The back row will come over and line up to the right of the ball. We have five on the sideline and five in the cluster. Now we have 25 seconds to decide what we want to do.

Our coach on the sideline will tell our kicker what we want. If you do not get over to cover the area on the sideline, we will bump the ball on the top and kick it to the sideline. We play tricks like that with the kicking game.

PAT Teams

The last thing I want to cover is the extra point. We line up in a formation that has no bearing on what we're going to run. We huddle on the hash mark and then shift over to the center of the field on our PATs.

Every year someone will ask me why we huddle on the hash mark on PATs. They want to know when we are going to run a trick play from that formation. I tell them we'll never run a trick play from that formation. But they know that this may be the year I come up with something new!

When you spend all of *your* time on *their* kicking game, you're trying to keep from getting beat instead of winning in the kicking game. If you want to start having fun in the kicking game, *you take control*. If you've installed the type of kicking game that will make the opponent prepare for your trick plays, it will take a lot of time away from their regular practice time. You force the opponents to spend time defending you while you're being creative.

1991 Summer Manual. Coach Walden was head coach at Iowa State University.

Pressuring the Punter
SPARKY WOODS

Perhaps more than any other single play, our punt return sums up our philosophy towards the whole game. We believe in the importance of turnovers, field position, and—more critical than anything else—we believe that tough guys win.

We feel that our punt return-block teams are possibly the most important teams that take the field each Saturday. We tell our players that the punt is the only play in our playbook, and in our opponent's playbook, that can average 40 yards. Because of that, we put our best athletes on the field and allow enough practice time to execute in the same fashion as we do any of our defenses or offensive plays.

Punt Return-Block Team

We block punts with *people*; a great plan with the wrong people won't do it. It's futile to ask a huge lineman to get himself into a position to block a punt. When we send our punt block team onto the field, it consists of defensive backs, linebackers, and defensive ends. This is positive in two ways: (a) It gives us the speed and quickness needed to get to the punter, and (b) it involves some nonstarters in a crucial part of the game.

We place our two quickest players on each side of the center. These players are usually defensive backs who can slip through a small seam.

We put our fastest players on the outside because of the distance they have to cover if they are going to be a factor. We position players with the best knack for making the block in the offensive tackle area on the LOS. The reasoning behind this is that they are close enough to get to the punter quickly and far enough away so that the personal protector is usually drawn by players closer to the ball.

In our alignment, we will always take a pressure approach, whether we have called our return or our block. A rush-return combination has worked better for us than a hold-up return approach.

By putting a strong rusher on the punter, we not only put pressure on the snapper to get the ball back to the punter quickly, but we also put pressure on the punter to get the ball off fast. The "look of pressure" also requires the coverage team to block before they release, giving our wall time to form and our punt returner time to catch the ball and get upfield.

Our punt block team has two defenses, one base and one blitz, which can be utilized according to field position and time remaining in the game.

When people talk about blocking punts, the first thing that comes to mind is an all-out 10-man block. We carry a 10-man block, but very seldom do we send all 10 men. In actuality, it only takes two men to block a punt. The first man must draw the personal protector's block while the other man makes the block.

Punt Block-Return Team Alignment

We line up 10 men on the line of scrimmage. This makes the punt team account for an all-out block. We number our positions, 1 through 5, on both sides of the center. If we do not want an all-out block, we will simply call out the numbers of the positions we want to fall off. For example, we might call "13," meaning the 1s and 3s drop off (see Figure 1). We can use any combination of numbers we wish. It is extremely important that the positions dropping out do so *as the ball is snapped*, so that they draw the blocker they are aligned over, not allowing their opponents to help out somewhere else.

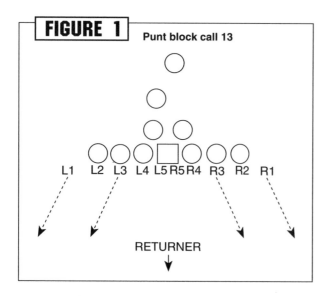

FIGURE 1 Punt block call 13

L1 L2 L3 L4 L5 R5 R4 R3 R2 R1

RETURNER

Adjustments to Punt Protection

There are basically two types of punt protections, and each requires different aiming points for the players attempting to block the punt. It is critical to determine which type of protection your opponent is using. The first, and most common, is an *outside zone*. In an outside zone protection, the blockers step out, protecting their outside gap (see Figure 2). On this particular type of protection, we ask our punt blockers to take a wider alignment and take an outside aiming point to create an inside-out stretch. If you were to take an inside rushing angle, you would be running into the blocker instead of away from him.

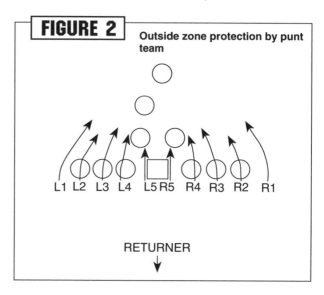

FIGURE 2 Outside zone protection by punt team

L1 L2 L3 L4 L5 R5 R4 R3 R2 R1

RETURNER

The second type of protection includes both the man concept and the *inside zone*. In an inside zone protection, the blockers step down, protecting their inside gap (see Figure 3). Versus these types of protections, we ask our blockers to take a tighter alignment and to take an inside angle or aiming point, much like an extra point or field goal block, to create an outside-in stretch. Once again, the reason for the inside angle is to run from where the block is coming and make people move their set foot.

Punt Block Technique

After we have taught our players to clear the blocker, we then turn our attention to the punt block technique. It is very important that we teach proper technique in blocking punts just as we teach technique in any other phase of football. We break our teaching into six different areas.

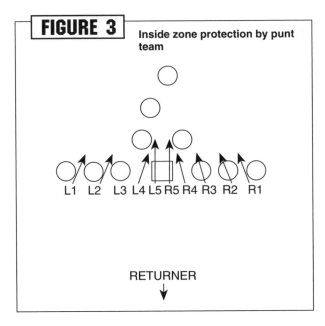

FIGURE 3 — Inside zone protection by punt team

L1 L2   L3 L4 L5 R5 R4 R3 R2 R1

RETURNER

• *Getting off on the ball.* We teach our players to key the ball and concentrate only on the ball. Teams will jump and shift in an attempt to draw us offsides, so we must be disciplined.

• *Running over the legs of the blockers.* This must be emphasized to avoid getting tripped up. We practice running over dummies to insure getting our legs up while keeping our feet moving forward.

• *Taking the proper angle to our aiming point is our next step.* We teach our outside players to clear the block, drop their inside shoulder, and take an aiming point in front of the punter. The aiming point will vary depending on the depth of the punter and how many steps he takes.

• *Eliminating the personal protector (fullback).* We tell the first man who clears the line of scrimmage to attack the personal protector's inside number. In doing this, we create a shorter angle for the people who clear later.

• *Blocking the punt.* We talk about hands. Our players put their hands together and look through them to the ball. This prevents the ball from going between their arms and emphasizes keeping their eyes open.

• *Leaving your feet is the next point.* We teach our outside people to extend their arms over their head and to jump across the punter. We teach the outside blockers to leap towards the foot (leap for distance and not height). Inside people are taught to jump up

instead of out and to extend their hands in front of their chest, not over their head.

• *Advancing the blocked punt.* Players should communicate and not fight over the ball. The first man calls for the ball and always scoops the ball in front of him, away from the line of scrimmage and toward our opponent's goal line. Everyone else should turn and find someone to block, making sure we do not clip, hold, or block below the waist.

Defending Against Fakes

We anticipate fakes, and work very hard to make a fake a dangerous gamble for our opposition. The most important thing in defending a fake punt is to believe your opponent will not only fake it, but will execute the fake well.

We have a checklist to prepare for fakes. The first item on our checklist is for our players to identify all eligibles, including the fullback (personal protector), punter, and interior slots. Besides having people drop off the line, we assign an extra player or players to guard against the screen. Out of the 10 men on the line of scrimmage at the snap, it is likely that 6 or more men are committed to defending fakes and only 3 or 4 to the block.

Some of the fakes to watch for each week are quite common, such as the fullback run on a down-block, kick-out scheme. We attack this play from both sides, and are quite proficient in defending the fake. Another fake, less common, is the option. The biggest advantage of the option from a punt formation is surprise, so when we work on it we assign option responsibilities and a secondary to rotate to it.

On our fake punt checklist, we also consider other "attacks" not usually considered as simple fakes. The third down punt tops the list here. Because we have had so much success at blocking punts, several teams have punted the ball on third down—with a punting team inserted—from the shadow of their goal line.

In order to make sure we are ready for a third down punt, our regular defense always has three returns, and they usually get as much or more practice time on them as our block team. As well as having a block, a regular wall return, and a "safe" return, we also prepare our defense for quick kicks. We don't spend much time working on blocking the quick kick because, if a block does occur, it usually happens quickly and with one rusher.

Rather than spending time on blocking quick kicks, we teach our defense how to return them. We practice two elements. First, we try to block the "kick chasers," usually wide outs, who attempt to down the ball. Second, we practice getting our players to change from a defensive to an offensive point of view. We teach our players to think of a quick kick as an interception. We believe we are capable of returning the quick kick for a score, and our players are convinced of it.

Other elements we work on every week include shifting and substitution attacks. We are always ready to move out to spread punt formations with our best personnel for coverage. We actually prefer to see spread formations because we think they are susceptible up the middle as well as affording short corners.

In order to confuse our substitutions, opponents sometimes hold their punt team to the last second and then rush them onto the field. Organizing and working against this attack of our punt team is a priority for us in practice. The second possible substitution attack is sending out the second offense with the punter, and then shifting into an offensive formation.

No one has successfully faked a punt on us since we have changed to our aggressive style. An opponent does not have much time to get a fake off because of our rush. We believe we can defend—through proper scheme and *practice*—the fake. We also know that our opponent is going to think hard about a fake when they see how often we rush the punt.

Because of our success in blocking punts, we feel that our return has also become dangerous. Teams often hold their coverage to insure getting the punt off. Most coaches believe that holding up the coverage is half the battle in returning

punts (see example of return in Figure 4). When we get a good return or two, the odds for making a block become much greater.

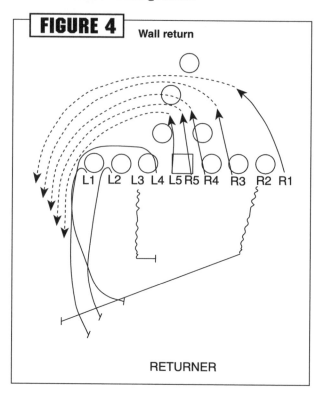

FIGURE 4 Wall return

RETURNER

The return and block must go hand in hand. One is not good without the other. *Pressure* is the key. We believe that the pressure will cause the situation we want, whether it's the return or the block.

The positive results we've achieved are the consequence of practice time, our use of personnel, and our overall football philosophy. Very simply, it takes practice time and people to pressure the punter well.

—*1987 Summer Manual. Coach Woods is offensive coordinator at Mississippi State.*

Blocking Kicks and Punts

CHUCK AMATO AND JIM GLADDEN

The kicking game has become the difference in more and more games. We want our players to have an *attitude* and belief that proper execution in the kicking game can produce "hidden" yardage as well as points on the scoreboard.

A blocked kick can provide the edge needed to win a game. The team that can consistently block kicks has a big weapon in its arsenal. Coaching the technique is important, but not nearly as important as selling players on the value of blocking kicks. There is no other phase of the game that gives a team a better opportunity for a big play. Every kick is a chance for a block or return.

Concentration and effort are essential. Our system of punt blocks and field goal blocks is not that different from other systems. We attribute our success to drill, practice time, and the attitude of our players; very simply, we attribute our success to *hard work*.

Rules for kick block/return team:

- Don't be offside.
- Don't rough the kicker or holder on extra points and field goals.
- Don't fall on a blocked kick unless it is third down.
- Don't let the ball hit the ground on returns.
- Don't clip.
- Don't block below the waist.

Punt Block

Our punt block scheme is a simple overload. We try to have one more man on one side that the opponent cannot pick up in its protection, whether it's a zone or man. We like to disguise our alignment and move immediately after the ball is snapped. We generally align with 10 men on the line of scrimmage and bring either 1 or 2 men out to play the pass or run.

As a rule, we pressure all kicks. All punt blocks are automatic returns; we return opposite the block. Our base scheme for block left is shown in Figure 1.

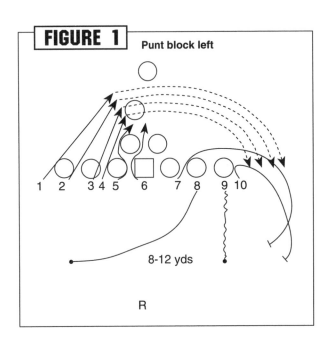

FIGURE 1 Punt block left

For our defensive punt unit, we attempt to leave as many regulars as possible in the game. We want experienced starters in the game. This is important, especially if the offense decides to fake or run patterns that an inexperienced player might not readily perceive.

In the early fall, we try to identify who will "lay out" to block a kick; then we'll find a way to place those players on the block units. The "lay out" is a *must* ingredient; without it, the entire blocking procedure can be nullified.

We number our personnel 1 through 10; the returner is designated as R. We number them for alignment purposes and flip-flop them with the call. The number system allows us to show several different looks, but the players always know where they have to end up when the ball is snapped.

In Figure 1, numbers 1 through 6 are selling out to block the kick. We designate a visual landmark that we refer to as the "spot" for all of them to aim for. Our number 7 and 10 play the fake on the line of scrimmage, and 8 and 9 will normally move before the snap to a depth of 8 to 12 yards and play the fake, positioned off the line of scrimmage. These are *crucial* coaching points on punt blocking:

- The spot for blocks is 5 yards in front of the punter and 2 feet to the right or left.
- See the ball from the snap. Don't take your eyes off the ball.
- Block the punt with the hands. Take it off the kicker's foot.
- Lay out for the ball, placing the body parallel to the ground across the spot.
- Do not hit the kicker!
- On fourth down blocked punts, pick the ball up and try to advance, regardless of risk. On third down blocked punts, cover the ball (do not try to advance it).
- A partially blocked punt that crosses the line of scrimmage is a punt. It is our ball, so get away from it.

Extra Point and Field Goal Blocks

The extra point and field goal blocks are either right or left. We usually have only one substitution (most of the time our primary block man). When our best blocker is on the base defense, we don't have to substitute.

Our block-side end is the key to the field goal or extra point block. He must draw (or pull down) the block of the upback (wing) so that the distance to the spot is reduced for our primary block man (corner; see Figure 2).

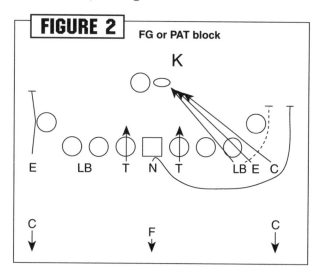

FIGURE 2 — FG or PAT block

The spot for the block is 2 feet in front of the holder. We will contain to the block side with either the linebacker or the noseguard and away

from the call with the end. The contain men must be alert, as there is always a danger of a high snap, a fumbled snap, or the holder pulling the ball up and out.

Drills for Blocking Kicks

Players need to be taught and drilled on how to block a kick. We usually begin our practice (first 10 to 20 minutes) with kick-blocking drills so our players appreciate the importance of the kicking game.

The first drill is very elementary. We line the players up 5 yards from the spot in their respective blocking position with a coach stationed on the spot and a mattress next to him. The player takes off and the coach tosses the ball up at different angles. The player simply runs through the spot and bats the ball with *both* hands, never leaving his feet. Through this drill, the player becomes accustomed to looking at the ball and redirecting his hands to the ball. This also teaches the blocker the proper angle he must take from his position to block a kick (see Figure 3).

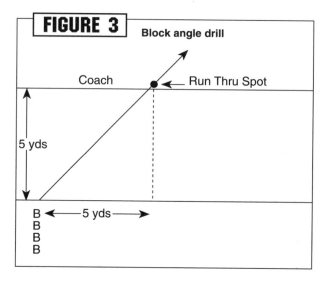

FIGURE 3 — Block angle drill

Our next drill is similar. We require a player to lay out on the mattress as he slaps at the ball. After the player hits the mattress, we require him to get up and scoop the ball toward the goal line. This creates a situation similar to an actual blocked kick and allows the players to practice a quick recovery and attempt to score (see Figure 4).

The next drill in our progression requires the punter to "pooch" the ball. This teaches the player to take the ball off the punter's foot, and how to adjust to the ball as it leaves the punter's foot.

We're finally ready to put the blocker in the exact position he will play. Have him go full speed

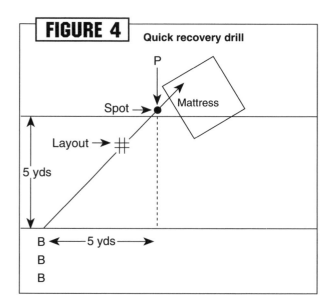

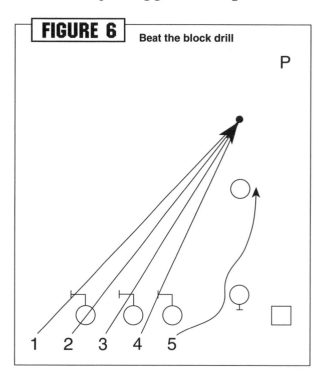

To modify this drill, you can (a) add a center and have players study the opposing center for a hitch or bend of an opponent's knee to get a jump on the snap, and (b) take the spot indicator away so the players automatically know where the spot is.

In our last drill, we place all our people in their proper position on one side of the center and have offensive people in front of them. We can now show our punt blockers the different blocking schemes our upcoming opponents use, so they're familiar with the players who will likely block them in the upcoming game (see Figure 6).

at the proper angle to the exact spot (indicate with play strip) to block a punt. We use a trailer in the drill to teach him to pick up the ball and run for a score (see Figure 5).

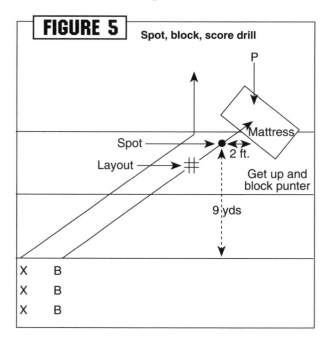

We want to emphasize the importance of working the kicking game every day and doing these drills religiously. Perhaps the primary ingredient these drills teach our players is that they *believe* they can go for blocked kicks without ever getting a roughing penalty.

—1985 Summer Manual. Coach Amato is defensive line coach and Coach Gladden is outside linebacker coach at Florida State University.

PART IV

Philosophy, Motivation, and Management

The Value of Football
BILL McCARTNEY

We're supposed to be living in very sophisticated times, with sophisticated young people. All worldly wise and knowledgeable. How can the game of football still be important in that context?

I feel it's more important than ever. What else have we got to anchor to? Where else can we walk out there even—everything the same—and compare? Look around. Maybe the football field's the only place left. Maybe we've already lost it everywhere else.

—Paul "Bear" Bryant

Is football the last outpost of discipline? The grind of the gridiron separates it from other sports. Where else—in what sport or activity—does a man line up directly across from another who could very well be bigger, stronger, smarter, older, and more talented? Yet, he is expected to compete intensely for 60 minutes. We ask him to give no quarter and take none.

It's been said that the most competitive men play the most competitive games. Coaches and players know the undersized men can win because nobody has a market on heart, desire, motivation, and will to win. Football reveals these qualities in men and rewards them.

Teamwork is necessary in all group sports. Yet, football digs deep into the true meaning of team, simply because 11 men must coordinate their efforts. Vince Lombardi said the best definition of team is "one heartbeat." To gain this requires total commitment, demands selflessness.

These qualities are not inherited and are rarely demonstrated in a laboratory or classroom. No, football develops them through the grind, the difficulty, the unity necessary to blend into one.

Have you noticed that a redwood tree can mature to a full 300 feet (the length of a football field) when fully grown? Did you know that its roots do not sink deep? Actually, they are very shallow. It would appear that any good wind could knock over any redwood.

Do you know why that doesn't happen? Redwoods grow in clusters. Their roots intertwine and grab one another—much like hands gripping on all sides. Our best football teams reflect the same dependence. A man learns to trust and depend upon others.

Bill Curry taught me the smartest definition of leadership. He calls it a powerful positive presence. If you are positive, your presence will be powerful. Think about it—everyone can lead under this concept. You need only to bring a healthy attitude to your squad every day and you are positively influencing your team.

There is a verse in the Old Testament, Deuteronomy 20:8: "Who is the man who is afraid and fainthearted? Let him depart and return to his house so that he won't make other hearts melt like his heart."

Did you know that when you are weak, you can make others around you weak? If your heart is melting, so will others. If you are strong, others will draw on your strength. Football has a unique way of building leadership. The very nature of our game depends upon leaders to emerge.

To me, no coach in America asks a man to make any sacrifice. He requests the opposite. Live clean, come clean, think clean. Stop doing all the things that destroy you mentally, physically, and morally, and begin doing those things that make you keener, finer, more competent.

—Fielding H. Yost

Think about it. Football has not really changed. Fielding Yost penned this quote some 80 years ago. It is still appropriate today. It is no sacrifice to play football. In fact, it's a distinct privilege, an honor, an opportunity of a lifetime.

I think we can look people in the eye and promise that if their son wants to play football, chances are good that they will see (a) improvement in his self-esteem, (b) renewed respect for authority, (c) willingness to cooperate with others, and (d) inclination to participate in everything more wholeheartedly.

I believe football develops character. There is no easy way to practice football. It is often the most difficult thing a man undertakes in his lifetime. It prepares him for the trials and struggles of life.

—1989 Summer Manual. Coach McCartney was head coach at the University of Colorado.

Priorities of Coaching

BILL CURRY

Every day you pick up the newspaper or listen to the radio or watch television, you are bombarded with information, a very high percentage of which is negative. And not just mildly negative; but facts, statistics, pictures, images, and suggestions that are so horrible that they can dominate your thoughts. They can make you into something that you never intended to be. And they can do it to you without your realizing it.

It's like if you run across rough ground enough, your body develops protective devices, calluses. You get blisters the first few days, but after a while your feet are tough; the callused surface protects them. In the same way, we think we're immune to the stuff that's flowing into our brains, but we aren't, and we change.

I have a son who's 19 years old. He is a normal American boy. He watches TV. He loves to watch the National Football League. He loves to watch you guys coaching. That means he has seen 100,000 beer commercials. One hundred thousand times it has been said to Bill Curry, Jr., "If you want to get a good-looking girl, you'd better drink

this kind of beer. Here it is. And here's the girl. Look at her. Whoa!"

What do you think he's gonna do? It scares me to death. He's a freshman in college. What do you think that child's gonna do with that many suggestions? How many times can I say to him, "When you drink beer, you're taking a risk." Maybe 150 times in his life? Look what we're competing against.

Learning and Repetition

I have a very difficult time learning. It requires many, many repetitions. I played football until I was 32 years old. I had the privilege of playing in the National Football League for 10 years, and I played on some of the greatest teams that ever played the game, and I played in some of the biggest games that were ever played. I played in Super Bowls I, III, and V, so every odd-numbered Super Bowl now, my body thinks I'm supposed to play.

I couldn't play middle linebacker, which was my dream. The people who were naturally quick mentally were the ones who played QB and middle linebacker. I just couldn't think fast enough. I could play center. If Johnny Unitas or Bart Starr told me what to do and told me what the snap count was, I could go up there, and I could make my calls because I knew where I was gonna go. I could hike the ball, and I could win on repetitions.

So, I've learned the value of quality repetition. If somebody could teach the drive block with 150,000 repetitions, and you could teach how to defeat the drive block with 150 repetitions, and that talent was equal, who do you think is gonna win?

My mom grew up on a farm. She walked along behind a plow and picked cotton, and was part of an agrarian society that we had not long ago. Our ancestors in their *lifetime* did not absorb as much information as you and I absorb in one day.

Let's not kid ourselves about what coaching is today. It is a lot more than it's ever been before. And it's a lot tougher. Players are exposed to more distractions and influences outside of family, team, and school than we were at their age.

Just think about what you're pumping into your brain and what's going into those players' heads. They're sitting there with those Walkmans on the team bus; you're wondering what in the world is going into their brains; your job is on the line in front of a national TV audience. You've prepared as best you can, but the competition—both from the opponent on the field and from the distractions facing your team—is awesome.

Personal Responsibility for Actions

Because we have so many outside influences and demands, it's easy to pass the buck when you fail. But excuses don't get you anywhere. I'm talking as a coach in football as well as in life. Understand this: You are today precisely what you had planned to be up to this point.

Bill Curry has determined what ever it is that I'm going to be today; I'm the one who has shaped that destiny. Nobody else. The instant you accept the responsibility for your life, you have the capacity to start to deal with the forces that are at work on your mind.

Until you do that, you are helpless and you'll be pulled from pillar to post and you'll wonder, "What in the world's going on? I wonder why I drink so much?" So many times you're not even aware. It's the subliminal influences. The same thing happens to the kids we work with.

I come from an environment where my players have been told, every single day, "Your coach is not good enough to coach you. He shouldn't be here. He's not qualified. He's not one of us." All those things.

That's nobody's fault. That goes with the territory. You may be going through something similar. So I'm not complaining. I'm just telling you about the environment in which I've lived. What it did was force me to do something that I find very, very difficult—listen.

Listening and Learning

I learned how to listen from my daughter, who was then 17 years old. She didn't speak to me for 6 months. This child, who has always been her own person and has a brilliant mind—she's just like her mom—decided her dad wasn't worth talking to. I didn't like that. We went through some hell together.

I went from being terribly offended, to being angry, to playing the adult role—the parent role. I tried to hammer her, change her, and tell her who she would and would not see. I tried to lock her up. I tried to shut off the telephone. I did all the stuff stupid dads do to beautiful daughters.

Until one day I said to her, "I love you more than my own life. I've given you everything I have. What is it that's wrong?" She said, "You tell me you love me, and I know you think you mean that, but I don't feel it when you say it. When I try to talk to you, you never listen. You're only thinking about what you're gonna say next." I wept. And I almost fell out of the chair, because she was right.

Then, less than a week later, I asked our coaching staff's opinion on a very important matter. One of the brightest football coaches I've ever known, Don Lindsey, is a guy who will tell you how he feels about things. You don't have to wonder about what's going on in Don's mind. He'll tell you exactly how it is.

Don was giving his thoughts on this subject and about halfway through a sentence he just stopped talking—end of conversation. I noticed it, but we went on about our meeting. Afterward I asked Don to join me in my office. I said, "Hey, Don, I asked your opinion, and you got about halfway through your thought and then you stopped."

He said, "Yes." I said, "Why would you do that?" He said, "Because I can tell when you stop listening. When you stop listening, there's no sense in me continuing to talk."

I was 44 years old and didn't know how to listen to another human being. How are you gonna learn anything if you can't listen?

Handling Professional Responsibilities

I want to encourage you to be enthusiastic about our profession, and help you understand that you have determined where you are today—not the alumni who don't like you, not the press who wrote an ugly article about you, not some big booster who talks to your president and keeps you from having full support.

That's all baloney. It's *your* responsibility what you are. It's Bill Curry's responsibility whatever has happened to me and my family and my team. It's absolutely my doing and no one else's because I have the capacity, the God-given gift, to deal with that situation, whatever it is. The moment you accept that, you begin to grow and understand.

We can make a *big* difference because the children who watch our games are the same ones who are bombarded by beer commercials and pornography. And they're more interested in what you're doing than some of the garbage. You can change lives by being what you're supposed to be.

Those children who watch you, those children who go over there and go through those offensive line drills, who've got big old fat stomachs and are 5-4 and 13 years old, they're gonna be like you. They're gonna be like you *talk*. They're gonna be like you *are*. And they're gonna know what you are. So please don't stand there and tell them, "Don't drink beer and don't get drunk" when you go out and drink 14 beers every other night.

They'll know it. They'll find out. They'll smell it. They'll feel it. And you will instantly be spot-ted for the phony that you are. You'll be discounted. You'll be out the window. And then they'll be victims on the television. You've got an awesome responsibility.

Dr. Viktor Frankl is a Jewish man who spent six years in a German concentration camp. He lived through that nightmare—the most brutal physical, emotional, and spiritual conditions in the history of mankind. He described the actions of some of the victims: "These towering, dignified figures moved through the hell of the Holocaust, giving their two-inch-square bread away to the weaker inmates, and they dragged us through it with their power. They showed us how to live and how to die; my life was never the same."

Dr. Frankl concluded, "Here's what I learned: No circumstance, no condition, no group of people, no negative idea, no killing, no nothing can remove from me the fundamental obligation I have as a human being, which is to choose how I will respond."

So, if you're spending your time pointing fingers and complaining and trying to decide who's trying to keep you from succeeding, maybe you ought to spend that time getting your body in shape. Maybe you ought to spend your time learning some more football. Maybe you ought to spend your time not feeling sorry for yourself, but feeling sorry for that youngster who lives down the street and doesn't have a mom and a dad. Maybe you need to spend your time doing those things, because it is in giving that you receive.

Not only will you win a lot of games but you'll win. God knows, you'll win because they'll die for you. You've changed some lives—and that's a privilege.

Integrity

Be honest even when the other folks are not. Don't be one to point the finger and say, "We can't win because they are cheating and buying players." Just be, in that moment, tough as nails by being honest when it's not fashionable to be honest.

You see, the real losers are the cheaters. God bless 'em. We've all cheated from time to time. There's nobody in this room who's pure as the driven snow, least of all Bill Curry. I'm ashamed of the years that I lived when I wasn't what I was supposed to be. And I'm not what I'm supposed to be now, but I know that I'm working toward being that, and I'm giving everything I've got to be that for the first time in my life.

I've finally figured this out: The cheaters don't want to find out how the game will come out if they play by the same rules as everybody else. So they don't. And they've never won a game! And you know something? There'll be a day when they know it. I look back on every lie I've ever told and every deceptive act and every stupid thing I've done out of selfishness, and I've paid many times, and I pay today with guilt and anguish.

I think the worst sin you commit today if you're a coach is to teach a youngster that it's OK to break a rule. Who's going to help that child 25 years from now when he's sitting across from the IRS and getting ready to go to jail and it crosses his mind, "My coach taught me it was OK to cut corners"?

I don't think I want that on my conscience. And that's tough and that's hard to swallow when you're getting your butt kicked in the football game and you know you're standing for a principle. Nobody cares about your principles. They only care about that scoreboard, and you'll lose your job or gain your job.

I hired a coach one time, and we had our meetings, and I said, "Men, we want to do this the right way. We're not going to break a single rule." We broke for lunch, and the new coach came up to me and said, "I need to talk to you, Bill. We're not gonna break any rules?"

I said, "That's right." He said, "You know, nobody does that." I said, "Yeah, I know. We haven't always done it, either, but we're fixing to." He said, "Every rule? We're gonna get killed. What if we lose our jobs?"

I said, "I've never heard it put that way. If we lose our jobs, we'll go get other jobs. We'll have our integrity, but we won't be swayed by a system that destroys children."

I don't think that's particularly noble. I don't think that makes me anything great. I think that's the American way, isn't it? Is that what we're supposed to stand for? Is that what America was at one time? Where in the hell did this happen, men? Why is it such a big story when somebody's honest?

Never quit on your principles. I'm not talking about you never changing jobs or changing directions. I'm talking about never quitting on what's right.

I sat in a house with a great player one night. I said, "Son, what do you want to do with your life? I'm here to help you." He said, "I want the car." I said, "Excuse me?" His mom was sitting there, his dad; God was watching, everybody. He said, "I want the car."

He'd already had keys offered to him by another coach. He said, "Coach Curry, I'm trying to make you understand. I want the automobile. You hear me? Read my lips." I was so shocked, I was sitting there with my mouth hanging open. I finally found an honest kid who told me the truth about what he wanted to do with his life. He wanted to drive a brand new car because he'd never had one. He was poor.

The dad took me outside and said, "I'm gonna do you a favor. I'm gonna reopen this discussion. I'm gonna go tell my young son that he's off the wall. He might take the car, but I'm gonna give you a chance to start over."

I sold that kid—and I've lost a lot more than I've sold. He bought the idea that he wouldn't sell his soul for that automobile, and he would buy his own car. And four years later, I swear I'm walking down the street, and I hear this rumble. It scared me, and I looked back and there's about a $40,000 black car with about 5,000 horsepower, and all I could see was teeth when I looked in there.

Pat Swilling smiled at me. He's a star in the National Football League, and he has a diploma from the Georgia Institute of Technology, and I'm proud of Pat Swilling. He bought his own car. He didn't let somebody buy his soul. He's a man. God bless him.

Rules and Discipline

We have two basic training rules:
- *Treat other people the way you want to be treated.*
- *Don't embarrass your family, our team, or our school.*

These two rules have worked for us, even when we went into situations where there had been a lot of problems. Our players take the responsibility to follow these guidelines and it helped us have a quality, disciplined program.

Focus on Priorities

When I was a child, I used to love to get those magnifying glasses out of Cracker Jack boxes and go out in the woods on a cold day. It fascinated me. The temperature would be 35 degrees but I could take the sun 93 million miles away and get those rays to where I could get a pile of leaves on fire.

I got in a little trouble around the neighborhood, but it fired me up. Those rays that emanated so far away that we can't even imagine the distance could be brought to a useful purpose by focusing that energy. Bill Curry can learn by repetition, properly directed and focused, and so can that young offensive center or young quarterback or child whom you're responsible for. As soon as you accept responsibility for focus, then you can begin to make progress.

In our program, or any program, there will be priorities. Now, you may scoff and say, "I'm not into all that priority-setting and goal-setting." Yes, you are.

Your goal may be to go out and chase women after practice. That may be what you love to do, and that's fine. We've all seen that, and we've all known that that's supposed to be associated with our profession. Your goal may be to go out and see how many beers you can drink. But you've got priorities, and those children are going to mirror your priorities.

Personal Faith

Here are our priorities. Number one, *personal faith*. It's critical to me that our players and our staff understand the fundamental realities of human experience, which is that each of us has faith. Again, you may scoff and say, "Well, I don't have faith. I don't believe in God. I'm an atheist."

That's not true. You believe in something. Maybe money. Maybe coach of the year honors. Or maybe even winning the national championship or the Super Bowl. I hope not, because when you get to all those places there ain't much there.

When you get there, you look at the world championship ring and say, "Well, is this it? What do I do now? I've got to win another one." It's not much. It's not what it's cracked up to be. But a personal faith is the rock in a foundation.

It took me a lot of years to learn that it is in Christ that I have anything significant to contribute to anybody. He has redeemed me and saved me from myself. He's my hero, and I thank Him every day for that.

That's a personal matter. I don't impose that on my staff or my players. I leave that for them to decide, but I want them to understand that they must make some kind of decision about that.

Family

The second priority is *family* and I learned that from Vince Lombardi. We were a family on the Green Bay Packers, and that's how I always think about them.

Lombardi said, "Great physical conditioning is absolutely fundamental to victory. Winning is not a sometime thing. You don't do things right some of the time. You don't win some of the time. You do things right all the time."

Why do you think I learned those things? I had no choice. I'd say, "If he makes that speech one more time, I'm gonna throw up" and a teammate would say, "No, you're not. You're gonna sit right where you are and you're gonna listen one more time."

When somebody told me that Coach Lombardi went to church every day, I said, "No way. Nobody who goes to church every day talks like that." His language could really shock you.

So I went to Bart Starr and said, "Does Coach really go to mass every morning?" He said, "Coach is such a devout Christian he goes to mass every single morning, but after you've been working for this man about three weeks, you're gonna understand this man *needs* to go to mass every morning."

Coach talked family, and he meant it. If you came to him with a family problem, he'd always take time for you. When I went to see him in the hospital when he was dying, he grabbed my hand. I said, "Coach, you've meant a lot to my life." He said, "You can mean a lot to mine if you'll pray." He wasn't about to give up to cancer. It was his faith in his family that mattered. All of the resentment I had for him—the hatred for having made me run so hard, the hard feelings for getting rid of me—all dissipated when I realized the man was real.

Do you want to know what a great football coach is and a great man? Vince Lombardi was a great man because of his pursuit of what God wanted him to be. That's what made him great.

Education

Education is a big part of the answer today. We can compete with the pornography and the booze and all the garbage with proper education. Any guy who goes through a major program and does not get a diploma has been ripped off.

Don't make excuses and say, "The athletes are better off than they would have been because they spent four years with us and helped us win a national championship."

That's baloney. They're not better off. I've got too many good buddies who played with me in the NFL who ended up without diplomas, and they're on the rocks because some college coach abused them and told 'em, "You'll be better off whether you get a degree or not."

That's garbage. That's a lie. Don't believe it. Don't ever say it. It's a lie. I don't want my son ripped off, and I don't want your son ripped off. Don't tell some minority youngster he can come to your school and help fill up a stadium and end up without a diploma and go out in the NFL. Without an education he's gonna lose whatever money he makes and wind up in a bread line or worse.

Football

The fourth and final priority is *football*. For a guy who wants to be a great football player, there's not going to be much time for anything other than those four things—faith, family, education, and football. If he wants to have fun, be in a fraternity, and do the party route, then he might not have a spot in our program, because it's hard. And we don't apologize for that at all.

Summary

Faith, family, education, and football are our priorities, and we will live with those. We will prosper or we will fall with those priorities.

None of these ideas is original with me. But I did come up with these from studying great people.

When I was 8 or 9 years old, like a lot of us here, I was what today they would call "hyperactive." In those days, they called it "problem child."

They sent me home from school. I had one teacher who tied me to my desk with a rope and taped my mouth shut with Johnson and Johnson because I just had too much energy. I thought since my dad was a boxing coach that I was supposed to box with any of the kids in the class—especially the smaller ones.

I stayed in trouble all the time. In the fourth grade the teacher put me in the back of the classroom so I wouldn't disrupt things too much. Back there was this incredible shelf full of biographies about some of the greatest people ever: Jackie Robinson, Babe Ruth, George Washington, Helen Keller, Thomas Jefferson, Winston Churchill.

I didn't pay much attention to what the teacher was saying, but I memorized those books—and it changed my life. I decided I wanted to be like those people, and I wanted to learn what it took for them to achieve.

Characteristics of Champions

Why was Vince Lombardi such a great coach? Because he had something that he talked about all the time, singleness of purpose. I've never known of a great achiever without singleness of purpose. And singleness of purpose means *singleness* of purpose.

That means you live it, and you breathe it, and you think it, and you learn how to focus, and you burn it into the brains of the people that you represent in as many ways as you possibly can.

Our purpose is to teach our young men how to be winners, in their spiritual lives, in their academic lives, in their family lives, and as football players. It all goes hand in hand. We want to win every single game. We don't care what the odds are. We don't care what the press says. We don't care what the oddsmakers say.

We intend to win every single contest, do well in every single class, to graduate every single player in a meaningful major. Those are our goals. Those are our purposes, and we will shoot for them while we breathe. We mean it, and anybody in our program has got to buy into that.

The second characteristic of real champions, as I studied the biographies of these great people, is that they're *unselfish*, which means they know how to give when it hurts to give. They know how to love when it's unconditional. The Master himself brought one fundamental principle of behavior, and that is loving people when they're unloving.

The reason I survived the National Football League is because Willie Davis and Bart Starr and Paul Hornung loved me when I was unloveable. I was the last draft choice. I was the 20th pick when they had 20 rounds. I had never been on a team with a black guy. And Willie Davis embraced me. The captain of the Green Bay Packers.

Willie Davis from Grambling State University, All-Pro, All-World, great player, decided to adopt the 20th-round draft choice from College Park, Georgia. Remember, it's 1965. Don't ask me why he did it. But he didn't just help a terrified rookie to make it in the NFL. He changed my life in a heartbeat because he cared when there was nothing in it for him.

If you're unselfish, your players will spot it. If your team is unselfish, you'll win games that you have no business winning—and that's a promise!

—1990 Proceedings. Coach Curry was head coach at the University of Kentucky.

The Game and Coaching
GRANT TEAFF

I am a great lover of history. I particularly like the Civil War and the Second World War. I spend a lot of time studying generals, and I think for you young coaches who aspire to be field generals, it is important to know the thinking of the real generals. One that had an interesting background and that you have to admire, whatever your political persuasion, is Douglas MacArthur.

Douglas MacArthur accomplished an awful lot in his lifetime; however, he touched me as he came to the end of his life, as he made two profound and inspirational statements—one to the Congress of the United States, "Old soldiers never die, they just fade away." I don't intend to fade away, I can tell you that right now; I want to serve until I die.

The second statement he made has become very large to me in recent weeks, as I have thought of this, my last year in coaching. General MacArthur went to West Point Academy to address the Corps in the waning days of his life. He stood before the Corps that he loved, in the hallowed halls that he admired so greatly as a young man, and he said to them that as his life would come to an end, his last thoughts would be of the Corps, the Corps, the Corps. I would say to you as a coach who loves the game that my last thoughts will be my family, my maker, and the game, the game, the game.

Without the game, I would not be here, standing in front of you. The game of football is what drives the machine of our profession. I would have never been a player had there not been a game; I would have never had the opportunity to serve the players in these nearly 40 years. Had there not been a game, there would be no profession—a profession of which I am very proud. No game, and there is no American Football Coaches Association. No way of gathering our thoughts, our dreams, and the ideals for our profession.

Roots of Love for the Game

There was always a cloud of cotton gin smoke hanging over Snyder, Texas in the fall. It was cool and we would play the game. To this day, when I smell the cotton gin smoke, I think of football.

Have you ever been in a town of 2,000, where they shut all the doors on game day? If we were going to Roscoe or Roby to play, all business workers and all those who owned stores would shut the doors and get in a car caravan and follow the yellow school busses to the opposing town. Snyder was a place where a young heart and mind was ready to be ripened, and the change that occurred in my life was when two coaches came to town.

Speedy and Mule

I had known Tommy Beane as the high school coach, and he influenced me to a degree, but I was too young and just watched him a little bit.

Then, when it came time for me to be of age to want to play the game, two men came to Snyder: Speedy Moffat and Mule Kizer. Both had played at Texas Tech.

When they came in, I immediately began to idolize them, because they talked about winning and the importance of winning. I knew how to work, but they knew what was important, and that was to win, not only on the field, but off the field. I rag-tagged around as a student, but when they came there, I rag-tagged no more.

The last day I played hooky, Mule whipped my rear from one end of the dressing room to the other. Pieces of paddle were flying everywhere. He wore me out and taught me a lesson about the importance of education. As long as I was going to be a part of that team, I was going to be a disciplined member of that team, on or off the field.

Mule said, "Be disciplined, Grant, be disciplined in everything you do." Be disciplined in your study of the game, in your approach to the game, and in the fundamentals of the game. Be disciplined, be tough.

He also said, "Grant, Speedy and I believe one of the most important parts of winning is effort. I know you are slow, and I know you are little, but if you give us effort every down on every day, in every way, we're gonna find a place for you to play."

And they did, and I never left the field from that day. I played both ways and was captain of every team I was ever on, because they taught me the fundamentals of success—discipline, toughness, and effort. Then they began to teach more. They began to take me, as a child, to mold me in a way that would change my life forever.

Not only did they say discipline, not only did they say effort, they said toughness—mental and physical toughness combined with caring. Care enough to be loyal to your teammates, care enough to be loyal to family and to yourself, but be tough. Be tough mentally, be tough physically. You don't have to take a back seat to anybody; be tough.

And then one day Mule Kizer pulled me aside and said, "If you really want to be successful, you got to be error free." I said, "What do you mean, error free?" He said, "You can't make mistakes. Other guys with more talent will make mistakes, and if you don't make mistakes you can win." Yeah, error free, no mistakes on the football field, no mistakes off the football field, seize your opportunity, take advantage of the time that you

have. Sit in that class and listen instead of day dreaming—error free.

What a fantastic piece of advice. He said one day, "You are tough, Grant, you are real tough, but you need to be aggressive, off the field as well as on the field." I said, "What do you mean?" and he said, "Well, just approach everything with the same aggression that you have on the field. You will stick your nose and face on anything that moves. You are not afraid of anything out there. Don't be afraid of anything off the field. Approach it like you are going to rob a bank: plan, discuss, dream, plan, discuss, dream, visualize, and communicate."

I began to use film like probably no other guy from Snyder, Texas ever used it. The film wasn't very good, but as they would get a film or two in on our opponent, I would sit for hours and study the way my opponent moved, how he lined up, and what he was going to do on the snap of the football. It allowed me to understand the game of football.

Finally, one day, I got into a fight on the football field. Mule didn't mind if we had fight in us, but he pulled me aside again and he said, "Look, it's okay to be willing to fight; there is nothing wrong with that, but you lose if you are not in control." Be in control of your mind and your body.

That was pretty hard to ask of a guy—to be in control of his body when he had a hard time running—but it was a point well made. He said, furthermore, to be in control of everything. Don't let somebody hit you in the back out on the football field, provoke you into a fight, and destroy what you have already gained. The second guy always gets the penalty.

It's a simple thought and a simple process, but be in control. Be in control as a father, be in control as a husband, be in control of your physical body, be in control of your natural instincts—be in control of your mind.

If you don't want to end up with an alcohol problem, be in control and don't drink. If you don't want to die of lung cancer, don't smoke. Be in control.

It was a revelation that changed my life. It came from a high school football coach. Be in control—I am the one in control. I control my own destiny. If I am going to control my destiny, I need to set goals. I need to know where I am going. How am I going to get there if I don't know where I am going?

Control of your own destiny—it's mine, it's not anybody else's. I can be what I want to be; I can do what I want to do. Control—what a fantastic revelation. I said when I get to be a coach, I am going to teach my guys that, too, because it changed my life.

What a wonderful experience, playing high school football in Snyder, Texas, for men whom I loved and admired. My life changed because I wanted to dedicate my life to the game, to coaching. I wanted to be just like them, so I made up my mind I was going to coach. That's what I wanted to do. I didn't know how I was going to do it yet, but I had to play this game to do it. I had to be an educated person, I had to get a degree, because I was going to coach.

Attracted to the Game

I remember the first football game I ever saw. That was in Colorado City, and I was about 6 or 7 years old. I might have been to a game before then, but I don't remember it. My dad liked high school football, though he didn't play. He took me to Colorado City, because Snyder was playing Colorado City, and I remember vividly being on the sidelines.

In those days, the men of the town always walked the sidelines. They didn't sit in the stands; they walked the sideline following the chain, so they could see what was going on. They could holler at the referees and the guys on the field, and all the way across the field to the fellows walking down the other sideline.

I remember driving over there and going out on the field, and there was a pretty good crowd. They evidently had a good game, and I kind of liked it, you know. First time I had ever seen it: Two guys line up and hit each other, then go tackle the guy with the football. I said this is good, and after the game we were on the side of the field. When the final whistle blew everybody ran to the middle of the field. My dad ran, and he is dragging me along. He's got me by the hand, and I am hanging on.

We get out to the middle of the field, and I look around, and everybody is squared up. They are all swinging away. The players fighting the players; coaches fighting coaches. These folks out of the Colorado City stands fighting the guys from Snyder. It was about three years before I realized that wasn't a part of the game of football.

Later my dad took me to see my first college game in Abilene; McMurry and ACC—what a rivalry. We hear about all the big rivalries, but there are men in this room that coach at some of the schools that many of us never hear about, but

their rivalry is just as intense as that of Michigan and Ohio State, Texas and Texas A&M, and all of the other big rivalries that you hear about, and so it was with McMurry and ACC.

When I saw the game, I was smitten. I loved that college game. They were bigger, they were faster. The coach had a strong influence and impact, so I decided on that day that's what I am going to do. I'm going to be a college coach.

The Coaching Trail

Leaving Snyder High School and going to college, I came under the influence of some other coaches. Max Baumgartner was at San Angelo College (it was a junior college). He was a guy that had fun with coaching, and I learned a lot from him. Max loved life and was a good kind man, yet wanted to win and believed in winning, and did win.

I was with Coach Baumgartner for two seasons. We seldom put on a pad except on game day. He believed in having fun, but I tell you, I learned something. When we stepped on that football field, we were ready to hit somebody.

Then I went to McMurry College where I played for Wilfred Moore. He was just out of the military. This was in 1953 when I started playing for Wilfred Moore. In 1947, he had guys out of the military, and many were older than he was, so he was tougher than the back end of a shooting gallery. Four hour workouts were nothing; head-on tackling at 20 yards apart was daily fare.

I mean to tell you, I learned so much from that man that I couldn't ever express it today. I also learned a lot of what not to do. I learned also that it is important to tell your players that they are doing a good job.

Coach Moore didn't say much, but what he said, you listened to. I thought he did not like me; I played every down for him, and he never said a word to me. He would just look at me. Then, on the last game that I played, we won. I'm in the dressing room trying to get my stuff off and I feel somebody behind me, and a slap on my ribs.

I turned around, and it was Coach Moore. He had just this little smile on his face, and he said, "Good job, Grant." Momma, Momma, Coach Moore said, "Good job!" I'm telling you, I would have run through a brick wall for him that day. I learned the importance of telling people that they did a good job, that they are doing good, that they are doing what you ask.

I think one of the things you soon understand when you decide to go into coaching is to determine what you want to do, devise a way to do it, and then do it. I'm a freak in the coaching profession by many people's standards. I never played for Bear Bryant or Bo Schembechler. I didn't coach for Frank Broyles or Darrell Royal.

I came up through small colleges, worked hard, dedicated my life to the coaching profession, and applied those very simple principles that those high school coaches taught me—discipline, effort, tough caring, being error free, aggressiveness, and control. It allowed me to reach a measure of success. I can say that I have done it my way, which is usually the hard way.

Game Under Attack

Never in the history of the game, even in the dark times when they threatened to expel the game from the college scene, has our game and our profession been under greater attack. I think I have the background and the knowledge to be believed when I say that. I served on every rules committee that has shaped our game. I have been chairman of the Ethics Committee for a long, long time. I am a trustee of the American Football Coaches Association, a trustee of the Fellowship of Christian Athletes. I worked on legislative committees for our association, for the CFA, and for the NCAA. I now serve on a task force called the Gender Equity Task Force that will affect every person in this room.

Media

The media in different areas and in different ways have chosen to attack our game, the people who coach it, and the players who play it. Some of those attacks are probably justified, but I am concerned that everywhere we turn all you read about is the bad things that happen. There are hundreds of good things that happen on a daily basis in our profession and with the young people we coach that nobody ever hears of because the media chooses not to publish it.

Another thing is that our radio and TV stations are filled with talk shows. We live in a society where everybody expresses their opinion, and they may not know beans about our job, but there they are, on the air, spouting their opinion.

Academic Standards

The NCAA in its infinite wisdom, in trying to do what is right for young people, the game, and for all athletics, has been a part of those attacks. I

work hard in the NCAA, and I will continue to do it in whatever capacity I am in, but we have been under attack, and you must recognize it. The Knight Commission has pointed out football as something that needs to be changed. They say there needs to be reform in all areas of our athletic world and, particularly, in football and in the coaching profession.

Football players are the most scrutinized segment of our society. Any one year, on my football team, a football player can be drug tested eight times, if he falls into the right category to be selected. Eight times! I know of no other student in any university that has to be drug tested.

The NCAA, under the urging of the Knight Commission, has attacked academics with a vigor. There is nothing in this world wrong with stressing academics, but my fear, my concern is for those young people with a poor background who strive for an education, particularly our young African Americans.

A 5-year review showed about half the recruits at Baylor would not have qualified. A high percentage of those have graduated from Baylor University. Mike Singletary is a very good representative, I think, of our program, the game, our profession, and football itself. Mike Singletary could not get in school under these new requirements. He graduated in four years.

I had a Prop 48 student-athlete that I let in because I felt concerned about him having an opportunity to get an education. He graduated in three and one-half years. Are we the ones to say to those young people that because you have had a weak background, you no longer have a chance to become an educated man and to have a degree so that you can do something for your family? I am deeply concerned about that.

I am one of the ones who has for a long time pushed for strong academics, tutorial help, working with the young people on campus. We lead the Southwest Conference in graduation rates, and it is not by accident. It is because we will take a youngster that qualifies, and we will do everything in our power to motivate and to assist him to get that education.

I see even our conference commissioners getting in this, by setting up ways and means by which we can cut back. There is even a proposal, get this, to eliminate walk-ons. Can you imagine? I sure wouldn't be here, as I went to college as a walk-on, to get a chance to coach. Max Baumgartner gave me a scholarship, but I had a chance and I earned it.

If we start eliminating walk-ons from this opportunity to be successful—that's not the American way. That's not the way this country was built.

Gender Equity

The Gender Equity Task Force that I serve on will affect profoundly every man in this room in the next few years. Gender Equity is above the law. There are proposals to cut scholarships to get everything equalized, without recognition of the importance of the sport and the game of football. I am scared, I am concerned.

The Presidents' Commission that I've had the privilege to speak to on two occasions has done some good things. Unfortunately, presidents have shorter terms than most coaches. I get concerned when people in high places make decisions without communicating with those in the field who, on a daily basis, have to fight the battles and have to win the wars.

I begged the Presidents' Commission on two occasions to listen to the coaches. You can trust us. We are men of integrity. When we tell you that we need "x" amount of days for phone calls, that we need "x" amount of days for recruiting, that we will do this or we will do that, you can count on us doing it. We have the American Football Coaches Association that is made up of men of integrity.

I have served on the Ethics Committee for a long time. I can tell you that my case load has gone from 15 or 20 cases to 1 this year. I was informed just the other day that over 100 members of the coaching profession are no longer in it because they decided they didn't want to go the way that we are all going, the way with integrity. I say good riddance, because we are the ones that those players look up to.

What if Mule Kizer had been a cheater—what would I have thought? A man of integrity taught me to have integrity, and that's what we all need to do every day—have integrity. I just want the Presidents' Commission to listen to us. Listen to us as an association. We'll tell you how to have a successful game and how to do it the most economical way, because we know how. Don't let some group of commissioners or somebody else dictate to us what our game is going to be, how we are going to play it, and who we play it with. I beg you to let us help make the decisions.

The NFL

We are under attack by the National Football League. We all love to watch the NFL. Our players are there, and we take great pride in our players being there, but I have been around long enough to tell you that we are under attack. We have banded together as a profession this year to make a loud statement to them. Some didn't stay with it, but the majority did, and they heard us.

Now is the time to let them know we mean business. We are in the education business, not in the business of providing tutorial help for the professional ranks. We want our young people to have the chance to play pro football and make those millions of dollars, but they must become educated men with degrees.

We need help in this area; we need to band together. We can't be splintered. We have something we have to do, and we have to do it together. That's what an association is—it is the gathering together of men of a like purpose and a like cause, going forward with those ideas and goals that are positive for the profession and the game.

Representing the Coaching Profession

We are the only profession I know who has very little control. And I say to all of you, loudly and clearly, we need to gain control. The only way we can do that is to recognize who will fight for us, who will make a stand for us as coaches. Your high school administrators, your Board, where will they be when the heat gets hot?

Who will stand tall and look them in the eye and say, "This is the way it needs to be." Who? Nobody, that's who. Nobody will stand, except you. You are the one who has to stand. You say you have only been in coaching for 2 years. Great, I hope you are in it for another 40, but if you want it to be as I've had it, as all my friends have had it—you must be willing to fight for it.

The game is being taken away from us by chipping away and whittling away. Don't let it happen; be willing to take a stand. But if you are going to take a stand, I must tell you what you have to do. You have got to fight—fight for the game, for the players who play the game, and for our profession. You have got to use this association as your association, not just as a social club, not just as a gathering once a year, but by being actively involved and caring about what happens.

You must be professional. Nobody is going to listen to somebody that is half-baked and shoots their mouth off one day saying one thing, and then turns the next day and says something else. You have to be professional and consistent.

Your appearance, your conduct, and your attitude have to be above reproach. The hard-drinking, tobacco-chewing coach is outdated and is no longer. I no longer see any more of those old nylon shorts and white socks that we all used to wear. It's an outdated thing, and we have to recognize it and take a stand for who we are. We are professionals.

You, as a professional, and we, as members of the association, need to apply those same principles taught by Speedy and Mule. You have to be disciplined, you have to be aggressive, you have to be caring and tough. You have to be error free.

Error free means you can't be in your community doing things that are unethical toward our profession, even though someone might not know about it. You have to be above and beyond reproach, and you have to be in control in all areas of your life. Control your own life, control your family life, be in control of your own children.

We need to walk softly, hold our heads up, be proud of who we are. We need to carry that big ole stick, we need to talk intelligently, and then I guess there is that point when you have to take out that big ole stick and knock the hell out of somebody that's trying to destroy our game. Who can do it? Only you.

At the outset, I shared with you Douglas MacArthur's words concerning his last thoughts on this earth, the Corps, the Corps, the Corps. To emphasize to you my love for our game, I said that my final thoughts would be of my maker, my family, and the game, the game, the game.

My statement was not entirely accurate. Because of my love for our profession and my love for those of you who serve in this profession, my final thoughts will also be of you.

—1993 Proceedings. Coach Teaff is executive director of the AFCA.

Taking Care of the Game
CHARLIE McCLENDON

Family and football have been my life, and I might have put football in front of my family sometimes. That's a mistake.

I have always felt that I owed the game of football something, and that I will never be able to pay back what it has done for me and my family and what is has done for a million or more student-athletes. You can bet on one thing—that I have tried to pay back and will continue to pay back to football for the rest of my life.

We have to care for our game of football or we will lose it. If we don't do the right things for our game of football, somebody is going to do it for us, and we won't like it. Years ago, nobody bothered our game of football. That day is gone.

Coaching Football

Beyond administrative action, perhaps the best thing we can do to ensure a bright future for football is to coach the game in a way that promotes respect and enthusiasm. If I were to advise a coach and could give him only three areas of emphasis, I'd pick these:

- *Philosophy.* Know what you really believe in, believe in it, and be sure your players can execute it.
- *Teach techniques in an effort to get the proper execution.* All of you assistant coaches, if you want to be head coach, you have to prepare yourself every day.
- *Management.* If you can't manage the people that surround you, then you can't win. Can I manage coaches, players? The normal answer is yes. But, can I handle the fans and media? If you can't handle them, it makes your job harder to accomplish.

Basic Reminders for Players

I reminded my squad every year of some basic things they needed to know:

- You must learn to adjust your lifestyle for us to cooperate as a team.
- You can't beat the system. It will catch up with you.
- Prepare yourself for constructive criticism. Our coaches may raise their voices at you to make corrections, and that should be okay. When we quit talking to you, you have a problem.

Play a Number of Players

When you went out for football in high school or college, what is the one thing you wanted to do? The players today are not any different. At LSU we were one of the first schools to start playing a number of players. There were several reasons for this:

- It was a great morale builder, because they knew they were going to get the opportunity to play. Therefore, they practiced really hard during the week.
- It made better players out of each player. Each had to prove he belonged.
- We realized the second unit was not as good as the first unit, but the second unit was fresher and quicker. I coached many all-star games after the season, and that was the one thing that players from opposing teams would talk about. They got tired of facing fresh players, especially in the fourth quarter.
- It made the program more fun.

Develop Self-Discipline

Have you ever let your players grade themselves from a game film? I learned that the players would grade themselves down, so I used that information in dishing out discipline. I would call them in, have them sit behind my desk in my chair, and present them with the problem as if I were the player and they were the coach.

You know what? They'll give themselves tougher discipline than you'd planned for them. I would stick with my regular discipline, but keep wondering out loud if I should do what they said. So when the player leaves, he's not griping to the other players. He accepts his punishment without a problem. He feels like he got a reprieve.

Positive Attitude Is a Plus

Our attitude in football has been that we don't care who gets the credit, but we've got to get the job done or we all go down the drain. The team concept. You will never lose communication with your squad if you have fun as you work. Attitude starts with you.

Simpler Is Often Better

I always wanted to make sure we weren't trying to teach too much. So, I asked myself, "Are they getting what you are coaching?" It sounds simple, but it's a very big, important question.

What some pro teams do is great, but most of our teams don't have the talent or the experience to do the things the pros are doing. Keep the game simple and uncomplicated so you can get execution.

—1994 Proceedings. Coach McClendon was executive director of the AFCA from 1982–1993.

Insights Into Coaching
WOODY HAYES

I shall start with some insights into the coaching profession that are taken from a book published in 1969. The author* has graciously given me permission to read from it. The name of it is *Hot Line to Victory*.

1. One of the most important characteristics of a successful coach is be yourself. It was Socrates who said, "Know thyself"; but it is up to the coach to be himself. Often a young coach will imitate one of his former coaches. It is excellent to emulate a former coach, but do not imitate him.

2. There are two qualities that a coach must have to a far greater degree than any other member of the teaching staff. First, the coach must have an intense and continuing interest in the welfare and in the all-around development of each player. With little reflection, the coach will realize that his own success is dependent on the attitude and the effort of those players. If he is successful, he certainly owes much to those players, and his continual interest and help to those young men becomes important and worthwhile.

   Second, the coach must have an extremely strong desire to win. However, it must be a "we" win attitude, not an "I" win attitude. He is the leader of the team, but he is also a member of the team. When he is confronted with defeat, he must never use the sick alibis, "if that pass hadn't been intercepted" or "if our end had caught the ball in the end zone." Such excuses are a reflection on the individual player and will be construed as an attempt by the coach to remove himself from the blame of losing. In time of victory there are enough plaudits for everyone, but in time of defeat, the responsibility must be taken by the most mature and most responsible man involved—the head coach.

3. There is one luxury the coach cannot afford—it is the luxury of self-pity. When the coach resorts to this psychological mechanism, his days in the profession are numbered.

4. The coach must assume a positive attitude toward his job. If he enjoys coaching, as a good coach will, he must realize that he gets paid for the headaches involved in the coaching profession. Headaches—such as morale problems, training problems, undue pressure—all of these are things tied in with the profession, and the coach must recognize them for what they are. He must anticipate these problems; he must not say "if they happen," but "when they happen"; and then he must take all precautions to keep them from happening.

5. The coach must win. There is a Roman expression, *Res nolunt diu male administrari*, which purportedly means "Things refuse to be mismanaged long." In the coaching profession there is no adequate substitute for winning.

6. Criticism must be regarded as impersonal, for it is an occupational hazard. Usually the critic is vocal only because the team lost, and this cannot be regarded as a personal criticism. The critic may not even know the coach, but he does know that the coach is the leader of the team that lost. Quite often this type of criticism is hardest on the coach who returns to his own college or to his own community. He must realize that the same person who patted him on the back as a player can change his aim and figuratively beat him over the head as a coach. The coach and his family who are not prepared for this will have bad times.

7. In high school the coach is hired for one thing and fired for another. One of the true anomalies in the high school coaching

---

*Mr. Hayes himself was the author of *Hot Line to Victory*.

profession is the fact that the coach receives a small percentage of his salary for coaching and a large percentage of it for his classroom teaching and other duties. However, he will rarely be dismissed for his failure as a classroom teacher.

8. The head coach's job security lies in three areas:

First, he must rely on his own abilities and resources.

Second, he must believe absolutely in the players and his coaches. This does not mean that the discerning coach does not recognize the weaknesses of each player and coach, but at the same time, he must recognize in them and in himself the opportunity for team victory. He must realize that you win with people, the right people, properly led.

Third, the football coach must cooperate with his administration. Coach Bear Bryant, one of the truly great college coaches of all time, would second this 100%. He goes further to say that a coach should always have a long-term contract. This cooperation with the administration is obviously a two-way street. Most administrators see in the coach and the athletic team a positive force for good attitude and good discipline in the school system.

9. The training of the coach must be an extremely broadening experience. In general, coaches feel that the most important coaching preparation is first, actual coaching experience after graduation; second, undergraduate athletic experience; and third, coaching schools and coaching clinics after graduation. Undergraduate work in physical education, psychology, education, and practice teaching are regarded by coaches as having relatively little value in preparation for coaching. With this in mind, it would appear that the coach upon graduation should make a strong effort to get on a good high school coaching staff or stay at his university, or some other university, for graduate work. Even though he works for "peanuts," it will be worth his while to be able to work on a good college coaching staff for a year or two. When a coach becomes a head coach, he must have a sound knowledge of all the phases of football. For this reason a young coach must be a fast and eager learner. Although we often say that there are things more important than drawing circles and X's, this is only partly true; for the young coach's first contact with the player is as an individual coach, and he must prove himself to be a good technician with a good knowledge of intricate football. He must be able to captivate the player mentally and to build within the player the desire to compete and to improve. The first impression the player must have is, "Here's a man who really knows the game and knows how to put it across." Considering first things first, the young coach must be a good technician.

10. Moving into college coaching, we find that almost always a successful high school coach has aspirations of moving into college coaching. Although there are many reasons for this, several seem to be the most important.

First, the coach wants to find the answer to the question, "How good a coach am I?"

Second, the college coach gets to spend more time on actual coaching and less time on other duties.

Third, the college coach gets more recognition, and, for this reason, to move into college is an advancement. The high school coach has seen his own players move into college ranks, and he has the desire to follow them there and to work with more mature athletes.

Fourth, he has the desire to excel and he believes he can achieve this better on the college level.

Fifth, higher pay standards are also a factor, although this is not always the case.

11. Much has been written and discussed about the coach and public relations. Certainly his most important qualification in this area is to live up to all the fine things for which football stands.

In this area he must be like no one but himself. In dealing with the press he should tell the truth, or say nothing. To mislead the press is neither ethical nor sensible. Most of these men are interested in sports and want to portray sports in a positive sense, and very often a coach can give them information that will help them do this. On the other hand, the coach has no right to expect these men to write exactly as the coach sees it.

One caution: The public relations image can be grossly exaggerated; for the coach who is spending much of his time associating with different groups is making a mistake. The alumni, the boosters, and your own close friends never win games; but a well-trained and minutely coached group of young men will win.

In educational circles very often the word "win" is given an evil connotation, because it is often implied that winning means breaking some rules, but this is certainly not true. On the contrary, winning means the bringing together, in a common effort, of all the physical and mental resources of the football squad and its coaches, which in no way warrants an apology.

If a football coach is successful, he will usually move up by changing positions some five or six times during his career. At each of these moves his interview with the selection committee is a very important step in his success. The job interview is rarely discussed, but it will suffice to say that the coach should go into this interview as well prepared as he can possibly be, having anticipated every exigency that will probably arise, for his future depends on his selling himself at this crucial moment.

12. Coaching is not a profession that offers great security; a coach almost always gives up active coaching before he is ready to retire. This phenomenon is equally true in high school and college and must be taken into consideration in the coach's life preparation.

Coach-Player Relationship

We feel that the single most important consideration is that the football player must get an education and that nothing short of a degree is considered a complete education. The help and encouragement that the coach can give the player is extremely important, particularly during the first year that the player is on campus.

So many youngsters at this time will be neither properly guided nor motivated, and since the coach has the closest contact with these players, he is in an ideal position to render real help. The coach who is intelligent enough to coach and teach

in a university must be intelligent enough to sit down with a student and tutor and help the student over his rough spots. Any college coach who is not capable or willing to do this should not be on a college staff.

In our program we believe the only way that we can repay a player for his efforts is to make sure that we do everything within our college rules that we can to help this man get an education. Only in this way can we make sure the college athlete is not being cheated. This is the basis of the coach-player relationship at Ohio State University.

At Ohio State we are aware of the enormous educational value of football. It has never been our intention to overemphasize football, but perhaps at some time we have done so. However, the longer a coach stays in college football, the greater weight he gives to the educational value of the sport. As he studies former football players in their varied careers, he realizes that a large part of the useful education that they take from the campus is directly or indirectly tied in with football.

To play football is to respect rules, for the game of football could not exist without rules. Rules may not be absolutes, but they are absolute necessities for group achievement. The football player must not only have great respect for rules, he must also have an equal respect for the necessity of a rule change when a rule is outmoded or fails to fulfill its intended purpose. The absolute should be orderly change. This implies the democratic process, a process that has recently been flouted on many campuses, but a process that in comparison to all other methods of change, stands out as the best. If this sounds like indoctrination, that is exactly what it is meant to be.

A good football squad is controlled better by attitudes than by rules. Attitude includes many things: First, the desire to improve individually, to warrant membership on a team; second, the desire to win as translated into team conduct; and third, the development of a high respect for the rights and privileges of others on the squad. On our squad there are two rules.

First, there is no place on the football squad for haters, either white or black. Second, each player has a right to approach any coach off the field without fear of recrimination, if the player feels he has a legitimate complaint. We feel that this is a necessary safety valve.

Standards for football players must, of necessity, vary from those of other students. His conduct must always be considered in light of the effect it has on other members of the football squad. In matters of dress, punctuality, and living habits, the football player leads a much more disciplined life and must realize that for the team to succeed, this is a necessity.

Another area in which the coach can be of great help to the player is in the player's selection of his college associates. We tell him when he starts to run around with some new acquaintance he should always ask himself, "Would this man (or woman) be welcome at my home for the weekend?" This may sound rather cornball, but we have found it quite effective.

We are continually stressing the importance of such things as appearance and associates, but we know that these students do not like to be harped at. In closing, I would like to recite a little poem through which we like to stress the importance of college associates. It goes like this:

> *It was sometime in November, in a town I*
> *   can't remember,*
> *I was carrying home a jag with maudlin*
> *   pride,*
> *When my feet began to stutter, and I fell*
> *   down in the gutter, and a pig came up*
> *   and lay down by my side.*
> *As I lay there in the gutter, thinking*
> *   thoughts I dared not utter,*
> *A lady passing by was heard to say, "You*
> *   can tell a man who boozes by the*
> *   company he chooses."*
> *And the pig got up and slowly walked*
> *   away.*

—1970 Proceedings. Coach Hayes was head coach at Ohio State University.

Putting Together a Winning Program
BO SCHEMBECHLER

My years in coaching have been unbelievably good for me, for my family, for my staff, and for the guys who have played for me. I've been very, very fortunate.

I was an assistant coach for 10 years before I became a head coach. I had the privilege of coaching for three of the greatest football coaches who ever lived: Doyt Perry at Bowling Green, Ara Parseghian at Northwestern, and Woody Hayes at Ohio State.

In 1969 Don Canham, the athletic director at Michigan, offered me the job at Ann Arbor. I was excited. I'll never forget when I told the staff we were going to Ann Arbor. Most of them had never been there.

Implementing the Plan

The plan was a simple one. And it was important to communicate our approach to those involved in the Michigan program. My staff came up with the slogan we would give our players: Those who stay will be champions.

We went into the season with the idea that we wanted to simulate, and to beat, the most effective, dominant program in the league. That program was run by Woody Hayes at Ohio State. We felt his program was so dominant that nobody in the league had been able to keep that team from running the football. In order for us to compete against that, we felt we must be able to stop the run, and for us to be able to stop the run we must be able to run ourselves, because Lord knows our defense was going to play against our offense more than it would any opponent's.

I believe in defense first. I don't think you can win championships, I don't think you can be successful, unless you have a great defense. I also believe very strongly that you must be able to block—I mean the one-on-one, basic, fundamental blocking in football—and that you must be able to run the ball. I am not opposed to passing. I've been accused of that on a couple of occasions. I just don't want to come up on short yardage, and I don't want to go to the goal line, and I don't want to get into circumstances where I need to control the football, and suddenly, I can't block anybody and I can't run with the ball.

So we went with an offense where we would use the base block and run the football. We would simulate what Ohio State did because we wanted to stop that Ohio State attack. We put in a defense that was based on speed and quickness so we'd be able to pursue and to tackle. We used an agile defense because we were not a big defensive team. And we wanted to win the kicking game every time we played. This may sound strange to you, but we zeroed in on the best team in the league, Ohio State.

Avoiding Lapses

We used the phrase "You get better or you get worse; you never stay the same." We used it constantly and talked to the players about it: "Every time you take the field to practice or play a game, regardless of the opposition or what we do, when we go off the field we're either better or we're worse. You're damned sure not gonna stay the same."

In the 1970s, we won our share of championships and our program was quite successful. We were running the football, we were playing defense, we had great, classic confrontations with Ohio State in the last game of the year.

Almost every year we played for the championship in the last game. Those games were something special. We were playing against the greatest football coach and one of the greatest schools—particularly the greatest football coach—the Big Ten Conference has ever seen.

We were successful and happy. And then I learned very quickly that you can't become self-centered. You can't take for granted that even after 10 years of success that the problems the losing teams have you can't have just as quickly—in the wink of an eye. I learned this great lesson in 1979, when we had probably the worst kicking game in the history of college football.

We'd always placed such emphasis on the kicking game. We spent 15 minutes a day on it, every day. We coached punting the same we've coached it for 20 years, and yet we had punts blocked, we had punts returned on us, and we averaged something like 36 yards a kick. We couldn't cover, we couldn't punt, we couldn't do anything.

Why did this happen? Because all of us coaches stood there that 15 minutes. We folded our arms. We didn't coach with the same enthusiasm and with the same drive that we should have, on a

play that doesn't change from year to year. I promised to never, ever let that happen again.

In the 1980 season, I gave every single coach on our staff a responsibility for a position on punts. I told them if there was a breakdown at that position on a punt that that coach was responsible—and that we had no long-term contracts at Michigan. We suddenly approached it with a lot more enthusiasm.

I took over the responsibility of coaching the punt return. I have kept that responsibility, and I will never relinquish it. The man responsible for the kicking game at Michigan is me! And if I'm responsible for it, all of those players look at that and say, "Hey, this is something special if the old man is going to take all the time to conduct all the drills and do all the talking in practice to make sure that kicking game is done right."

In 1980, because of what happened to us in 1979 and the renewed emphasis on the kicking game, we led the nation in net punting. We were the finest punting team in the United States of America.

You've got to teach it every single day. Once you take for granted that you're gonna have a great team because you've got great talent, you've got another thing coming—because the single most important factor is attitude. And the only way you're gonna have a great attitude is to coach it every single day on and off the field!

Keys to Winning Programs

- Organization
- Mastery of basics
- Work ethic
- Courage
- Loyalty
- Integrity

Organization

If I were to tell you today how to win, this is what I'd tell you. Be an organized guy. I would have those practices well-organized and the staff well-organized, and everybody knowing what they're gonna do.

If you don't have organization, and you're not prepared, your team will never be competent. They're only competent when they know you have done a great job of simulating what's going to happen to them in a game. And you can't do that unless you're properly organized.

I had Bill Walsh at my clinic last summer. Walsh is a great coach. He's proved that. He was telling those coaches out in the audience how he'd won a game. He felt he'd won it because of his organization, because he closed every offensive practice session with a play that he'd run if it were fourth down and 25 from his own 30-yard line with 30 seconds left on the clock.

How many of you coaches work on that play? That is not a real good situation to be in if you're trailing. But he works on it. It's a special play where he puts three wide receivers out on one side and puts this guy (Jerry) Rice out on the other by himself.

If they cover these three receivers over here and leave one guy on Rice, they're gonna throw the ball to Rice. Walsh worked on that. They got into a game that year in which a very similar situation occurred, and he told the guys to run that pass play.

And all the guys said, "Hell's fire, we practice this. We've got a shot. We might possibly hit this play because we work on it." And damned if the guy didn't go back there and throw the ball to Rice on a streak route for a touchdown and they won the game.

Now that isn't gonna happen all the time, but it damned sure never would have happened had he not practiced that situation. You must anticipate and organize and practice every single thing that possibly could happen in a game.

Mastery of the Basics

The second thing to do is master the basics, the basic fundamentals of blocking and tackling, and you teach 'em with great enthusiasm. The greatest teacher I have ever been around in college football—by far, no one has ever compared—was Woody Hayes.

Woody Hayes was the advocate of the old fullback off-tackle play. All old coaches knew Woody was gonna run 26. He had all kinds of blocking adjustments up there to do it. I coached with him for 6 years. For 6 springs and 6 falls, as we put in the offense on the first day, the old man would go to the board and, as if it was the greatest invention in football, he would describe to the staff the 26 play.

Because he taught it with such enthusiasm, you sat there and watched every move and you learned something different—every time. Maybe it was just a slight lateral step of the fullback, or maybe you were really gonna change the play and have a new blocking adjustment up front.

When he took that play to the players, he taught it with great enthusiasm. When the play-

ers were in the huddle in a game and the play came in and it was 26, there wasn't a damned one of 'em—and you can talk to any guy who played Ohio State football—who didn't feel they were gonna gain yardage, because he had sold those men that no one can stop 26.

To me, that's important if you want to win—if the play's sound and you teach it that way. It would have been easy for him to say, "OK, we're gonna run 26. You all know how to run it." No! That isn't the way Woody put it in. He put it in so everyone would think, "This is the greatest thing we could do."

Motivation and Courage

The next thing you've got to do to be successful is be willing to work. There's no substitute for hard work. There's no substitute for careful planning. There's no substitute for putting in the time.

Motivation! You must have your heart in your work so you can motivate others—your coaching colleagues and the players on your team. You must set goals. Any team that's not a goal-oriented team is not going to have much chance at success.

There's no substitute for hard work. I admire coaches who are willing to put in the time. It's not a part-time job. Even though you may have other responsibilities to your school, as I have to mine, coaching football is a full-time job, and you don't punch a time clock to do it.

In order to win, everybody on the staff must understand that his job is important. One of my pet peeves is the assistant coach who is always looking for the big break or the next job or the next head coaching job.

Anybody who wants to become successful in football should become the greatest coach, at whatever responsibility he has, and he should be happy doing it! I can say to you in all sincerity, I never had a bad job. I never had a job I didn't like, whether I was a graduate assistant, or coaching the guards or tackles or center, or whatever it might be.

I talked about discipline and the importance of it. I want teams with great courage, teams that are able to play under great pressure. That's important. There's pressure in Michigan football. There's pressure in your place. If you've ever taken a teenage kid and run him out in front of 105,000 people and say, "We want to win . . ."

That's pressure. That takes courage. Football teaches that. And when it's done properly, it's a great teaching aid for these kids, because later on they're going to have to make some decisions more important than whether they're gonna block or tackle somebody.

Loyalty

I believe in loyalty, loyalty to yourself and loyalty to those who depend on you. The greatest example of that I've ever been around was many years ago when Texas A&M was trying to hire me. I was going to help Bear Bryant coach in the East-West Shrine Game.

He was going to be the head coach. He'd just become the winningest coach in history in Division I; he was the greatest of all time. He and I had coached in some all-star games before, and when they asked him to be the head coach, he said he'd do it if I'd come—because he knew he would have me do all the work.

I got out to San Francisco and met him at the Shrine Hospital we were visiting. I said, "I've got to talk to you, coach." He said, "Yeah, I been reading the papers about you. You and I better sit down and have a little talk." I said, "Great, as soon as we get back to the hotel." He said, "I'll give you a call."

He called and came down to my suite, sat down, and started to talk. He looked over and said, "Aren't you gonna offer me a drink?" I got a bottle of bourbon. He poured himself a drink and said, "Texas A&M wants to hire you, eh? I'll never forget when I was down there."

He went on and on. He told stories and reminisced about all his background and his coaching. Finally after about an hour and a half, he looked over at me and said, "Well, Bo, we've talked about you enough. Now we're gonna talk about my problems."

I said, "What kind of problems do you have?" I thought he was gonna say something about his health. But he said, "Bo, I don't want to go back to the office. I don't want to call the office. I don't want to recruit one more kid; I want to quit."

I said, "Bear, everybody in the world expects you to quit at your age. You've just broken the record. You've done everything you could possibly do. It's time for you to quit. Why don't you just go ahead and do it?" So I put on a little show. I grabbed the phone and said, "Here, let's call your president right now."

He said, "Oh, no. It's not that easy. You're gonna find that out some day. I've got 47 people back there that I hired at the University of Alabama. What's gonna happen to them if I quit?"

You know the story: He went back and coached again. He didn't want to. He was sick, and he was old and tired. He coached one more year, finally quit, and soon afterward was dead.

That, to me, demonstrated loyalty. He wouldn't just walk out on his job. It wasn't that easy. Now, gentlemen, I call that loyalty. I see guys flying around, jumping around, leaving people sitting cold and not knowing what they're doing. Bryant couldn't do that. When he finally did leave, I'm sure there were people who were out in the cold.

Integrity

I believe in honesty and integrity. As you deal with your players and your coaches and everybody else connected with football, gentlemen, you must be honest and you must do it with integrity.

I don't feel sorry for those people who get caught and put on probation. I don't feel sorry for people who get the death penalty. We have rules and regulations we have to operate under, and when you break those rules you must pay the price.

There's enough criticism at every level across the country that we as coaches cannot afford to operate any other way than with honesty and integrity. That's your job, and if you can't win legitimately that way, maybe you shouldn't coach.

If you're in a situation where a great season is winning half your games, realize it, and make sure the people around you realize it. We must conduct ourselves so that we are above reproach. That's the only way to sell your program.

And that last thing I believe is that when we coach, every single one of our players must feel, when his career is ended, that it was one of the most meaningful experiences he's ever had or ever will have. If it is not, then we're at fault.

All of us coach for one reason, and only one reason: what effect it has on the guy we coach. I don't mind filling that stadium at Michigan. I don't mind making millions of dollars. But I'm gonna tell 'em one thing: We're only gonna do it if it's in the best interests of those guys who play.

That's important. If they come back and say, "Hey, this was the greatest thing that ever happened to me," then it was all worth it.

—1989 Proceedings. Coach Schembechler was head coach at the University of Michigan.

Things I've Learned From Coaching
JOE PATERNO

I'll never forget the first time I spoke at the Atlantic City coaches clinic way back in the old days, when Dr. Harry Scott was running it. He set me up one night. We had a little dinner, and Harry said, "Joe, I've been reading everything you have had to say about football. I've been watching you, the way you have coached, and I've asked a friend of mine who is an author to put together a book, and I want you to have this. The title of the book is *What I Know About Football* by Joe Paterno." I could hardly wait to get at the book. I opened it up, and there were 200 *empty* pages. I still have that book.

The first clinic I went to was back in 1950, when I was in my first year of coaching at Penn State. Four of us got in the car and drove all night from State College to Dallas, and we were going to stay at the Baker Hotel. The university gave us $50 each for expenses. We rented a room and shared the expenses of the car. We walked into the Baker Hotel about twelve or one at night, and

there was a whole crowd of people in the lobby. There was this kind of heavy guy holding court, running the clinic. That was Woody Hayes.

Woody had just had an undefeated season at Miami of Ohio and was in the process of being interviewed for the Ohio State job. He was in there talking about how he blocked the off-tackle play. We were there until four in the morning, and I was fascinated. That was my introduction to the American Football Coaches Association clinic.

About Teaching

I know most of you may have heard this before, but first and foremost, what I have learned is that a coach must be a teacher. I was able to learn this from a person who I truly believe to be one of the best coaches and teachers ever: Rip Engle. Rip would never let us put in more than the kids could handle. He was constantly evaluating the assistants to determine how much new material they were putting in and how quickly the kids were comprehending it.

I can't tell you how important that is. The minute you have to play a kid that can't learn quickly, can't handle some things you want to do, all of a sudden your whole scheme has come down. We couldn't do some things we do in our secondary if we didn't have four bright kids back there who could handle some of the adjustments, the checks, the change-ups on coverages. We can only go as fast as the slowest learner.

About Players

In evaluating personnel, I've always believed that the first thing was consistency, the second thing was the RBI—the guy that can make the big play and win the game for you—and the third thing was the guy that makes the major error. You can't play him. I try to remember what players can do well. If you have a player that can do something particularly well, don't forget it. In the clutch, that's what you want to use.

About Coaches

In evaluating coaches, there are certain things that I've tried to look at when hiring them or keeping them. First, can he live without it? I'm only repeating what Coach Bryant and some other people have said, but if you can live without coaching, then I don't know whether coaching is for you.

The *NCAA News* had an article once about this great musician that Bobby Knight invited in to talk to his team. This world-renowned cellist, named Janos Starker, talked to Bobby's group and explained how he didn't want to play a cello, but his mom stuck the instrument in his hands, and he was forced to learn how to play it. Then all of a sudden, he realized that he didn't want to go one day without thinking, doing, making music. He said, "Anyone who can go through a day without wanting to make music or hear music is not supposed to be a musician." Starker became a true professional—not a dilettante, but a man who committed his life to music.

I don't think any of us who've been coaching very long ever gets up in the morning without thinking something about football. I don't know if there has been a day in my life of coaching that I haven't thought about football or my team, and I try to evaluate my coaches in the same way.

I think coaches have to be willing to make any sacrifice to win, except their families. You've got to be willing to make any sacrifice, and you've got to have self-discipline. You have to be in there when you're supposed to be, and you have to do the things you are supposed to do because you can't fool kids. You can't talk to kids about being disciplined and not be disciplined yourself.

About Developing Young Players

One of the greatest mistakes I've ever seen in coaching was made one year when we had a great freshman kid from upstate New York who was a 6-4, 215-pound fullback that ran (in those days it was a good speed) a 100-yard dash in 10.0. He came down to our place, and we could hardly wait to see what he could do. He was a pretty good runner, but not a great one.

So during the following spring practice, we matched the kid up against Dave Robinson, who played with the Green Bay Packers for years and was as good a football player as we ever had. We can't wait to see how tough the young kid was, so we put him in there against Robinson for a dive drill. The point was we didn't have any guy on the football team—there wasn't a football player on our team who, in that situation, Robinson couldn't pick up and throw on his back. Robinson was that good. The first time the kid comes, Robinson takes and throws him on his back. The next time, same thing.

The kid was so frustrated. And you know what happened? That kid never showed up to practice again. All we did was take a great prospect who wasn't ready for that kind of challenge and destroyed him. If we had led him along, given him some success, we may have been able to develop him into a good football player.

I'm not in a hurry to play young players. My staff knows how I feel. A lot of times kids think they're ready to play. I'd rather be two weeks late in playing a kid than one day too soon. Because until a kid is comfortable, until he has had an opportunity to feel good about himself, until he really knows he's ready to go, until the whole squad says to themselves, "When are you going to play that kid?" I'm not sure I'd like to play him. After they have some success, and once they believe in themselves, then they can become winners.

About Winning

People often talk to me about developing individuals into winners. I always wanted to be around Paul Bryant because I thought he did as good a job as anybody in creating a winning mentality around his players. We played a couple of his teams, going back to the 1959 Liberty Bowl, when we had a great team and he was in his first year at Alabama. We struggled like dogs to beat him and got lucky to score on a screen pass in a 7-0 football game. We outmanned them, but they were winners!

The only difference between winners and losers is that the winners believe in themselves. They've had success. They haven't been knocked around. Things have turned out well for them up to a point, and they keep thinking it's going to continue to turn out well for them. They expect things to happen because they have had that success.

—1987 Proceedings. Coach Paterno is head coach at Penn State University.

Fifty-Plus Years of Coaching Football

EDDIE ROBINSON

One of the best things that's happened to me in my lifetime is that I've heard the best coaches who have ever walked. From 1941, when I first went to coaching school, I've heard them all. You name them, and I have a piece of every one. And when I leave here today, I'll have a piece of those who will talk today.

At Grambling, we don't do a whole lot of things that other people haven't done. We come here and we get the plays. I've had your plays; you know that. I got the Wing-T from (Forest) Evashevski, from (Dave) Nelson. I picked their brains. This is what it's all about. You can't come here and walk in the halls and hang around like I see some of the guys. When someone gets up here to speak, you need to be in here to hear him.

For example, back in the '50s, we were trying to change plays at the line. I'd gone all over the country trying to talk with people who changed something at the line. At one clinic, an unknown speaker came up after Frank Leahy had spoken, and while the other coaches were walking out, this guy said everything I wanted to know.

Why Coaching?

To paraphrase the late Alonzo Stagg: "The coaching profession is the most rewarding profession in the world, and no man is too good to coach in America." It's a great profession, and this is what you need to tell the young coaches. Work hard, and promotions will come. You can't work at one job, looking to go to another job. You've got to have commitment.

I agree with coach Stagg wholeheartedly, and I have for some 49 to 50 years, to the extent that at this point, if I had a decision to make about a vocation, I wouldn't have to take a second guess—it would still be the coaching profession, because I know that football builds character in young men.

When I look at you, I see people who can make winners out of losers. I see people who can be a plus to our society. I see people who are looking

at the young man instead of the record. You've got to look at both—you don't have a record, you get fired—but you're dealing with America's most precious possession. These great men who I heard kind of shaped my philosophy about things like this, that football builds character in young men.

Football Lessons

Coaches in the past have said this about football, and I believe it, too. Football makes young men strong enough to know when they're weak and brave enough to face themselves when they're afraid. Football will teach them to be proud and unbending in honest failure, but humble and gentle in success. Football teaches men not to substitute words for action, nor to seek the path of comfort, but to face the stress and spur of difficulty and challenge.

Football will teach them to stand up in the storm but to have compassion on those who fall; to have a heart that is clean, a goal that is high. It will teach them to laugh, yet never forget to weep; to reach into the future, yet never neglect the past; to be serious, yet never take yourself too seriously; to be modest so that you will remember the simplicity of true greatness—the open-mindedness of true wisdom.

We've got some great minds here. The players have great minds, too. At Grambling, we have a man who's our leader, our president; I've had the distinct pleasure of coaching two players who are now college presidents. Great minds. That's why I want you to leave here with a commitment about this game and the young men you coach.

A boy can't come to my office and tell me, "Coach, I don't want to waste your time." He doesn't waste my time. It's our time. I don't flunk anybody, and I'm not running the football, and I'm not catching it. So, these athletes are the most important people in the world to me.

It's all right for a man to be a man, but you put him down there in a one-on-one situation, and this guy will find out how good he is, just like the other one will. I could be wrong, but I think football and athletics in general have made our nation the best fighting force in the world.

I don't like people who substitute words for actions. When a team whips us, and the boys are in the dressing room, I walk in, and I'm asked, "What about the game?" I say, "We should have stayed at home. They outplayed us, they outblocked us, and they outcoached us."

Taking Responsibility

I learned so much from football. I learned how to win from football. I learned how to lose from football, to lose without offering excuses.

No assistant coach of mine can say Coach Robinson said that a boy lost a game, or that an assistant coach lost it. If anybody loses a game, Eddie Robinson does.

At one time early in my coaching career, when I'd get up in the morning, I'd say, "Eddie, you're a hell of a coach, boy, you're coming on," but that didn't last long. Now, you've got offensive coordinators, coaches with defenses. Back then, I was coaching it all.

For all these years, I've ridden on the shoulders of the athletes, the football players, and the coaches. Whatever we have achieved, or will achieve, then the athletes and coaches should share. I don't believe that I could have done that by myself.

The football players and the football coaches have been good to me. I don't have enough time at my age to pay them back. It's so important to give something back.

I've never walked off from an autograph. I don't allow it. We had a crowd of 55,000 against Temple in Tokyo. When the game was over, we were on the bus, getting ready to leave, and were about an hour late. The guys were all mad, saying Doug Williams was not here. He finally came about 10 minutes later, and he stepped on the bus, and he told them, "I don't make the rules; Coach makes the rules, and he said, 'don't come out of the dressing room if you're not going to sign them.'"

Ask anybody on our team. I don't want to see any kid running to somebody asking for an autograph and not get one. Stop and sign it. This is what you need to do.

Coaching School and the AFCA

I went to my first coaching school at Northwestern. I don't think anybody's old enough to know

about the *Chicago Tribune* all-star game, where I think they bought glasses for the underprivileged. At that time, they held the game at Northwestern. The all-stars played the professional champions. In 1941, I went to this coaching school, after I'd been hired at Grambling.

The coaches who were there—you've probably read about them—were Fritz Crisler, Carl Snavely, and Lynn Waldorf. I still remember some of the things that were said during that coaching clinic. What Fritz Crisler said was true then and still is true. The essence of offense is blocking. On defense, it's tackling.

Most of you've read about coach Crisler. He was a disciplinarian. He was tough, with a deep, commanding voice, and he was a man that was respected. When he talked, you could hear a pin drop in the stadium.

Coach Waldorf was one of those guys you could get close to. He'd tell you in his own gentle way that one method of coaching doesn't go for all ballplayers. They have individual differences. And you can give a guy with more ability more things to do.

Crying, Dreaming, and Doing

I'm a crier. I cry over good things. When I was a boy, I didn't have a great deal. I remember when they played the first Sugar Bowl game, I was sitting on the steps of an Italian store, listening to it on a borrowed radio. I listened to the Rose Bowl.

Like Martin Luther King, I had a dream. I wanted to coach. And when Grambling played a game in Pasadena in the Rose Bowl, I walked on the field and I cried, because I couldn't realize when I sat there listening many long years ago that I would ever coach a game there.

When we got the first chance to put 76,000 people in the Sugar Bowl, I cried again, because I realized that only in America could this happen to me. I'll tell you one thing: I can sell Americanism. I believe Eddie Robinson is as good an American as any other American. And I'll always want to be the best coach, or among the best.

When I was introduced, I had all those nice things said about me. But something that wasn't said was that nobody in my family before me finished elementary school. There's a price you have to pay.

What you young coaches have to understand is that I wasn't as fortunate as you are. I live in Grambling. In order to get to Grambling, you got to be going to Grambling. You can't go through Grambling to get to any other place. From 1941 to 1955, I didn't know anything about the American Football Coaches Association. But on the average, I went to one to three coaching clinics a year since 1941.

In 1956, I went to my first AFCA convention. When I got there and walked through that door and saw the people there and all the famous names on their badges, I became a badge freak. I was looking at all the coaches that I had read about, heard about—that's this guy, there's that guy. I was just so excited about being there for the first time.

Meeting Coach Stagg

At my first AFCA meeting, Ray Eliot, the president, was introducing some people. When he said "Alonzo Stagg," it was just like putting on an alarm. Everybody wanted to shake his hand.

I had read about coach Stagg, and how he wrote to his 14-month old son, and if he would die, how he wanted his son to treat his mother, and what kind of man he wanted him to be. I read about all the changes he had made in the game. He was just about a football god to me.

Just like that, everybody was coming up to shake hands with coach Stagg. The line circled all the way around the room. It took me about 30 minutes to work my way up there. Finally, after reading about this guy for so long, I was going to meet him. I couldn't imagine what he would look like up close—figured he had three ears, two noses. I don't know what he had, to be the kind of guy he was. So, by the time I got to him, and extended my hand, I wanted to get a good look at him—possibly looking for that third ear, or something that made him superior. The guy behind me finally said, "Hell, Eddie, kiss him and move on."

Developing a System

When I was leaving the coaches' school, I waited until everybody had left, and I went in the locker room where coach Waldorf was. And when I walked in, he had his back to me. He took a quick glance and said, "Yes, Eddie, what do you want?"

When this gentleman called my name, it really nailed me down. With all these people, how does this man know my name? Calling my name made me know right there that I needed to know the first name of my ballplayers. When your name is called, when a man comes up to you in a strange town and calls your name, it means something.

And I said to him, "Coach Waldorf, what is your advice to a young coach on his first job?" He said, "As a new coach, you need to get a system."

I said, "A system?" He said, "Yes, you need to get a system."

"Well," I told him, "I just got through playing football, and I don't really have a system."

He said, "Well, we can handle that. What do you play, what is your offense?" and I told him it was double wing and single wing, and the defense was a 6-2.

So he said, "Eddie, you can take the plays that you used in college, and then whatever you heard here related to what you play, and take that back to Grambling. Get it mimeographed and give it to your players. And tell them this is your system, and make them play it." The train couldn't get to Grambling fast enough for me to get this system home, and in the first meeting I had with my players, I told them this is our system and this is what you have to play.

Cosell and Grambling QBs

Back in the 1970s, we had several outstanding quarterbacks. At this time, the question was whether any black could ever play quarterback for the NFL. We were in New York, and Howard Cosell (who helped us quite a bit, helped our teams, helped get a lot of people drafted, helped us get our game in New York) told me he wanted me to be on his show. I told him, "Howard, I don't mind being on your show, but I don't want you to ask me all those crazy questions."

He said, "Well, I won't ask you any questions like that, that you have to answer." Now, on the show: "Ladies and gentlemen, I have Eddie Robinson. Eddie, do you think, with your vast experience and the number of years that you have coached, that you could prepare in four years a young man who could play football in the NFL and direct the team?"

What was I supposed to say? I'm a coach. I said yes. I was just trying to hurry and get off. When I got on the airplane and left New York, I went straight to James Harris' house. He's 6-5, 210 and I told James Harris, "I am recruiting you to play quarterback in the NFL." He took the challenge. James Harris stepped out of school and was the first one to start in the NFL, in Buffalo.

After that, I wondered if in my lifetime, with my years running out, will I live to see a Grambling QB in the Super Bowl? So I've never been more satisfied than seeing Doug Williams get off the ground and win the Super Bowl for the Washington Redskins.

Since 1941, there have been so many things to be pleased about at Grambling. We have three people in the pro football Hall of Fame. We have Willie Davis in the '50s, and Willie Brown and Buck Buchanan in the '60s. Vince Lombardi said Davis' quickness, power, and intelligence made him the best defensive end that he'd ever coached. We've had television coverage, great teams, and great players.

But with all the success Grambling has had over the years, sometimes you still have to ask somebody for help. You probably won't agree with this, but George Steinbrenner helped us keep our program going. When the Urban League couldn't sponsor the game in New York anymore, he stepped in and guaranteed the guarantee. Since he's been connected with this group, the Yankees have played at Grambling two times, and 46 kids graduated from college on the funds that we received from those games.

Leadership

You young coaches have to create in the men you are coaching a real love for the game and a spirit for work. You have to give them the will to win, because that's the deciding factor in close ballgames. After you teach the fundamentals of blocking and tackling, you have to teach them to execute. You have to have morale and create a good feeling among the teams.

All coaches must be absolutely sincere to the work ethic. You cannot win the confidence of the men you coach unless you are dead honest in what's going on. You can't fool the kids if you are not sincere, if you're not doing the work.

Each practice should be carefully planned in advance, with room for modification. You've got to know exactly what is to be done on the field. Before you go on the field, you have to be ready.

The game will be won or lost by what the players know, not what the coaches know. Coaching is repetition, explanation, illustration, imitation, correction, repetition, and that is the way that you'll do it.

Hello, Remember Me?

I'd like to leave you with something I always finish with when I speak somewhere:

Some people call me Old Glory, others call me by the Star-Spangled Banner, but whatever they call me, I am your flag of the United States of America. Something has been bothering me, so I thought I might talk it over with you, because it is about you and me. I remember some time ago, people lined up on both sides of the street to watch the parade and, naturally, I was leading every parade, proudly waving in the breeze. When your daddy saw me coming, he immediately removed his hat and placed it against his left shoulder so that the hand was directly over his heart, remember?

And you, I remember you. Standing there straight as a soldier. You didn't have a hat, but you were giving the right salute. Remember little sister? Not to be outdone, she was saluting the same as you with her right hand over her heart. Remember?

What happened? I'm still the same old flag. Oh, I have a few more stars since you were a boy. A lot more blood has been shed since those parades of long ago. But now I don't feel as proud as I used to.

When I come down your street, you just stand there with your hands in your pockets. I may get a small glance, and then you look away. Then, I see the children running around and shouting; they don't seem to know who I am. I saw one man take his hat off, then look around. He didn't see anybody else with theirs off, so he quickly put his back on.

Is it a sin to be patriotic any more? Have you forgotten what I stand for and where I've been? Anzio, Guadalcanal, Korea, and Viet Nam. Take a look at the memorial honor rolls sometimes, of those who never came back to keep this republic free, one nation, under God. When you salute me, you are saluting them.

Well, it won't be long until I'll be coming down the street again. So, when you see me, stand straight, place your right hand over your heart, and I'll salute you by waving back, and I'll know that you remember.

You are the greatest people, and this is the greatest profession. Keep making these young boys be good Americans.

—1991 Proceedings. Coach Robinson was head coach at Grambling State University.

Motivation—The Difference-Maker in Coaching

LEE CORSO

When you talk to football players, you'd better believe in what you're talking about. They can sense it! They know that when the coach says, "I want you to do this," that he believes it. If not, they're not going to play for you, they're not going to perform for you, and most important, they're not going to respect you!

You know what we do the first two weeks of our spring practice, both on the field and in meetings? We work on the mind. We try to figure out what we can do to stimulate these young men. We have different young men every year. You've got to motivate them in different ways. I've seen guys try to motivate one football team exactly the way they did another, and that's difficult. They're not the same. And I believe in the basic right and dignity of every man to be different. Every man has the right to be himself and to be his own man, no matter what he believes in.

Flexibility

You've got to change. There's one thing I learned from the United States Naval Academy, if they taught me nothing else. I learned to "I & A"—improvise and adjust. That's exactly what it takes in college coaching, in high school coaching, or in life.

Coaches should be ready at any moment to adjust their philosophy, if necessary. You better have rules with a little outlet. You must be ready to move quickly, to improvise, and to adjust every moment in your life when you're dealing with men 15 to 20 years old, because they're changing! They're changing from year to year, from week to week, from day to day, and from hour to hour. Evaluate whatever you did last year to motivate your people to see if it is feasible this year. Every Sunday afternoon we look at what we're going to do to motivate our guys this week. And it changes every week. But there are some basic principles that I'd like to go over.

Responsibility

Before you can motivate anyone in this world, you must have their respect. Coaches have a lot more responsibility than teaching kids to run off-tackle. They've got one of the most responsible jobs in the world! Sure, the X's and O's are important in winning games. But a coach's main responsibility to a football player is to teach him to be a better man. If it isn't, why not let him play some other sport, or let him hang around the corner, or let him go to the biology teacher? That is to me the most important responsibility of a football coach today—to take his football players and motivate them, mold them, and teach them to be better men.

There are a lot of fathers sitting at home, playing golf, working, or flying all over, who turn their sons over to the coach and say, "Whatever you do, make them better men, because I don't have the time." When you look at it like that, it's a tremendous responsibility and privilege. And that's exactly the way I feel about coaching as a profession.

Self-Confidence and Optimism

The first thing is they must believe in themselves. You're putting in their minds, a little at a time, the magic of believing in themselves. You see a guy, for example, walking into a room and people will say, "I don't know who that guy is, but he must be a winner." This is because he moves, looks, and acts as if he believes in himself. If you don't believe in yourself, don't ever expect any man to believe in you. They won't do it. You've got to have that inner belief first.

Never downgrade a man. You've got to have a personal inner pride. You've got to get it out of him—it's inside. How? You keep telling him he's got it there. You tell him he's got more pride than you've ever seen in anybody! The player will end up saying, "I do have that personal pride, and the other guy doesn't, and when it gets down to the fourth quarter, I'm going to win!" You may think that won't work, but it will.

When I got the job at Louisville, in three days I spent more money on football uniforms than my predecessor did in five years. I said to the players, "Gentlemen, you now look like what we're going to be—champions. You've got the finest uniforms in the world. You look like a champion! You're going to play like a champion!" You know what happened? They looked at each other and said, "You're right! You're damned right, we do look better! We're a lot better team than we were last year!" In their minds, they felt like they were better!

After you snap the ball, you can't promise anybody anything. That's when the other guy's talents come into play. But on your side of the line, you can do anything you want. And they can't hit you! Stop and think about that sometime: How long have you spent on your pregame warmup? Our guys take pride in their pregame warmup. They actually think it helps them win! They actually think it's worth a touchdown at the end! It doesn't make any difference whether it is or isn't—what's important is that they think it is.

Another thing we've learned is that there's no use worrying about the other guy's talent. There's nothing you can do about it. You cannot control the other man's team, and 90% of the coaches worry too much about what the other guy's got. You can't do anything about it. Worry about what you've got, and make them the best.

We run into a lot of negative thinking in football—there's always something wrong, always something bad. We don't allow one negative phrase in our whole organization. We've got the world's worst dressing room, but it's close to the practice field. That's positive thinking. Always sell this positive attitude. If you think things are bad, go by the cemetery.

Self-Discipline

We have two training rules. The first one is to *treat every man as you want to be treated yourself.* That's all we ask you to do. And you know what happens? You'll find a beautiful family starting to develop. Because when a guy starts to say something to somebody else, and he realizes, "I wouldn't want him to say that to me," it comes as a reaction because they feel it in the heart.

The second training rule is to *act like a man and you'll be treated like a man.* Act like a bum

and people will treat you like a bum. You might say, "What does 'act like a man' mean?" Players know! Let them use some of their imagination. You get those two principles across to them, and they'll play. And when they get to respecting the coach, then he can motivate them.

All coaches are looking for discipline, and no matter what anybody tells me, the first thing you've got to have in order to discipline a man is his respect of you as a person. We've tried a different approach to the normal rigid discipline. We tell our players that we want them to be disciplined from the inside out, exactly the way you try to heal a wound. The real danger is when you discipline by commands, as if the players are robots.

If you regiment players and tell them everything to do, they'll do it, but it won't be part of them—inside of them. When it gets down to the fourth quarter, and it's fourth-and-1, they'll quit a lot of times. They'll say, "To hell with it! I don't believe in that guy anyhow!"

Try to avoid the extremes if you can. Don't go all the way in one direction, letting them do anything they want to; and don't go all the way in the other direction, telling them they can't do anything! Try to hit, in your own way, a happy medium.

Respect

I've heard college coaches say, "Run the deadwood off." If you do, you're not gaining anything there—you're losing a possibility. You're losing a guy who could possibly help in some way. And when the guy you run off is on the fourth team, guess who his best friend is? The star! And the star says, "Some day, coach, I'm going to get you for running my best friend out of here." So, be respectful to the guy with less ability, because you are usually judged by the team on the way you treat your reserves.

You must believe that the most important people in the world besides your family are your players, because that's what you want them to believe about their coach. Every day, do something respectful toward a player. Some day it will come back to you. We try to do that.

The challenge coaches face is a tremendous one. We can only succeed if we continue to go over the relationships and duties with our players with the same aggressive and progressive attitude that we have doing X's and O's on the blackboard.

—1972 Proceedings. Coach Corso is a football analyst for ESPN.

Getting Your Team Ready to Play
KEN HATFIELD

Back in 1982 at the Air Force Academy, a week after we'd defeated Brigham Young, 39-38, we were playing Colorado State with a chance to win our very first Western Athletic Conference championship. It was an exciting game—one in which we had 19 plays of 10-plus yards on offense—but we lost because we turned it over six times.

As I looked at the film after that game and saw that on many of the turnovers we just dropped the ball and really weren't ever hit, I started to question my own coaching ability and whether I was overcoaching people. The week of that game, because it meant so much, I'd been up twice at 3:30 in the morning, trying to get a little extra film work just to be sure we had the right game plan.

Obviously, it didn't work. And I remember saying after that ballgame that from now on, whatever happens, our team will be mentally and physically fresh at kickoff.

So we changed our philosophy, cutting back on practice. No drills on Monday, no drills on Friday, and no meetings on Sunday. It really paid off for us, as we won 18 of our next 21 games.

The second lesson came while playing the University of Hawaii in a big game, also in '82. We ran our basic triple option play.

As the quarterback read the tackle, who happened to loop out, he handed the ball off to our fullback. The defense did an echo stunt and the end folded back inside to try to tackle the fullback. Our tough, short fullback lowered his shoulder and knocked the defensive end down. As soon as that happened, the offside linebacker was coming across and hit our fullback as hard as he could, but our fullback kept his feet churning and knocked him down, and then about 5 yards later met their free safety head-on in the open field. The FB knocked him down too and went 44 yards for a touchdown.

As I stood on the sideline and looked at my assistant, Fisher DeBerry, I thought about how the defense had read the play correctly, but our fullback had just run over three people. I said, "Football players win games, not football plays."

A fresh football player, who is eager and anticipates the game on Saturday, will play harder and make more big things happen than if he works on a play 15 to 20 extra times, and winds up being too tired before kickoff.

Along with those two lessons—be fresh at kickoff and football players win games, not football plays—we try to make sure our players enjoy playing the game, that it's fun for them. Football is a fun sport, and the thrill of competition has to be enjoyable each and every day. If they look forward to playing the ballgame, then they will play their hearts out, and that's all you can ask, come Saturday.

Free Day

I am indebted to a high school coach—Tom Grant of Jacksonville Wolfson High School in Jacksonville, Florida—for something he taught me, and that's to give players some time to themselves during the season. After I talked to Tom one spring during recruiting, I came back and told our coaches from then on we would not meet with our players on Sunday.

Well, you can imagine the rebellion that brought about. But I said these kids need some free time to themselves; they need some time to make their decisions, to sleep, to go to church, and just relax on Sunday if they want to. We instituted the program and have continued it, and it has been the No. 1 best thing that we have done.

It allows the player a chance now to sleep, to go to church, to watch pro football, to study, or do really whatever he wants to on a Sunday, and have one full day where he doesn't see any of his coaches. We find that by Monday, he is really eager and ready to learn everything that he should have learned in the game the previous week, and he is ready to go on from there.

The second benefit we've found is that now the assistant coaches don't have to rush through everything they're doing on Sunday. We no longer have to hurry and grade the film before the players come in, or hurry to make corrections or adjustments on new things they are going to do. We all were used to hurrying through everything, and, as a result, never really thought things out completely. This way, we're able to take our time, grade the film, determine as a staff what corrections need to be made, and then make the corrections with players on Monday.

I told our staff that a player doesn't need to see the mistake he made if he made the same one 10 times. He just needs to see it once or twice, so there's no real need for him to see the whole football game. He just needs to see the one or two mistakes he made, how he is going to correct them, and go from there. Don't keep harping on the same mistake.

Enthusiasm, Not Emotion

Another thing that helps our players be consistent week in and week out is to learn to play with enthusiasm versus emotion. Everybody has seen an emotional team. A team that plays with high emotions usually has great highs and great lows, because it is hard to sustain a high emotion at all times. Every game doesn't bring out the high emotions in you, and many times teams that play the great high emotional games are very susceptible the next week to getting knocked off by an inferior opponent, who itself is very high emotionally.

We think that if you learn to play with enthusiasm, that enthusiasm never wears out, and that's why we emphasize playing your best this play. The motto or the foundation to our program is to play our best this play in practice, because if a player learns to do that every day in practice, when there's no band or cheerleaders, or nobody out there watching him, and he is in that dirty old uniform, and repeating plays 15 or 20 times, then I know what he'll play like on Saturday, with his folks there, with that clean uniform on, out on that field, representing all those fans in the stands that came to see him play.

Enthusiasm never wears out. If you play with enthusiasm each and every day, it never wears out, and that enables you to play your best each and every week also.

Goalward Bound

A final suggestion to keep in mind when trying to play your best each week is to set a new goal each week. Last year our goal was to improve each week so that we could win a bowl bid.

We kept that as a goal, and we tried to prepare for each game to improve from week to week. If you lose during the season, then you've got to sell your kids on the importance of improving for that next ballgame, because when the kids believe in something, you've got the tiger by the tail. We won the bowl bid.

These have been some of the basic ideas that we feel are important in preparing a team to play its best each and every week, week after week throughout the season. The main thing is to keep the joy and enthusiasm in the game of football, so the kids look forward to coming out there each and every day. When kids have fun, and they want to compete, and they want to be the very best, then you'll play well every Saturday.

—1989 Summer Manual. Coach Hatfield is head coach at Rice University.

Turning a Program Around
GLEN MASON

Like most coaches, I moved into this job and was offered an opportunity because the situation was not great. That's why a coaching change was made. It's a situation of "catching up and turning things around," or more appropriately, "turning things around and catching up."

Anyone who has ventured into a turnaround situation will attest that you can feel overwhelmed by the job at hand. Here are some guidelines I'd suggest to get started.

1. *Evaluate present status.* Objectively evaluate what condition your program is in. Once you've done this, forget about it and concentrate on where you're going. Some coaches spend too much energy covering what has gone wrong in the past and second-guessing their predecessor.

2. *Don't worry about things you have little control over.* You have the job now. Don't become overwhelmed on what you don't have in the way of facilities, funds, talent, etc. Spend your time on the things you have a chance to control—your coaches and your players.

3. *Emphasize improvement.* Too often, all we talk about is winning. However, when asked the question, "how do you win?" we have no consensus on the correct answer. Therefore, set your sights on improving your team as fast as possible. You must believe that if you do a great job of improving, winning will take care of itself. If you improve as much as you can, and you still don't win, there isn't anything else you could have done.

4. *Be enthusiastic and positive.* When a program is down, everyone will be reminded of the bad things—the media, fans, alumni, etc. Do not reinforce their negatives. Get your hands on the good things and run with them. Enthusiasm is contagious, and nothing great can be accomplished without it.

5. *Set your sights high.* Yes, I already recommended that the emphasis should be on improvement. However, don't lose sight of where you want to end up.

6. *Don't lose faith in yourself.* The road will be bumpy. You will get knocked down many times—floored a few times. Stick to what you believe in, and stay strong and confident.

A formula for success is diagramed in Figure 1.

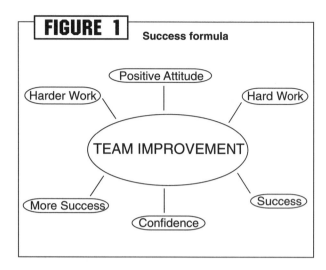

FIGURE 1 Success formula

Key Part of the Plan

There must be a basic plan or philosophy that everything spins off of. These become very detailed; however, here are some of the most important elements:

- Hire a quality staff.
- Set practice guidelines for practice.
- Establish a style of football.
- Develop your players.

These four areas of development and improvement are emphasized.

- *Attitude:* Never be outhit or outhustled.
- *Conditioning:* Be in the best possible condition.
- *Technique:* Teach, practice, evaluate, and stress the fundamentals.
- *Knowledge:* Teach the whole picture so players know the why behind the system. We'll gain an edge by using our brain.
- Clarify player expectations.
  Make certain each player in the program knows what his most important responsibilities are to the program.
  - Do your best (academically, athletically, and socially).
  - Do the right thing.
  - Be honest.
  - Be totally committed and loyal to our program.
  - Take great pride in your performance and our team performance.

The most important factor in "catching up and turning things around" is people. Surround yourself with the right people, and you are on your way. It will be just a matter of time—and it will be well worth it.

—1992 Summer Manual. Coach Mason is head coach at the University of Minnesota.

Coaching Duties and Opportunities
BILL SNYDER

About 80% of all college football coaches are assistants. I was a college assistant for 15 years. Any success I have had as a head coach is due to the work of assistant coaches. I am grateful to all of you who serve in that capacity and I want to share these quick thoughts with you.

I didn't completely understand the position of a head coach, nor his true relationship with his assistants, until I had the opportunity to serve as a head coach for a few years. There are some serious misperceptions about both positions and their roles that I seriously doubt anyone can truly appreciate, until they have served in both capacities.

My experience as a head coach has allowed me to realize that I wasn't nearly as good an assistant as I could have been. I think that the perception of the head coaching position often stands in the way of proper communication and interaction between a head coach and his assistants. If I were to offer any suggestions to assistant coaches at any level, they might be the following:

- Understand that the big picture is larger and more significant than each part. Decisions (even though not always to our liking) should be accepted and supported based on that premise.

- Trust the instincts of those more experienced than yourself. Just like players, experience means a great deal, and as detailed as we get, instinct plays a key role in daily success and failures.
- Genuine concern and caring for each other, and for all parties and facets of a program need to be combined (in a proper blend) with strict discipline. These two entities can co-exist.
- Assistants must carry out the discipline of the program and accept and want the responsibility for their players. Too often, assistants sidestep discipline for the sake of "making friends" with their players.
- Accept the responsibility for success and failure (winning and losing).
- Realize that all problems can be solved if two people (or however many are involved) truly want to solve them.

We're all blessed with the opportunity to impact young lives. Not only must we see it as an opportunity, but equally as a responsibility. This is a most difficult time for young people in the age groups with which you work.

Young people have greater access to information and, at the same time, more difficult decisions to make than you and I at the same age. For these age groups, this is the most difficult and complex time in the history of our society. These young people need you. They need to understand a process by which they can make good decisions about how they choose to conduct their lives and react to the daily choices laid out before them.

In many cases, you and you alone have the power to teach them such a process. In addition, you are capable (if you will) of influencing these young men to positively influence the lives of others in their communities. You can (if you will) teach them leadership, you can teach them to affect the decisions of others younger than themselves, but susceptible to the same pressures and choices. Many young black people, in particular, need leaders, role models, people who care, and people who can influence their decision-making process and guide them out of darkness.

Who better to be that guiding light than the young men you coach? You can influence them to become that guiding light: to save a life, prevent a rape, prevent a killing, prevent an unlawful act, prevent an additional addict. It's amazing what a positive impact we could have on this society by networking through our players to the vulnerable youth of our country.

—1994 Proceedings. Coach Snyder is head coach at Kansas State University.

▪▪▪▪▪▪▪▪▪▪▪▪▪▪▪▪▪▪▪▪▪▪▪▪▪▪▪▪▪▪▪▪▪▪▪▪▪▪

Coaching Philosophy and Objectives
DON NEHLEN

▪▪▪▪▪▪▪▪▪▪▪▪▪▪▪▪▪▪▪▪ ▪▪▪▪▪▪▪▪▪▪▪▪▪▪▪▪

In every decision I make as a head football coach with my team, the most important thing to me is the morale of my staff and our football players. I think there are a lot of ways to throw the post or whatever you want to do, but the only thing that really matters is the attitude of the guys who get that done for you.

If any of you have followed our football team, the only thing that you'll find out is that folks normally will say, "They come to play." They come to play because that's what I work on the most.

We do an awful lot as far as motivation is concerned.

Establishing Priorities for the Program

Right off, our kids understand the mission of our football program. First, to each a degree and to all an *education*. When you're not teaching this, you're teaching something else, and that something else is wrong. If that's not your priority, then you're going to take shortcuts and you're going to do some things you shouldn't be doing with those young guys.

The No. 1 thing that our kids have to understand is that this is what we're in the business for. We're going to do the best job we possibly can do to help these kids graduate. Don't misunderstand me—we don't bat 100%, but I think we do a pretty good job.

When somebody asks me about our graduation rate, I tell them, "Every one of those guys who wants to," and right now, about 7 and 1/2 out of every 10 guys want to. We've got to get a little better, but that's our mission, and our kids understand where we're coming from.

The values that we have are character through discipline. We want character on our team. You all know when its fourth-and-1, you've got to have the right kind of guys playing for you. We're going to discipline our kids; we're not going to harass them. But we're going to make sure they do what's right when they're supposed to do it. If we have character, guys, then we've got a chance to win. It's important that they understand if they lack character, they're not going to last in our program very long.

The second thing we talk about is our *family*. This is our family. We don't have black guys. We don't have white guys. We don't have short guys. We don't have fat guys. We've got a team. I'm the head of the family, and what I say in that team meeting stays in that team meeting.

There's awesome power in 100 guys all going in one direction, but when you've got guys jumping outside that framework, then you've got a problem. They understand that our family is the name of the game.

It's our football family, and we're going to hang tough. You know and I know that when you lose a football game, the student newspaper is after you and it's very, very important that your kids hang together. Lots of folks will try to get them to scatter. Our family is the second value that we work extremely hard to preserve.

Next is our *commitment*. Our players have to understand the commitment that they have to make to play at our level. We don't have a lot of players in West Virginia—we've got a lot of trees—but the players we have are tough and the commitment they have to make is big league. They have to understand that in order for us to win, they're going to have to lift, they have to run, they have to do all the things all you guys expect your players to do in order to play. They have to make a great commitment to that program.

Football is no longer a game that's played in September, October, and November. Football is all year long. I can't wait to get back to school. We left the Sugar Bowl—and you know I wasn't too happy about that—and I've been on the road since. I can't wait to get back to our football team. They have to make sure that they have the commitment, because we've already started our program for next year.

Our next value is *loyalty*. You can't build a program without loyal coaches and players. Our players know I'm going to fight. I'm going to scrap. I'm going to scream for every one of them. My coaches know the same thing. I expect that the secretaries, the janitor, the third-string quarterback, and the graduate assistants all have the same loyalty.

One thing I know about coaching football or about running an organization is that you can't have loyalty if your employee or your football player lies to you. I can't support my guy if he's going to lie. Our kids understand that. Loyalty is the most important ingredient that anybody can bring to any organization. Loyalty starts at the top. It works on down and right back up through. If they understand that, then I think you've got a chance to motivate your players, and you've got a chance to win.

Establishing a Style of Football

I want our players to understand our style of football. Number one, we're going to be *physical*. I want them to understand how we're going to be physical. I want them to understand how we're going to practice. In the spring, we're going to hit every day, and we're going to hit in the fall on Tuesdays and Wednesdays. They're going to have to be physical if they're going to play in our program.

I used to worry all the time about injuries, because of the way we played. I coached for coach Schembechler at Michigan. I said, "Coach are you sure we're doing what's right? We're going to have to play with the third-string guard." And he said, "Don, if he can survive this week, he'll be good enough on Saturday. That's your basic problem, Don. You're soft. Our team will play on Saturday with whoever is left."

And you know what? He was right almost every time. Whoever played in that game was ready to play because they had commitment, they had loyalty, and with that week of repetition, they got it done for us.

Second, you've got to have *tenacious* guys on your team. I have a little story I tell our team. There's a guy at the bottom of a well, and he's a

Mountaineer. He climbs his way to the top of the well. Our biggest game is Pitt, so the guy at the top who keeps pounding his hands and making him slip back down is a Panther. The Mountaineer climbs up and gets pounded back down about 500 times. But the 501st time, he climbs up, and the Panther gets tired of hitting him. That's when the Mountaineer grabs him and chokes him to death.

That sounds a little farfetched, but our kids start to understand about playing football and being tenacious. Hanging on with great effort is the name of the game.

Number three, I want a *classy* football team. I don't want a bunch of bums. I want a team. I want guys who understand they represent themselves, their family, our university, and our coaching staff.

When we travel, everyone wears a coat and a tie. When we eat, everyone wears a coat and a tie. In the dining hall, nobody sits down until the captain says grace. Today, earrings are a big fashion, and that's fine, but on Fridays they take them out and they don't put them in until after the game. They understand that—we're not harassing anyone—but they understand what we're trying to do. We're trying to be a classy football team.

A lot of times when we go away from home, nobody tells us we're very good, but they always tell us how well behaved our kids are. That's what we're trying to teach our kids. We're in the education business, not the entertainment business.

Lastly, with our style is *confidence*. We want our kids to believe before they ever take the field that they're going to win. If you don't believe that, gang, you have a major, major problem. We won 11 football games this year and we were picked

fifth in our league. Five years ago, we also won 11 games. So I know some of this stuff works if you work at it long enough and hard enough.

I love the X's and O's. I don't think there's any question they're important. But, if you are fundamentally sound and your kids are motivated and they have great morale, you've got a great chance to win.

Our goals are not fancy. Our goal this year was simple—just play and play hard. The only time the scoreboard matters is at the end of the game. We don't know which play is going to be the one that wins it, so play hard on every play until the end. You play as hard as you can on every single play.

Every decision I make is based on how it is going to affect team morale. That means the first-string quarterback, the third-string quarterback, the starting tackle, the fourth-string tackle. They have to understand their roles on the football team, and how important they are to the success of that football team.

If you've got 100 guys on your team and they don't all feel like they're important, then you aren't going to win them all. I believe that's the job of the head coach. He has got to do a good job making sure that all his kids believe that they're special.

We also work hard at bringing our team together. One thing we do is have a superstars contest. Our kids love it. That's the first thing they ask me when we get back together each season, "Coach, when are we having the superstars contest?" It's fun. We have a dance. We have a casino night. We do something at the bowling alley, things to have fun as a team.

—*1994 Proceedings. Coach Nehlen is head coach at West Virginia University.*

Since it was founded in 1922, the American Football Coaches Association has striven to "provide a forum for the discussion and study of all matters pertaining to football and coaching" and to "maintain the highest possible standards in football and the coaching profession." These objectives, first declared by founders such as Amos Alonzo Stagg and John Heisman, have been instrumental in the AFCA's becoming the effective and highly respected organization it is today.

The AFCA now has more than 7,000 members, including coaches from Canada, Europe, Australia, Japan, and Russia. Through three annual publications and several newsletters, the Association keeps members informed of the most current rules changes and proposals, proper coaching methods, innovations in techniques, insights in coaching philosophy, and the business conducted by the Board of Trustees and AFCA committees. A convention held each January gives members a special opportunity to exchange ideas and recognize outstanding achievement.

The Association promotes safety in the sport, and sets forth strong ethical and moral codes that govern all aspects of football coaching. In addition, the AFCA is involved in numerous programs that ensure the integrity of the coaching profession and enhance the development of the game. The Association works closely with the National Collegiate Athletic Association, the National Association of Collegiate Directors of Athletics, the National Association of Intercollegiate Athletics, the National Football League, the Canadian Football League, the National Football Foundation and Hall of Fame, Pop Warner, and other organizations involved in the game. Indeed, one of the many goals of the Association is to build a strong coalition of football coaches—TEAM AFCA—who will speak out with a unified voice on issues that affect their sport and profession.

The AFCA is *the* team for the football coaching profession. All current and former football coaches or administrators who are connected with the game are encouraged to join. To become a member of the American Football Coaches Association, please write or call:

AFCA
5900 Old McGregor Road
Waco, TX 76712
(817) 776-5900

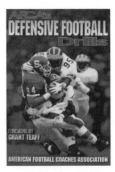 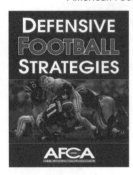 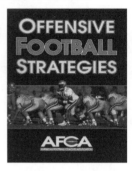 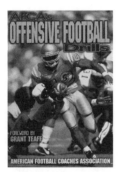